Global Themes in World History Since 1500

Global Themes in World History Since 1500

Written and edited by Elizabeth Sundermann,

Mario J. Azevedo, and John P. Dunn

cognella®

SAN DIEGO

Bassim Hamadeh, CEO and Publisher
David Miano, Senior Specialist Acquisitions Editor
Michelle Piehl, Senior Project Editor
Abbey Hastings, Production Editor
Jess Estrella, Senior Graphic Designer
Trey Soto, Licensing Coordinator
Natalie Piccotti, Director of Marketing
Kassie Graves, Vice President of Editorial
Jamie Giganti, Director of Academic Publishing

Cover images: Source: https://commons.wikimedia.org/wiki/File:Jacques_Bertaux_-_Prise_du_palais_des_Tuileries_-_1793.jpg.
Copyright © 2009 Depositphotos/georgios.
Copyright © 2014 Depositphotos/karelnoppe.
Copyright © 2014 Depositphotos/frizio.
Copyright © 2014 Depositphotos/2630ben.
Copyright © 2009 Depositphotos/odua.

Printed in the United States of America.

3970 Sorrento Valley Blvd., Ste. 500, San Diego, CA 92121

Brief Contents

Detailed Contents

Chapter 2   Empires and Imperialism   45

Chapter 3 The Global Industrial Revolution   83

ACTIVE LEARNING

This book has interactive activities available to complement your reading.

Your instructor may have customized the selection of activities available for your unique course. Please check with your professor to verify whether your class will access this content through the Cognella Active Learning portal (http://active.cognella.com) or through your home learning management system.

Acknowledgments

Elizabeth Sundermann: I would like to thank my coauthors and Michelle Piehl, Senior Project Editor, and David Miano, the Senior Acquisitions Specialist, and all Cognella staff who contributed to this textbook. Michelle and David particularly, have been incredibly patient and helpful in bringing a multiyear project to fruition in its first edition.

I would also like to thank colleagues, students, and friends who supported my work on this textbook. A big thank you to my history students Joshua Scullin and Nathan Patrick for carefully reading and commenting on several chapters of the text. Their "student-eye view" was vital. I would also like to thank my THIST 151 "World History: II 1500 to Present" students who read and commented on the preliminary edition of this text I tested in class. Your feedback was helpful in improving the textbook. Many of my colleagues at UW Tacoma have provided support either directly or indirectly by answering my questions about their specialized fields, supporting my world history teaching and scholarship, or simply offering encouragement when I was frustrated with the writing and publication process. A number of world history colleagues from a variety of institutions also provided support, including helping outline the text's themes and topics and helping me grow as a world history instructor: Thanks go to my professors at UC Davis who initially trained me in a world history teaching field; UW Tacoma's School of Interdisciplinary Arts & Sciences, who first hired me to teach world history; and members of the World History Association who have inspired me, specifically Candice Goucher, whose scholarship, collegiality, and friendship have been invaluable to me as a world historian and instructor. Of course, the authors take all responsibility for any errors in the textbook.

Mario J. Azevedo: I wish to express my heartfelt thanks to Michelle Piehl, our Senior Project Editor, and David Miano, the Senior Acquisitions Specialist, who worked diligently and patiently with us, guiding us over the past two years with a firm but gentle hand, and my colleagues Elizabeth Sundermann and John Dunn, without whom the work would not have been done as professionally as it has been. To Elizabeth, in particular, my sincere gratitude for her support and encouragement when things were not moving as fast as they should, and for never taking her eyes off the prize—namely, the timely completion of the manuscript. It has been a pleasure knowing you and working with you.

John P. Dunn: To my coauthors, who both helped improve my contribution, I express my sincere thanks. I also appreciate the hard work of Valdosta State University's Library staff, who cheerfully found many data sources. If there is quality to my sections, it must be shared with the above-mentioned friends; if there are problems, they are my exclusive property.

Introduction

Global Themes in World History Since 1500

What Is World History?

It may seem strange to students that historians debate the definition of world history. Like any interpretation of history, however, historians' ideas of what world history is, and should be, have changed over time and place. Historians debate when world histories were first written and, to make matters even more complex, also differentiate between world history, global history, international history, transnational history, and **Big History**. All these debates are valid, and it is worthwhile for historians and students of history to consider the different arguments. As your textbook authors, we offer our take on world history.

While historians have made efforts to write world histories since antiquity, a noticeable shift in history writing took place in the twentieth century. Events and ideas related to decolonization and globalization shifted scholars' (and the public's) attention away from traditions of nineteenth-century national histories (often Eurocentric in nature) to examining patterns in human history and interactions and exchanges among and between groups of humans around the world. This led to a post–World War II breakout of the now-established field of world history and its companion genres (e.g., global, international, and transnational histories). We view world history in its broad parameters, following the model of the World History Association, which suggests that world history, like any history, can and should be studied and interpreted in a variety of time and geographical frameworks.[1]

Mission Statement

Like other historians, we have made certain decisions about how we frame world history's vast periodization, geography, and patterns of human history in one textbook. This text is designed for modern world history university courses' conventional starting point in the sixteenth century—around 1500. We recognize, however, that this periodization is one of convenience rather than a definitive historical break, and thus make efforts to address people, events, and patterns that led to global transitions that took place before 1500. Our main goal is to present a concise, thematic world history textbook to appeal to college-level world history students and their instructors. We focus on selected topics and themes representative of global patterns in world history, but the chapters are framed to allow each author to emphasize their specific and diverse interests: Mario J. Azevedo's (Jackson State University) teaching and research

---

1   World History Association, "What Is World History?," https://www.thewha.org/about/what-is-world-history/

interests include the history of Africa, the African diaspora, infectious tropical diseases and health care with geographical focuses in Africa, and specifically Francophone and southern Africa. John P. Dunn's (Valdosta State University) teaching and research interests include the Middle East, Eastern Europe, China, and World Military History. Elizabeth Sundermann's (University of Washington, Tacoma) teaching and research interests include Modern Europe, twentieth-century Britain, and World History (prehistory to present), history of education, empire and imperialism, food, and cultural history. We also consulted with other world history college instructors as well as interdisciplinary colleagues and a variety of primary and secondary sources as we developed the text.

Topics and Themes

A significant feature of our textbook is Azevedo's chapter devoted to "Africa on the World Stage." In our experience as world history instructors, we have found that African history continues to be glossed over in many world history textbooks and courses, and if covered, typically focuses on issues related to the Atlantic Slave Trade. While the slave trade is a crucial topic in world (and African/African diaspora) history since 1500, it does not adequately cover the history of modern Africa, nor its diverse connections and contributions to world history. We hope Azevedo's chapter will help foster increased attention on African history in the world history classroom. He argues, "Notwithstanding the nefarious impact of the slave trade, European colonialism and imperialism, and the natural geographic barriers, Africans have survived, and are catching up with the rest of the world in every sector of life, including the sphere of technology and science." Azevedo's "Africa on the World Stage," with a focus on the twentieth century, reveals Africa's modern world history following the key themes of our textbook: Geography and Environment; Material Culture; Science and Technology; Gender and Sexuality; and War, Peace, and Diplomacy.

These themes serve as the connecting threads for each chapter in the text. In addition to "Africa on the World Stage," we describe "Atlantic World," "Empires and Imperialism," "Global Industrialization," and "The Twentieth Century." Each chapter examines these themes from a world history perspective, but also from the expert perspectives of each author. The emphases on these themes reflect important transitions in world history research and writing to include topics such as food studies and interdisciplinary work (archaeology, anthropology, cultural studies) related to material culture. We also refer to historiography in our chapters but gear these discussions toward undergraduate readers. Students and instructors should note that unlike some textbooks, the authors have included footnotes to help guide readers to sources that may be helpful in identifying scholarly arguments and debates and additional reading. We believe that undergraduate students can better understand and appreciate history if they become familiar with the idea that history, while based on primary source evidence, is also based on historians' interpretations of that evidence, and that historiography (like history) changes through time and place.

Textbook Features

The textbook contains elements meant to aid both students and instructors. The text is divided into five chapters, and each chapter is divided into five thematic sections. We hope this will allow students and instructors flexibility in using the text as each chapter may be read independently; the textbook may be read following themes that appear in each chapter; or the text may be read in its entirety following a broad chronology from the early Atlantic World to the twentieth century (and some references to the twenty-first century). Each chapter features an introduction to a chapter topic and its relation to the themes of Geography and Environment; Material Culture; Science and Technology; Gender and Sexuality; and War, Peace, and Diplomacy; suggested student learning goals; and a timeline of selected dates related to the chapter's topics. Chapters provide selected primary sources, discussion questions, images, timelines, glossary terms identified in bold, and suggested additional readings and media we have successfully used in our own classrooms or in research for this text.

Chapter 1

Atlantic World

Introduction to Chapter Themes

This chapter focuses on the Atlantic World—the rim lands and islands of the Atlantic Ocean and the intersections of people, cultures, trade, and goods that shaped this **world system** after 1500. While the Atlantic World was first imagined by Western scholars as a largely European world system, world historians have pointed out that the Atlantic World—indeed, much of what characterizes modern world systems—would not have existed without intersections of peoples and cultures from Europe, Africa, and the **Americas**. This chapter examines the Atlantic World through the themes of this textbook: geography and environment; material culture; science and technology; gender and sexuality; and war, peace, and **diplomacy**. Geography and environment are discussed in reference to human geography, the **Columbian Exchange** and its aftermath, **Ecological Imperialism**, and the relation of both to the Atlantic Slave Trade. Material culture and science and technology are illustrated through discussions of Caribbean cuisine and the science and trade of botanical specimens—both connect back to the Columbian Exchange and its aftermath.[1] Sections on gender and sexuality examine intersections of race, class, and gender in the colonies, as well as revolutionary female leaders. Sections on war, peace, and diplomacy follow these women and other leaders during revolutions—including those in Europe and the Americas—that swept across the Atlantic World.

Student Learning Objectives

After reading this chapter students should be able to describe and discuss:

- The complexities in scholarly definitions of the Atlantic World.
- Diversity and cultural hybridity in the Atlantic World.
- The causes and effects of the Columbian Exchange in its positive and negative aspects.

---

1 The Columbian Exchange, themes of ecological imperialism, and the Atlantic Slave Trade will be revisited in Chapter 2 through the lenses of European protagonists.

Timeline of Selected Dates

1508	Spanish explorer Juan Ponce de León colonizes Puerto Rico
1519	Smallpox arrives in Mexico from Europe
1773	British Tea Act imposed on American colonies
1562	John Hawkins sells enslaved African peoples in the Spanish Caribbean
1803	Denmark is first European country to ban the slave trade
1836	Portugal bans the slave trade
1688–1689	Glorious Revolution (England)
1775–1783	American (US) Revolution
1787–1799	French Revolution
1791–1804	Haitian Revolution
1810–1823	Venezuelan War of Independence

Why the Atlantic World?

In 1949, renowned historian Fernand Braudel published his groundbreaking *The Mediterranean and the Mediterranean World* using **Annales** methodology, an influential French-led interpretation of history with a more global and comprehensive focus on human history. These ideas translated into new historical thinking and methodologies of the deepness of geographic and environmental history, the landscape of collective histories and memories, and the sharp peaks of great events and individuals. Braudel envisioned the Mediterranean World as a grand historical vista rather than a place that could be understood by a traditional **historiography** that limited its scope to arbitrary units of time and space. Braudel understood the history of the Mediterranean World took interdisciplinary and transnational scholarship.

Braudel's work influenced scholars who embraced his idea that a nexus of history could be a body of water—the Mediterranean, the Indian Ocean, and the Atlantic—and their rim lands connected in historical processes. This scholarship gave rise to new methods of thinking about space and time outside of national histories and traditional (Western) **periodization** and geographical boundaries to help scholars move toward our current understanding of the Atlantic World. This chapter attempts to look at a broader and more diverse reading of the Atlantic World as a crucible in which diverse peoples, including indigenous Americans, Africans, and Europeans were brought together, although often, specifically in the cases of indigenous Americans and Africans, by force. Through innovative and often violent interactions, a new world—literally the meeting of two separate worlds, **Afro-Eurasia** and the Americas—was made in what we know today as the Atlantic World.

Geography and Environment

The Atlantic Ocean is the second largest of the world's oceans, covering roughly a fifth of the world's surface. It connects major landmasses—including the Americas, Europe, and **Africa**—as well as numerous islands—the Caribbean island chain being most notable (Figure 1.1). Scholars tend to focus on the events of the fifteenth and eighteenth centuries in identifying the Atlantic

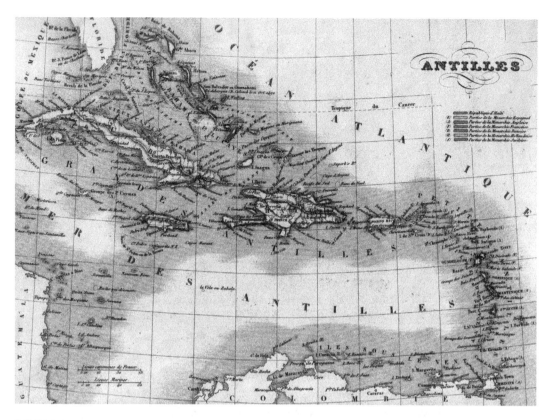

FIGURE 1.1   French map of the Caribbean.

World, although certainly the history of the Atlantic stretches further back and forward in time. The physical geographies and environments of the Atlantic World are diverse, as are its modern populations. This chapter will focus on aspects of geography and environment including human geography. This includes not only how indigenous, African, and European peoples came to interact with one another in the Atlantic World after 1492, but also how they shaped ecosystems and resources and how ecosystems and resources shaped them.

The African Diaspora

Investigations of the diverse human geographies of the Atlantic World are tied to how its history of race, ethnicity, class, and gender intersected to shape the Atlantic World by shifting early Atlantic history away from white (male) Western narratives to those that considered the **African diaspora** as well as reasserted a basic tenet of Atlantic World history—as a single, yet multifaceted, unit of analysis. The British scholar Paul Gilroy coined the phrase "the Black Atlantic" in his 1993 book, which sought to take race, nationality, and identity through the lenses of the African diaspora and the Atlantic World and transform those concepts into transnational ideas of modernity as culturally hybrid. While historiography of the Black Atlantic, like that of a broader Atlantic World, is complex, Gilroy's conception of a "Black Atlantic" allows for historical interpretation that recognizes that African peoples were diverse at home and in diaspora, and that they played an active role in shaping the Atlantic and the modern worlds.

Olaudah Equiano was captured into slavery as a boy but eventually gained his freedom and became a noted abolitionist, author, and traveler. His autobiography gives a firsthand account of his capture transport across the Atlantic, and slavery, as well as his travels in the Atlantic World, including Central America, the Caribbean, and England. This excerpt of his time on the Mosquito Coast (coastal region of modern-day Nicaragua and Honduras) and interactions with white colonists and indigenous peoples provides a unique perspective of Atlantic World history through the eyes of an African man with deep personal experiences in the systems of that region.

Excerpts from The Interesting Narrative of the Life of Olaudah Equiano, or Gustavus Vassa, the African.

Olaudah Equiano

[O]n the eighteenth [of February 1776 we] arrived at the Musquito [Mosquito, Meskito or Miskito][1] shore, at a place called Dupeupy. ...

We then sailed to the southward of the shore, to a place called Cape Gracias a Dios [on the Musquito Coast between Honduras and Nicaragua], where there was a large lagoon or lake, which received the emptying of two or three very fine large rivers, and abounded much in fish and land tortoise. Some of the native Indians came on board of us here; and we used them well, and told them we were come to dwell amongst them, which they seemed pleased at.

So ... Doctor [Charles Irving, Equiano's employer and a noted British scientist] and I, with some others, went with them ashore; and they took us to different places to view the land, in order to choose a place to make a plantation of. [Equiano planned to serve as Irving's overseer and arrived with slaves he had helped purchase.] We fixed on a spot near a river's bank, in a rich soil; and, having got our necessaries out of the sloop, we began to clear away the woods, and plant different kinds of vegetables, which had a quick growth.

...

However, we went on with the culture of the land. We used to make fires every night all around us, to keep off wild beasts, which, as soon as it was dark, set up a most hideous roaring. Our habitation being far up in the woods, we frequently saw different kinds of animals; but none of them ever hurt us, except poisonous snakes, the bite of which the Doctor used to cure by giving to the patient, as soon as possible, about half a tumbler of strong rum, with a good deal of Cayenne pepper in it. In this manner he cured two natives and one of his own slaves.

---

1   This name comes from the indigenous Meskito or Miskito people of the area, not the insect.

Selections from Olaudah Equiano, "Picking up Eleven Miserable Men at Sea in Returning to England," *The Interesting Narrative of the Life of Olaudah Equiano, or Gustavus Vassa, the African.* 1789.

The Indians were exceedingly fond of the Doctor, and they had good reason for it; for I believe they never had such an useful man amongst them. They came from all quarters to our dwelling; and some *woolwow*, or flat-headed Indians, who lived fifty or sixty miles above our river, and this side of the South Sea, brought us a good deal of silver in exchange for our goods. The principal articles we could get from our neighbouring Indians, were turtle oil, and shells, little silk grass, and some provisions; but they would not work at any thing for us, except fishing; and a few times they assisted to cut some trees down, in order to build us houses; which they did exactly like the Africans, by the joint labour of men, women, and children.

...

The women generally cultivate the ground, and the men are all fishermen and canoe makers.

...

The natives are well made and warlike; and they particularly boast of having never been conquered by the Spaniards. They are great drinkers of strong liquors when they can get them. We used to distil rum from pine apples, which were very plentiful here; and then we could not get them away from our place. Yet they seemed to be singular, in point of honesty, above any other nation I was ever amongst. The country being hot, we lived under an open shed, where we had all kinds of goods, without a door or a lock to any one article; yet we slept in safety, and never lost any thing, or were disturbed. This surprised us a good deal; and the Doctor, myself, and others, used to say, if we were to lie in that manner in Europe we should have our throats cut the first night.

...

The Indian governor goes once in a certain time all about the province or district, and has a number of men with him as attendants and assistants. He settles all the differences among the people, like the judge here, and is treated with very great respect. He took care to give us timely notice before he came to our habitation, by sending his stick as a token, for rum, sugar, and gunpowder, which we did not refuse sending; and at the same time we made the utmost preparation to receive his honour and his train. When he came with his tribe, and all our neighbouring chieftains, we expected to find him a grave reverend judge, solid and sagacious; but instead of that, before he and his gang came in sight, we heard them very clamorous; and they even had plundered some of our good neighbouring Indians, having intoxicated themselves with our liquor. When they arrived we did not know what to make of our new guests, and would gladly have dispensed with the honour of their company. However, having no alternative, we feasted them plentifully all the day till the evening; when the governor, getting quite drunk, grew very unruly, and struck one of our most friendly chiefs, who was our nearest neighbour, and also took his gold-laced hat from him.

...

The Musquito people within our vicinity, out of respect to the Doctor, myself and his people, made entertainments of the grand kind, called in their tongue *tourrie* or *dryckbot*. The English of this expression is, a feast of drinking about, of which it seems a corruption of language. The drink consisted of pine apples roasted, and casades chewed or beaten in mortars; which, after lying some time, ferments, and becomes so strong as to intoxicate, when drank in any quantity. We had timely notice given to us of the entertainment. A white family, within five miles of us, told us how the drink was made, and I and two others went before the time to the village, where the mirth was appointed to be held; and there we saw the whole art of making the drink, and also the kind of animals that were to be eaten there.

I cannot say the sight of either the drink or the meat were enticing to me. They had some thousands of pine apples roasting, which they squeezed, dirt and all, into a canoe they had there for the purpose. The casade drink was in beef barrels and other vessels, and looked exactly like hog-wash. Men, women, and children, were thus employed in roasting the pine apples, and squeezing them with their hands. For food they had many land torpins or tortoises, some dried turtle, and three large alligators alive, and tied fast to the trees.

I asked the people what they were going to do with these alligators; and I was told they were to be eaten. I was much surprised at this, and went home, not a little disgusted at the preparations. When the day of the feast was come, we took some rum with us, and went to the appointed place, where we found a great assemblage of these people, who received us very kindly. The mirth had begun before we came; and they were dancing with music: and the musical instruments were nearly the same as those of any other sable people; but, as I thought, much less melodious than any other nation I ever knew.

...

At night there were great illuminations, by setting fire to many pine trees, while the dryckbot went round merrily by calabashes or gourds: but the liquor might more justly be called eating than drinking. One Owden, the oldest father in the vicinity, was dressed in a strange and terrifying form. Around his body were skins adorned with different kinds of feathers, and he had on his head a very large and high head-piece, in the form of a grenadier's cap, with prickles like a porcupine; and he made a certain noise which resembled the cry of an alligator. Our people skipped amongst them out of complaisance, though some could not drink of their tourrie; but our rum met with customers enough, and was soon gone.

The alligators were killed and some of them roasted. Their manner of roasting is by digging a hole in the earth, and filling it with wood, which they burn to coal, and then they lay sticks across, on which they set the meat. I had a raw piece of the alligator in my hand: it was very rich: I thought it looked like fresh salmon, and it had a most fragrant smell, but I could not eat any of it. This merry-making at last ended without the least discord in any person in the company, although it was made up of different nations and complexions.

Discussion Questions

1. Equiano has been described by scholars as having a transnational [crossing national boundaries] identity because his identity was formed across the Atlantic World [in Africa, the Americas, and Europe]. What does this excerpt suggest about Equiano's transnational identity and how it shapes his actions and his descriptions of White Europeans and indigenous peoples?

2. How does Equiano's depiction of the Musquito Coast suggest the meeting of technologies and cultures in the Atlantic World—what signs of European and indigenous technologies and cultures are revealed by Equiano? Keep in mind that technology encompasses manipulation of resources and the environment as well as applied science.

3. Equiano refers to a number of commodities including flora (plants) and fauna (animals) in this excerpt. Where do they originate? What are these resources and what are they used for?

The Indigenous Atlantic

As scholarship on the Atlantic World has progressed, scholars have increasingly begun to recognize the multiculturalism of the region—peoples native to the Americas (North, Central, South, and the Caribbean), Africans, and Europeans all participated in the making of this Atlantic World after 1500. While a variety of African and European peoples participated, so did a wide variety of indigenous peoples—for example, the Caribbean **Taino**, the South American Tupi, Central American Mayan, and North American Pamunkey. All these groups were diverse, much more so than the homogeneous names Europeans gave them, including "Indians."

The Taino, for example, a subgroup of the Arawak indigenous to South America and the Caribbean, had a large population spread over many islands including modern-day Cuba, Jamaica, and Puerto Rico, long before the arrival of Europeans to these islands. The ruins of Taino *bateyes*, or ball courts, for a rubber ball game played between two teams (Figure 1.2) suggest the transmission of traditions from Mesoamerica to the Caribbean.

The Taino developed into regional cultures across the Caribbean, distinguished by each group's geographic place in the Atlantic—but are generally known for their intensified agricultural practices and well-developed material culture. They also interacted with diverse indigenous cultures in the Atlantic World, and, after 1500, with Europeans, Africans, and other immigrants to the Atlantic World. The Taino also lived on **Hispaniola** (modern-day Haiti and the Dominican Republic), where Christopher Columbus met them on his arrival to the Caribbean.

FIGURE 1.2   Caguana Ceremonial Ball Courts Site, Utuado, Puerto Rico.

The European or "White Atlantic"

The White Atlantic typically refers to the European history of the Atlantic, told from a **Eurocentric** (focused on European history and superiority) perspective. This may include stories of Columbus's "discovery" of the Americas, European imperial conquest of the Americas, including the Caribbean, to modern understandings of the Atlantic World as a (White) Anglo-American space represented by NATO (the North Atlantic Treaty Organization). Bernard Bailyn, in his deep analysis of the concepts of the Atlantic World, argues the term "White Atlantic" owes its origins to American journalist Walter Lippman.[2] Coined by Lippman in 1917, the term further developed in the early- to mid-twentieth century as a response to the World Wars. The White Atlantic tends to focus both on colonial and nation-state history of Anglo-America (and sometimes other European) interactions in the Atlantic and has become less fashionable with the shift from national to transnational and world history. The history of the White Atlantic, taken with the increasing complexity of Atlantic World history, remains an important part of the story of this area, its peoples, and its changes through time after 1500. If it receives less attention in some cases in this chapter, that is because its story has been told frequently in many other sources.

---

2   Bernard Bailyn, *Atlantic History: Concept and Contours* (Cambridge, MA: Harvard University Press, 2005), 4–6. Bailyn rejects historiographical comparisons between the origins of Atlantic World and Braudel's Mediterranean.

Atlantic Exchanges

The Columbian Exchange, a term popularized by historian Alfred Crosby in his 1972 book of the same name, argues that much of post-1492 world history is a result of the exchanges of flora and fauna, as well as humans and microorganisms, that occurred with the opening of Atlantic trade routes between Afro-Eurasia and the Americas. As scholars have argued, differences in evolution of flora and fauna on the two sides of the Atlantic (as well as differences elsewhere) created vastly different systems of **agriculture**, based on what scholar Jared Diamond has identified as "packages" of plant and animal life ripe for **domestication**.[3] Humans, regardless of where they developed agricultural practices, have proven remarkably capable of carving out sustainable lifestyles in a variety of ecosystems and biomes from tundra to tropical. Although not all agree with Diamond's thesis of an environmental determinism for the relative successes and failures of human societies, vastly different "packages" of flora and fauna evolved in Afro-Eurasia and the pre-Columbian Atlantic World and humans domesticated those they found most useful.

The Columbian Exchange, dated from Columbus's arrival in the Americas, saw the transfer of plants such as daisies and domesticated animals like horses from Afro-Eurasia to the Americas. The Americas sent potatoes, **cacao**, and turkeys, among many other plants and animals, to Afro-Eurasia. Because of these exchanges, societies, cultures, economic and political systems, and the world's environment, experienced dramatic and long-lasting changes. An arguable positive outcome of the Columbian Exchange was the development of increasingly complex and tasty cuisines around the world—for example, Indian and Thai cuisines added the heat of American chili peppers to their now globally popular dishes. Regardless, much of Atlantic World history was racist and violent as human beings were forced into slavery, often to produce goods for the growing commercial viability of the Atlantic European–dominated trade of sugar, **cotton**, and other goods. In addition, the spread of biological invaders—diseases, weeds, and pests—across the Americas led to long-term changes in American environmental settings.

Weeds, Pests, and Diseases

While weeds such as dandelions seem ubiquitous today, they spread from Afro-Eurasia to the Americas and beyond during the Columbian Exchange. Diseases, including the common cold, also spread from Afro-Eurasia to the Americas early on. Pests, including the gypsy moth, whose caterpillar defoliates and thus kills a wide variety of American plants, including oak and aspen trees, arrived on the East Coast in the 1860s and on the West Coast in the late twentieth century, and both varieties prove problematic for modern forests. The spread of Afro-Eurasian diseases wreaked havoc on peoples and their societies: Smallpox decimated indigenous populations, while Afro-Eurasians contracted and spread syphilis after contact with indigenous peoples. The introduction of new diseases to unsuspecting populations who lacked immunities and medical practices specific to the new diseases—sometimes referred to as "virgin soil phenomenon"—allowed the diseases to spread quickly and kill millions of indigenous peoples in the Americas.

Smallpox is a global disease with a long history stemming from agricultural revolutions some 10,000 years ago. It has killed hundreds of millions of people around the world since its origins

---

3 Jared Diamond, *Guns, Germs, and Steel: The Fates of Human Societies* (New York: Norton, 2005).

in Africa (likely Egypt) and the Indian subcontinent. Spread along trade routes, smallpox ravaged Afro-Eurasia and then, in 1492, as new global trade routes emerged across the Atlantic Ocean, sailors unwittingly carried germs along for the journeys. Within a decade of Columbus's arrival in the Caribbean, smallpox took its toll on indigenous Americans. Within three decades it reached the mainland where it decimated Aztec (Mexica) and Inca (Inka) civilizations before reaching North America. Smallpox and other diseases introduced by Europeans to indigenous peoples killed millions, and estimates suggest that 90 percent of indigenous populations in the Americas died because of exposure to Afro-Eurasian diseases. Smallpox also reentered Africa from the Atlantic (and earlier by caravan trade) as the Portuguese and other European sailors made contact with a variety of African groups along the Atlantic coast of Africa. Smallpox as a disease plagued Africans living under European colonial powers well into the twentieth century. There is another link, however, between smallpox and African peoples—the Atlantic Slave Trade. Scholars argue that the decimation of indigenous populations was a factor in European interest in Africa as a site for finding slave labor to replace indigenous Americans to benefit European commercial interests in the Americas.

The Atlantic Slave Trade

The Atlantic Slave Trade was the most nefarious of Atlantic exchanges—a process in which peoples from Africa were literally treated as goods and in the process taken from their homes and families and forced west across the Atlantic Ocean to the Caribbean islands and mainland Americas. The Atlantic Slave Trade was unique and a transformation of existing practices of slavery. Slavery was not new in fifteenth- and sixteenth-century world systems, including those in Africa. Nor was the Atlantic Slave Trade the only slave system in the period between the sixteenth and nineteenth centuries—for example, the Dutch East India Company ran a slave trade in the Indian Ocean during the seventeenth and eighteenth centuries, with parallels to and differences from the slave trade in the Atlantic.[4]

Slavery in the African continent had deep roots, as slavery does in many areas of the world, and the origins of African slave trades existed as both domestic and transcontinental systems. This is a reminder that the history of the African continent and its many diverse peoples—especially for this chapter's purposes, those who occupied the Atlantic coastlines—have complex histories outside of the Atlantic Slave Trade. A world history of slavery, however, is no apologia for the horrors of the trans-Atlantic trade.

The complexity of the Atlantic Slave Trade is staggering. It involved at least four continents (Africa, Europe, and North and South America), millions of people who moved—many by force—between those continents, and who became a part of the region's political, economic, social, and cultural history. Thus, the history of the Atlantic Slave Trade has played out across a global historical landscape so vast that even world historians can only relate this story in pieces. Although, as discussed above, slavery itself had a longer global history than the Atlantic Slave Trade, specific differences mark the trade after 1500. The Atlantic system was based on **chattel slavery** (chattel

---

4   Markus Vink, "'The World's Oldest Trade': Dutch Slavery and Slave Trade in the Indian Ocean in the Seventeenth Century," *Journal of World History* 14, no. 2 (2003): 131–77.

refers to personal, movable property), which allowed enslaved people to be bought and sold and took from those sold in slavery—and their descendants—their rights as human beings and left them with virtually no hope of ever regaining their freedom. Human beings literally became property in an emerging capitalist system where forced and unpaid labor became key to an economic system which relied on intensive **plantation agriculture** as well as extractive work such as mining.

The Atlantic Slave Trade was distinctive in its scale and use of racism. Familiar statistics of scale include the generally agreed-upon number of 12.5 million Africans forced across the Atlantic Ocean to the Americas. Distance also characterizes the scale of the Atlantic Slave Trade—the journey took up to three months over some 5,000 miles. Racism is another unique characteristic of the Atlantic Slave Trade—like slavery, concepts of differences in human features, cultures, and religions existed long before this slave trade. The Atlantic Slave Trade, however, was based on a fallacy of White supremacy in economic, social, cultural, and biological spheres that infected the Atlantic Slave Trade and its aftermath.

The British were early—and heavily—involved in the forced transport of Africans to the Americas (including North and South America and the Caribbean) (Figure 1.3). As early as 1562, John Hawkins had the dubious distinction of being the first British merchant to sell enslaved African peoples in the Spanish Caribbean. By the mid-seventeenth century, with Atlantic trading patterns

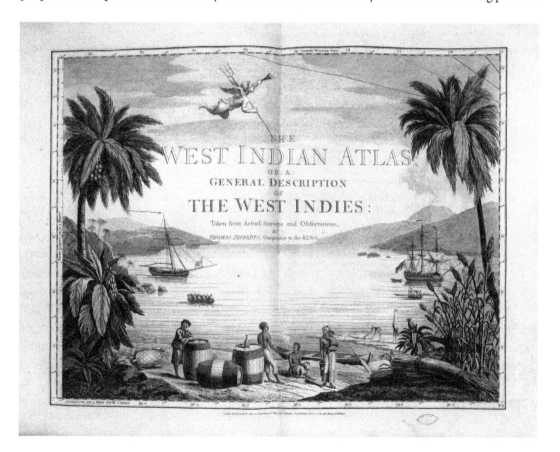

FIGURE 1.3 Representation of the Caribbean from "The West Indian Atlas," published in London in 1775.

well established, British merchants and consumers of sugar, tobacco, and other goods became wedded to the commercial system of slavery, which was crucial to the rise of the British Empire and the rise of a consumer economy. This economic system, as seen by the granting of royal charters, was not only sanctioned, but fought for and maintained by British leaders and politicians. The West Indian lobby (West Indian refers to the Caribbean), for example, whose vested interests in the slave trade bled into their roles as members of Parliament, sought to protect their wealth and the political power it afforded them. In the 1760s, the Society of West India Planters and Merchants formed to promote their economic interests in Parliament related to sugar imports and other interests in Caribbean **plantations** worked by enslaved peoples. The pro-slavery lobbyists would counter a small but growing interest in the abolition of slavery.

By 1787 the Committee for the Abolition of the African Slave Trade, a small group made up of **Quakers** and **Anglicans** (both refer to Christian denominations) led by Granville Sharp and Thomas Clarkson begin work to suppress the slave trade. They successfully persuaded Member of Parliament William Wilberforce to join the cause. Although Wilberforce has been lauded as a key player in British abolition efforts, others, including the former enslaved man Olaudah Equiano, helped publicize the need for the end of the slave trade. British women also participated in abolition movements with actions such as tightening their domestic purse strings to imports such as slavery-produced sugar. Fighting against the British government and wealthy merchants, abolitionists faced a long and challenging fight. In 1790 and 1792, two bills for abolition failed in Parliament. Events outside British interests, however, also challenged slavery, including an enslaved peoples' rebellion that eventually led to the establishment of Haiti as the first independent black state outside of Africa.

Finally, in 1807, the British Parliament abolished the British domestic involvement in the Atlantic Slave Trade. Slavery, however, took longer to dismantle. Not until 1833 did the British Parliament pass the Abolition of Slavery Act, eradicating the practice of slavery in all British territories. This act took several years to be effective in British colonies, and an international trade continued.

There is no argument that the Atlantic Slave Trade was an appalling era of human history. Historians, however, are charged with examining changes through time, and, as discussion of the Atlantic World suggests, offering evolving interpretations of the past based on evidence and interpretations of that evidence. While the history of the slave trade is one of exploitation, violence, and racism, scholars now understand that enslaved peoples were more than just victims—they were also participants, however unwilling at times—in the making of the Atlantic and the modern worlds. The slave trade led to many developments now taken for granted—**the rise of the West**, **capitalism**, and **industrialization**. It also led to the creation of new cultures in the Americas, including what is known as Atlantic World **Creole** culture(s). These creative processes, despite their shameful origins, created a material culture that helped to shape the modern world.

Conclusion

The Atlantic World was a diverse and complex system that served as a crucible in shaping the modern world. Africans, Europeans, and indigenous people all made contributions to the development of Atlantic World cultures, such as the Caribbean Creole cultures that developed as a result of European entry into the Americas where indigenous peoples lived and thrived before 1492, and the forced migration of African peoples through the Atlantic Slave Trade. In addition, an exchange of flora and fauna between the Americas and Afro-Eurasia led to the Columbian Exchange, which had radical effects on populations, cultures, and landscapes. A crucible is defined as "a situation of severe trial, or in which different elements interact, leading to the creation of something new."[5] The Atlantic World was a place of severe trials, especially for people of color, yet the interactions in the Atlantic World made it a laboratory of modernity.

Material Culture

Material culture is defined as physical evidence (e.g., objects and architecture) made by humans. Although the term has most often been used in archaeological and anthropological studies, its use by historians has grown in popularity with deepening interest in world history methodology. The study of Atlantic World material culture, especially of indigenous and enslaved cultures, is one that is still developing. In addition, world historians realize, much like the history of the Atlantic World itself, that the separate cultures within the Atlantic World (e.g., indigenous, African, and European) cannot be studied in isolation. The Atlantic World was the epicenter of the **creolization** of European, African, and indigenous cultures. Creolization, the blending of these cultures, however uneven it may have been at times, has been difficult to separate, and localized, nationalized, and ethnical distinctive studies—for example, that of locating **Africanisms** (culture or language identified as African in origin) without adaptions to new environments has been fraught with difficulties. Understanding Caribbean creolization requires an examination of the origins and blending of diverse cultures into processes of **cultural hybridity.**

Significant contributions by different groups—metallurgy from Africans, botanical knowledge from indigenous peoples, livestock from Europe—resulted in aspects of the Columbian Exchange that are specifically Caribbean. This Caribbean crucible is illustrated below by a discussion of the Caribbean kitchen—the literal spaces, the ingredients grown, borrowed, and blended there, and the distinctive Caribbean (or Creole) cuisine that emerged.

The Caribbean kitchen is one element of what some scholars have started to refer to as an Atlantic Creole Architecture. It seems while scholars may not agree on what specific architectural constructions are Creole, they can agree Creole architecture represents a blending of European, African, and indigenous characteristics in Atlantic World settings. This is illustrated in the history of the detached kitchens, yards, and gardens.

Kitchens, Yards, and Gardens
Evidence of detached kitchens, yards and gardens—cooking and agricultural spaces located outside houses—reveal domestic and agricultural material culture in the Atlantic Caribbean. *Yard* is a broad term for areas outside main buildings where a variety of activities related to domestic and manual labor and recreation might take place within a demarcated area that was outside, but part

---

5 "Crucible," Google Dictionary.

of, the main domestic spaces, marked by borders or fences. These yards might include detached kitchens and "slave gardens."

Records of the use of detached kitchens are found in European history, but in Atlantic colonial spaces, detached kitchens probably owe their existence to imported African traditions, though based on African social, not environmental concerns, within a traditional African family compound. When Africans became enslaved cooks and servants to Europeans in the Caribbean, they also introduced their traditions for how and where food was prepared. Atlantic colonial detached kitchens likely also served specific Caribbean social and environmental conditions: Cooking in an outbuilding kept its smells, heat, and threat of fire out of the main house. In plantation settings, it would also keep enslaved people who served as cooks and servers out of the main house to do the bulk of their work. Perhaps ironically, scholars have noted that for these domestic enslaved peoples, detached kitchens, relegated to the outskirts of the main house, may have served as spaces of some privacy and power.

While plantation kitchens were often located in yards, African and indigenous peoples also kept outdoor kitchens and cooking pits in their own yards, including gardens where enslaved men and women could raise crops and animals for their own use and often to sell in local markets; grow herbs and other plants for medicinal and cosmetic purposes; and cook, either in open-air cooking pits or in detached kitchens. These yards and gardens not only reveal what scholars call Africanisms but have allowed archaeologists and other scholars to study the history of enslaved people's day-to-day lives in new ways—allowing them a more personal identity than had been traditionally given in Western scholarship to enslaved people.

Plantation and Subsistence Crops

Early indigenous Caribbean peoples hunted wild game, gathered plants, and fished. Later, groups developed settled agriculture and ate manioc (cassava), corn, chili peppers, squash, arrowroot, peanuts, and sweet potatoes, along with plentiful seafood. This early diet overlapped with cuisine developed after the sixteenth century as imported goods reached the Caribbean through the Columbian Exchange. While Europeans and Africans were familiar with some indigenous Caribbean foodstuffs and adapted and adopted new foodstuffs, they also remained desirous of their own traditional foods and using traditional cooking methods for comfort in their new homes and lives. The mixture of indigenous, African, and European ingredients and cooking techniques encouraged agriculture and trade in the Atlantic World and the development of a Creole Caribbean cuisine. Some Europeans balked at changing their dietary habits and thus imported, or in the case of wheat, tried unsuccessfully to grow familiar crops in the Caribbean. Others, particularly those in the lower social classes (thus without the means to import foods), used familiar forms of cooking with new ingredients. Africans as well brought culinary traditions and tastes to the Caribbean.

The traditional focus on plantation crops and goods, including sugar, rum, and cattle ranching, in the Caribbean is ubiquitous; however, archaeologists continue to unearth evidence of the parallel agricultural cultures of subsistence and crop farming, notably Caribbean enslaved peoples and **maroon** (*maroon* refers to people of mixed African and indigenous ethnicity) gardens near plantations and in the forests beyond.

Primary Source 2

Two views of gardens, kitchens, and yards reveal the smaller-scale agriculture of enslaved peoples and indigenous Caribbean peoples during colonialism. These sources also reveal the Creole culture that developed on the edges of plantations and away from White planter culture.

On the Topography and Geology of Santo Domingo
William M. Gabb

Little is cultivated on the hills beyond the food necessary for the sustenance of the scattered population; though ... good crops of tobacco are raised for sale ... The men occupy themselves principally in the raising of horses, cattle, goats and pigs, the cultivation of their little garden-patches ... the women, besides their very simple domestic duties, find abundant employment in plaiting the leaf of the "guana" palm into ceroons for tobacco, which command a ready sale in Santiago. ...

Selections from William M. Gabb, "On the Topography and Geology of Santo Domingo," *Transactions of the American Philosophical Society,* vol. 15, no. 1, pp. 54-55. 1873.

Primary Source 3

A Practical View of the Present State of Slavery in the West Indies
Alexander Barclay

The house is divided into three, and sometimes four apartments. The room in the middle, occupying the whole breadth of the house, has a door on each side, to admit a circulation of air. This is the sitting apartment, and here the poorer class make fire and cook their victuals; the more wealthy have a separate kitchen at a little distance. The smaller houses have the sitting room in one end, and two sleeping apartments in the other. Behind the [slave] house is the garden, filled with plantains, ochras, and other vegetables, which are produced at all seasons. It abounds also with cocoa-nut and calabash tree. A good cocoa-nut will be a meal to a man, and boiled among the sugar ... would be a feast to an epicure. It contains also about a pint of a delicious juice, called 'cocoa-nut milk;' the leaves, which are thick, and twelve or fifteen feet long, are shed occasionally all the year round, and not only make excellent fuel, but are sometimes used for thatch. The nut also yields oil for lamps, and the shell is made into cups. Thus one tree affords meat, drink, fuel, thatch, oil for lamps, and cups to drink out of! No wonder it is such a great favourite that every negro [sic] village looks at a distance like a cocoa-nut grove.

...

Selections from Alexander Barclay, "Houses and Gardens of the Negroes, Their Mode of Life, &c" *A Practical View of the Present State of Slavery in the West Indies.* 1827.

They have also their hogsties: poultry houses are not wanted; the chickens are carefully gathered at night, and hung up in baskets, to preserve them from the rats. The fowls lodge at all seasons in the trees about the houses. The premises belonging to each family are commonly surrounded with a fence; their provision grounds are generally at some distance.

...

When they get up at day dawn, the first thing each does is to take his breakfast to the cook. It consists of plantains, edoes, or yams, or a few of each, with a little fresh or salted fish, or crabs, which are very abundant. These articles are sometimes boiled plain, sometimes made into a soup with some other vegetables, according to the various tastes and means of individuals.

...

At twelve o'clock at noon the shell is blown, and they disperse to enjoy two hours of rest, or to employ the time at their own concerns—mending their fences or hogsties, fishing, bathing, washing, carrying home fire-wood, cane-tops, or hog-meat, &c. A few roasted plantains, with a little fish, is all they seem to care about eating in the middle of the day; breakfast and supper being their chief meals. At half-past one o'clock the shell is blown again, and they re-assemble in the field at two.

...

Besides the regular physician who visits the hospital two or three times a week, or oftener if there is occasion, and examines all the patients individually, there is on every estate an 'hospital doctor' and a sick nurse; the former is an intelligent man (most commonly of colour), who, acting for years under the directions of the white doctor, acquires a sufficient knowledge of the common complaints of the negroes, to be capable of administering some simple medicines in cases of slight indisposition ...

Discussion Questions

1. What do these excerpts suggest about the daily lives of enslaved Caribbean peoples outside their forced working hours?
2. List all the flora and fauna mentioned in Primary Source 3; using the internet, find where each originated. What do your results tell you about the effects of the Columbian Exchange on the Caribbean?

Conclusion

The Atlantic World and Columbian Exchange were not just European phenomena—Atlantic **foodways** in places like the Caribbean developed in a melting pot of American (North, South, and Caribbean), European, and African goods and tastes, reimagined in the colonies of the Caribbean

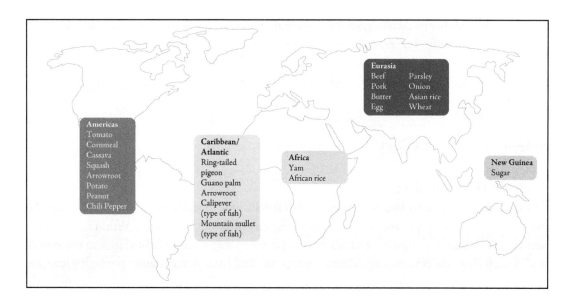

FIGURE 1.4   Origins of selected ingredients.

(Figure 1.4). The material culture of agriculture, cooking, and the spaces they were performed in shaped the Atlantic World early on and developed into important contributions to trans-Atlantic foodways, as two primary sources attest. R. R. Madden gave high praise to Caribbean cooks and cuisine in his 1885 "Life in Jamaica":

> I would back the Sambo [sic] cook of Mr. Cockburn, or the chief de cuisine of his Excellency the Governor, against a synod of French cooks, for serving up a dinner of turtle and calipever, mountain mullets, ring-tailed pigeons, black crabs, and wild guinea-fowl. ...[6]

Julia Davis Chandler's 1905 article, "Food and Cookery in Jamaica," published in *The Boston Cooking School* magazine introduced this trans-Atlantic cuisine to a twentieth-century American audience. Her description of the Jamaican use of salt fish (likely introduced by early Europeans fishing off North American coasts who air-dried and salted the fish to preserve it before shipping hundreds of thousands of tons eastward) reveals how Atlantic fish were combined with a variety of American, European, and African foodstuffs:

> [Despite] the island [being] supplied with varieties of fresh fish from both the ocean and the mountain streams, also with lobsters, shrimps, and crabs, ... Jamaicans are [very fond] of salt fish. It is popular with the natives, and often eaten by the more favored classes. It is prepared in a variety of ways, for instance: curried and served with rice balls; made into a sort of scrapple with cornmeal; baked with yams ... adding plenty of

---

6   R. R. Madden, M. D., "Life in Jamaica," *Atkinson's Casket (1831–1839)*, no. 12 (1835): 687.

butter and chopped parsley; scalded and then fried with onions and tomatoes; baked with eggs, herbs, butter, and tomatoes; and with tomatoes, eggs, skellions, allspice, and parsley made into fritters.[7]

These dishes reveal the bounty of ingredients to be found in the Creole Caribbean kitchen.

Science and Technology

Ecological Imperialism

The ingredients Chandler lists to accompany salt fish include foodstuffs that originated from the Americas, Africa, Europe, and beyond. Part of the creativity of the Atlantic World interactions was the melding of these goods and traditions, yet there was a serious imbalance in the power and wealth these encounters engendered. Europeans and their descendants, through processes of slavery and capitalism, tended to control the political and economic power in the Atlantic World during most of the period this chapter examines (Atlantic revolutions, which began some shifting of economic and political power in the Atlantic World, are discussed below.) In his 1986 *Ecological Imperialism: The Biological Expansion of Europe, 900–1900*, Alfred Crosby argued that the Columbian Exchange's imbalances allowed Europeans, at least in part, to achieve the world power and domination they possessed in the aftermath of the initial European entries into the Americas. Crosby noted the successes of Europeans in transporting their flora and fauna to the Americas, where diseases decimated indigenous populations, creating what appeared to Europeans as open spaces for their settlements and agriculture, allowing their crops to flourish, aided by the coerced labor of enslaved African peoples.

The world history of the spread of luxury consumables like sugar across the globe and their connections to European **imperialism** and the Atlantic Slave Trade led historians like Crosby to craft the term *Ecological Imperialism* following the exchanges of flora, fauna, peoples, and diseases in the Columbian Exchange. The theme of Ecological Imperialism is one that connects to myriad histories: here it is examined as part of science and technology, including agricultural, medical, and botanical sciences and methods.

The Science of Domestication

In a world where many people no longer must think about how their food got from field to table, the long and difficult processes of domesticating plants and animals for maximum human benefit is taken for granted. Furthermore, the global importance of seemingly humble and now ubiquitous foodstuffs—potatoes, for example—has been forgotten. The domestication of plants such as potatoes and corn in the Americas took centuries. Indigenous Americans carefully developed both into reliable crops. Potatoes, for example, preserved by the Inca as *chuño*, held a long shelf life and are surprisingly nutritious.

---

7   Julia D. Chandler, "Food and Cookery in Jamaica," *The Boston Cooking School Magazine of Culinary Science and Domestic Economics* (1897–1914) 9, no. 7 (1905): 372.

Europeans (and others) eventually benefited from American crops, including corn and potatoes, which added an important source of nutritious calories to the diets of peoples around the world. Some historians, including Crosby, argue that adoption of potatoes as a common foodstuff across Europe aided, in no small part, to the "Rise of the West." This rise refers to the relatively rapid rise of Western powers after 1500. The domestication of flora and fauna is a prehistory of modern agricultural and botanical sciences and technology. As flora and fauna spread across the Atlantic during the Columbian Exchange, plants found beneficial to humans led to developments in agriculture, botany, medicine, and food preservation. The materials of this science—plants—came, like the people, from different continents, and in the Caribbean, they too became creolized in the laboratory of colonial science. Like many developments in the Atlantic World, Europeans tended to manipulate the earliest benefits from the exchanges, borrowing from indigenous and African goods and knowledge. European successes in trading, preserving, transplanting, and codifying plants and their uses in the Atlantic World led to both Ecological Imperialism, as Europeans remade American ecosystems for their own uses, and profits, and to developments in medicine and botany, as well as economic gains from new foodstuffs and beverages, medicines, and other crops. The development of botanical gardens, key to these developments, would also lead to conservation efforts stretching into the modern day.

As Europeans encountered plants native to the Americas, they learned from, borrowed, adapted, and sometimes stole through bioprospecting, or **biopiracy** (the use of botanical resources without official sanction), knowledge about, uses for, and even the plants themselves. Thus, bioprospecting and shipping of specimens within the Atlantic World developed as a part of European trade after 1500. An often-overlooked necessity of trading botanical specimens was the need to preserve live or dried plants and their seeds in unstable ships' environments. Sea travel was rife with danger for plants that may have experienced heat, cold, drought, exposure to salt water, harm by shipboard pests (insects and rats), or simple neglect by their shipboard caretakers. Thus, naturalists had to develop new techniques for transporting specimens across the Atlantic from protecting seeds from rot and germination to understanding the specific moisture and soil needs of different plants, as well as techniques to successfully transplant and maintain plants in new environments. This led to communications between naturalists across the ocean, the professionalization of botany (still an emerging field at the time), and the development of Atlantic networks of botanical science and technology. Although much of this knowledge was codified by Europeans, indigenous Americans and others contributed to this knowledge by sharing and teaching Europeans existing agricultural practices, domestication of species, and use of plants for food and medicines.[8] Enslaved African peoples also made crucial contributions as collectors of specimens.[9]

Medical knowledge for treatment of tropical diseases often came from existing indigenous remedies, and Europeans often adapted medicines and treatments they learned (and sometimes

---

8   See, for example, Londa L. Schiebinger, *Plants and Empire: Colonial Bioprospecting in the Atlantic World* (Cambridge, MA: Harvard University Press, 2004) and Daniel Headrick, "Botany, Chemistry, and Tropical Development," *Journal of World History* 7, no. 1 (1996): 1–20.

9   Sam Kean, "Historians Expose Early Scientists' Debt to the Slave Trade," *Science*, April 4, 2019. https://www.sciencemag.org/news/2019/04/historians-expose-early-scientists-debt-slave-trade

coerced) from indigenous and enslaved peoples. Shamefully, White doctors also experimented on slaves to test and develop new treatments for White colonists. At the same time, Africans brought their traditional medical knowledge with them, including medicinal plants and seeds brought intentionally and unintentionally on slave ships. Native Caribbean practices added to creole Caribbean medical practices and contributed to new understanding of injuries, such as bites from indigenous poisonous species, to the use of medicinal plants, such as the Jamaican pepper plant *pimenta dioica*, more commonly known as allspice. Allspice has long been used in the Caribbean for a variety of maladies, including aches and pains and indigestion. It is recognized today for those uses as well as showing potential for some cancer treatments. Enslaved peoples not only treated themselves and their communities with traditional or local cures, but their medical prowess often became legitimized in their owners' eyes, and some were given responsibilities as doctors, nurses, or midwives in plantation systems.

Botanical Gardens

From the exchanges of flora and fauna in the Atlantic World, biological sciences blossomed, and botanical sciences in particular became institutionalized in the spread of botanical gardens, which served both as venues for entertainment and education, where visitors could see plants from across the ocean, and spaces where botanists could classify, attempt to adapt, and finesse technological, medicinal, and consumptive uses of plants caught up in the Columbian Exchange. Botanical gardens sprang up in Europe and the Caribbean, as the examples of Kew Gardens, just outside London, and the St. Vincent Botanical Garden in the Caribbean (Figure 1.5) illustrate. These gardens served as public displays of **empire** and **colony,** as well as laboratories and greenhouses for scientists—today they are often on the forefront of conservation efforts.

Aided by indigenous and enslaved peoples, European explorers collected plants and seeds during their travels into the Atlantic World. They also learned hands-on botany in caring for what to Europeans were exotic plants. British botanists learned that some plants could only thrive in hothouses or environments similar to their native environments. As interest in "exotic" flora grew, spurred by economic and scientific interests, groups like the Royal Society of Arts offered financial prizes for successful cultivation of colonial flora. This spurred the development of botanical gardens.

In St. Vincent, for example, General Robert Melville and Dr. George Young established a botanical garden by 1773. The infamous mutiny of HMS *Bounty* played a role here as well—William Bligh's mission included delivering breadfruit to the garden, and on his eventual return to England, he delivered 465 pots of plants to Kew Gardens outside London.[10] In 1775, Jamaica established a botanical garden in response to the successes in St. Vincent. Trinidad opened botanical gardens in 1818 and by 1897 held vast species of plants for sale, including nutmeg. These gardens, following contemporary practices, engaged in specimen collection via biopiracy: botanical cargo was seized from indigenous peoples or even rival botanists to add goods such as mango, cinnamon, and plums to the gardens' wealth.

---

10   Botanic Gardens Conservation International, "St Vincent Botanical Garden." http://www.bgci.org/garden.php?id=314

FIGURE 1.5   View of the Botanical Garden in St. Vincent.

Botanical gardens in the Atlantic World spurred significant agricultural experimentation and innovation in the domestication of cash crops, foodstuffs, and flora that offered economic and scientific (often medical) findings. These plant products often came with great financial rewards. Strains of sea island cottons, for example, cultivated in places like the St. Vincent garden, produced a sought-after luxury cotton cloth. St. Vincent was also the largest producer of arrowroot starch, used as a gluten-free flour or thickening agent, and its production and export from the island remains a viable industry today.

Conclusion

The spread of agriculture, flora, and fauna in the Atlantic World during the Columbian Exchange was a facet of science and technology in this world system. Europeans, however, monopolized the benefits of the Columbian Exchange creating what scholars have defined as ecological imperialism, in which Europeans directed agriculture, botany, and resulting commerce and industry to the detriment of indigenous peoples and landscapes. In addition, the contributions of indigenous peoples and enslaved Africans to Atlantic World agriculture and botany were discounted, and these groups did not reap the benefits of their labor. Despite these inequities, the Columbian Exchange and legacies made significant contributions to modern science and technology.

Gender and Sexuality

Intersectionality: Gender, Sexuality, Race, and Class

The diverse human geography of the Atlantic World created complex social and political settings. Historians note the crisscrossing or intersectionality of gender and sexuality, race, and class in colonial spaces. Gender, sexuality, race, and class became significantly complex among diverse colonial populations who also possessed different ancestral origins. Identity groups were often unbalanced: Europeans were outnumbered by people of color—including indigenous and those of African descent— and White men tended to outnumber White women. This led in part to the growth of a new "mixed-race" population, which created new tensions related to the intersections of race, class, sexuality, and gender.

Some White men raised their mixed-race children as heirs; this led to concerns over the rights—political and social—of mixed-race populations who were granted, or demanded, increasing social and political equality in colonial settings. Tensions also arose between European-born colonists and people of European descent born in the colonies; between White women and women of color; and between free and enslaved people of color. These tensions played out in social, legal, and cultural settings.

Colonial Mexico's *casta* paintings provide fascinating insight into Spanish attempts to order and control diverse populations and reveal their attention to issues of race, class, gender, and sexuality within a mixed-race society (Figure 1.6). Using pseudoscientific methods misapplied from scientific methods for classifying species, *casta* paintings contained sets of frames, each depicting a separate caste based on race, lineage, and social standing. Each frame typically portrayed a father, mother, and their child in domestic scenes that included depictions of local flora and fauna, landscape, and domesticity. The paintings reveal Spanish desires for a racial hierarchy based on race, keeping those of "pure," or White, Spanish blood ascendant. They also suggest Spanish norms for gender and social roles. Scholars note that these paintings did not reveal reality in the colonies and that identities, because they were intersectional (based on race, class, and gender) were more fluid than the *casta* paintings suggest.

The 1808 novel *The Woman of Colour: A Tale* also reveals standards and fluidity in race and gender in Atlantic colonial settings. Olivia Fairfield, the novel's protagonist, is the mixed-race daughter of a White slave owner and a Black woman who lives on his plantation. The story follows the orphaned Olivia on her way to London to marry her White English cousin and secure her inheritance. The novel explores Olivia's experiences and reflections on gender, race, class, and citizenship in the British Empire. Olivia's story illustrates ideas and tensions prominent in the early nineteenth century, including debates about the abolition of slavery. Olivia herself reveals the complexities and contradictions in gender and sexuality in racialized spaces. Olivia, as an upper-class, mixed-race woman, is depicted as beautiful, virtuous, and light-skinned—at the time, characteristics associated with White women rather than women of color. Olivia reveals how identities could shift dependent on specific situations in colonial societies.

Español con India.
Mestizo.

Mestizo con Española.
Castizo.

Castizo con Española.
Español.

Español con Negra.
Mulato.

5

6

7

Mulato con Española.
Morisco.

Morisco con Española.
Chino.

Chino con India.
Salta atrás.

Salta atrás con Mulata.
Lobo.

9

10

11

12

Lobo con China.
Gibaro.

Gibaro con Mulata.
Albarazado

Albarazado con Negra.
Canbujo.

Canbujo con India.
Sanbaigo.

13

14

15

16

Sanbaigo con Loba.
Calpamulato.

Calpamulato con Canbuja.
Tente en el Aire.

Tente en el Aire con Mulata.
Noteentiendo.

Noteentiendo con India.
Tornaatras.

FIGURE 1.6   Eighteenth-century Mexican *Casta* Painting, Museo Nacional del Virreinato, Tepotzotlán, Mexico.

FIGURE 1.7   Agostino Brunias, *Linen Market, Dominica*, Google Art Project.

Colonial women were classified not just by their gender and class, but by race, and by race in various modes of sexuality (Figure 1.7). White middle- and upper-class European women tended to be idealized as sweet, innocent, and compliant, if not overly intellectual, with unblemished fair skin. This was in contrast to creole White women, those born in the colonies, who were viewed as degraded by their experiences in the colonies—in gender, race, and class—by their exposure to mixed-race, indigenous, and Black men and women, as well as the tropical climate. Black women were often viewed as harsh, headstrong, and wanton, although often sexually desirable as mistresses—not wives—for White men.

White men, who far outnumbered White women, described this desire as fraught with danger—White men, sources reveal, found Black women both wildly attractive and noxiously repellent—but it is clear from the growing mixed-race populations in the colonies that **miscegenation** (a historical term for a sexual relationship between people considered to be of different races) was widespread. Upper-class White women were often instrumental in creating stereotypes about lower-class White and Black women to protect their own social standing in the colonies.

The tensions of gender, race, and class would, however, also lead to calls for abolition, emancipation, and revolution in the Atlantic World, and women, regardless of race or class, played a role in all three—from British sugar boycotts protesting slavery to women's rights efforts that included female freedom fighters in revolutionary movements for women's rights and **decolonization**.

Women's Rights in the Atlantic World

Women engaged in the Atlantic World in a variety of ways. As noted, British women participated in abolition movements through sugar boycotts. French women, like Olympe de Gouges, called for women's rights during the French Revolution. In fact, the Atlantic Revolutions saw women such as Abigail Adams and Manuela Sáenz (Figure 1.8) (Americas), Mary Wollstonecraft and De Gouges (Europe), and Cécile Fatiman and Nanny (Caribbean) demanding new rights. Each woman will be discussed in more detail below.

Adams used her influence in the US Revolutionary War and Continental Congress to advance claims for securing more power and protection for married women and achieving better educational opportunities for women. Her often-used and memorable argument to "remember the ladies" would be echoed by other revolutionary age feminists. Sáenz, like Adams, used her social standing

FIGURE 1.8   Manuela Sáenz.

in South American society and political spheres to advocate for women's rights, as well as to engage through salons (private intellectual and political gatherings) and written correspondence with leading revolutionary leaders as South Americans rebelled against Spanish rule. Her work not only benefited the series of revolutions that swept Spanish-controlled South America, but aided in stabilizing new nations like Peru, and, through her work, she actively challenged gender norms that relegated women to the private, rather than public, spheres of society.

If middle- and upper-class women were forgotten by revolutionaries in the Atlantic World, so were lower-class women and in the colonies, women of color. Cécile Fatiman and Nanny, both

Primary Source 4

Mary Wollstonecraft and Olympe de Gouges worked to reshape women's rights in Europe. In France, De Gouges's "Declaration of the Rights of Woman" (1791) and in England, Wollstonecraft's "A Vindication of the Rights of Woman" (1792) pointed out the hypocrisies of calling for freedom and equality and "the rights of man" but continuing to leave women out of the public sphere. Both Wollstonecraft and De Gouges argued that women should be educated, allowed to seek professions outside the home, and granted political and social rights in the public sphere— only then could the newly enlightened and revolutionary societies of Europe reach their full potentials.

A Vindication of the Rights of Woman: With Strictures on Moral and Political Subjects

Mary Wollstonecraft

Chapter II. The prevailing opinion of a sexual character discussed

To account for, and excuse the tyranny of man, many ingenious arguments have been brought forward to prove, that the two sexes, in the acquirement of virtue, ought to aim at attaining a very different character: or, to speak explicitly, women are not allowed to have sufficient strength of mind to acquire what really deserves the name of virtue. Yet it should seem, allowing them to have souls, that there is but one way appointed by Providence to lead *mankind* to either virtue or happiness.

If then women are not a swarm of ephemeron triflers, why should they be kept in ignorance under the specious name of innocence? Men complain, and with reason, of the follies and caprices of our sex, when they do not keenly satirize our head-strong passions and groveling vices. Behold, I should answer, the natural effect of ignorance! The mind will ever be unstable that has only prejudices to rest on, and the current will run with destructive fury when there are no barriers to break its force. Women are told from their infancy, and taught by the example of their mothers, that a little knowledge of human weakness, justly termed cunning, softness or temper, *outward* obedience, and a scrupulous attention to a puerile kind of propriety, will obtain for them the protection of man; and should they be beautiful, every thing else is needless, for, at least, twenty years of their lives.

Thus Milton describes our first frail mother; though when he tells us that women are formed for softness and sweet attractive grace, I cannot comprehend his meaning, unless ... he meant to deprive us of souls, and insinuate that we were beings only designed by sweet attractive grace, and docile blind obedience, to gratify the senses of man when he can no longer soar on the wing of contemplation.

How grossly do they insult us who thus advise us only to render ourselves gentle, domestic brutes! For instance, the winning softness so warmly, and frequently, recommended, that governs by obeying. What childish expression, and how insignificant is the being—can it be an immortal one? who will condescend to govern by such sinister methods! 'Certainly,' says Lord Bacon, 'man is of kin to the beasts by his body; and if he be not of kin to God by his spirit, he is a base and ignoble creature!' Men, indeed, appear to me to act in a very unphilosophical manner when they try to secure the good conduct of women by attempting to keep them always in a state of childhood. Rousseau was more consistent when he wished to stop the progress of reason in both sexes, for if men eat of the tree of knowledge, women will come in for a taste; but, from the imperfect cultivation which their understandings now receive, they only attain a knowledge of evil.

Selection from Mary Wollstonecraft, "The Prevailing Opinion of a Sexual Character Discussed," *A Vindication of the Rights of Woman: with Strictures on Moral and Political Subjects,* pp. 39-41. 1792.

Children, I grant, should be innocent; but when the epithet is applied to men, or women, it is but a civil term for weakness. For if it be allowed that women were destined by Providence to acquire human virtues, and by the exercise of their understandings, that stability of character which is the firmest ground to rest our future hopes upon, they must be permitted to turn to the fountain of light, and not forced to shape their course by the twinkling of a mere satellite.

Discussion Question

1. How does Wollstonecraft believe men view women? Why? How does she suggest this view might be changed?

women of color in Caribbean colonies, used their Creole culture and social status in revolutionary actions against European imperial powers. Fatiman, a voodoo priestess, is credited with leading a 1791 ceremony in Saint Domingue (Haiti) that marked the beginning of the Haitian Revolution. Although born to an African mother and Corsican prince, Fatiman had been sold into slavery as a child; she married Louis Michel Pierrot, a leading revolutionary and later president of Haiti. Nanny, as she is known, like Fatiman, was also a spiritual leader. Her leadership of Windward Maroons (escaped enslaved peoples) in Jamaica, however, also included cultural and military leadership: From "Nanny Town," founded in 1720, she directed hundreds of people engaged in preserving their Afro-Caribbean culture, freeing enslaved people, and ending British rule in Jamaica. Her successes—she is credited with freeing hundreds of people—made her a national hero in Jamaica. Her image graces the Jamaican $500 bill.

Conclusion

Gender and sexuality played important roles in Atlantic World societies and cultures. They were also tied to issues of race and class, especially in the colonies. Although some groups—White women and men and women of color—faced inequality and inequities as a result of their gender or race, or in the case of women of color, both—women played important roles in shaping Atlantic World societies, cultures, and politics. Women also played important roles in revolutionary movements for women's equality, abolition of the slave trade, and emancipation movements for marginalized peoples.

War, Peace, and Diplomacy

Global Warfare in the Sixteenth and Seventeenth Centuries

Constantine XI (r. 1449–1453), last of the Byzantine emperors, witnessed a formidable Ottoman army preparing to attack in April 1453. Many of the troops carried weapons and armor that would not have surprised Emperor Constantine I (r. 306–337), who laid the foundations for Constantinople, an imperial capital protected by nature and powerful walls. These defenses repelled numerous enemies; the city was only captured by outsiders once before in 1204, during the Fourth Crusade.

Both Constantines would have recognized the spears, swords, bows, chain mail armor, shields, and other military gear carried by the soldiers of Sultan Mehmet II (r. 1451–1481). Massive **bombards**, using gunpowder to hurl large stones with considerable force were another matter altogether. While Constantine XI had a few small cannons, these were dwarfed by the gigantic Ottoman siege guns.

Such artillery could knock down even the vaunted walls of Constantinople. The bombards' weak point was the lengthy time needed for reloading. The defenders, directed by the Italian adventurer Giovanni Giustiniani (1418–1453), could repair breaches before they became large enough for the Ottomans to send their more numerous infantry into the city. Still, the need to continually repair, plus casualties, including Giustiniani himself, sapped Byzantine morale. Although the siege lasted nearly two months, the city fell on 30 May 1453.

While gunpowder weapons were only partially responsible for the Ottoman capture of Constantinople, the story of Mehmet's giant cannon pulling down the legendary defenses of the city spread far and wide. The victory was not only dramatic; the fall of Constantinople opened the Balkans to greater Ottoman aggression. Renamed Istanbul, this was now headquarters for the sultan and his government. Their presence focused Ottoman energies toward Budapest, Vienna, and Kraków. The subjugation of Constantinople in 1453 fits the bill for calling this a decisive battle in world history.

It also connects us to the story of gunpowder, which started in China circa 1000, when the explosive powder was first used to make weapons. Within three centuries this technology had spread across Eurasia to the Middle East and Europe. Although the new gunpowder weapons were mainly designed to kill soldiers, commanders soon realized that enough explosive power could knock down defenses.

Zahir-ud-din Muhammad Babur (r. 1497–1530) used Turkish gunners and musketeers to defeat the Lodi Kingdom at Panipat (1526). Babur's access to gunpowder technology was a deciding factor in this battle, causing both casualties and fear among the defenders, who lacked such weapons. Here is another example of a decisive victory, for Babur's success allowed him to establish the Mughal Dynasty—a political force in the Indian subcontinent until 1857.

Gunpowder weapons were just as effective in Europe. One often thinks of the English with their long bows winning victories during the Hundred Years War at Crecy (1346) or Agincourt (1415), yet Joan of Arc and succeeding French commanders used gunpowder weapons to overturn these victories. At Castillon (1453), French soldiers armed with cannon defeated the last major British force, ending this conflict in favor of France.

Even on the seas, gunpowder created decisive advantages for smart admirals. This was evident during Japanese efforts to conquer Korea in the 1590s. **Yi Sun-sin** (1545–1598), serving Korea's Joseon Dynasty, designed the **Geobukseon** ("Turtle Ship"), the first armored warship in history. Armed with cannon and incendiary weapons, these destroyed several flotillas of Japanese invaders.

With gunpowder playing a part in so many different victories, the message was clear: embrace the new weapons system or place your troops at a considerable disadvantage. Taking on a technology could be as simple as Babur obtaining Turkish mercenaries and their gear. That was a start, but the founder of the Mughal Dynasty next invested considerable resources to train technicians who could cast cannon, construct matchlock muskets, or produce gunpowder. He also needed to teach soldiers how to successfully operate the new weapons, and since these were more complicated than swords or **pikes**, there was also the need for officers capable of employing more sophisticated tactics. Extra expenses required taxes, bureaucrats to collect them, and ministers to supervise their work. Gunpowder enhanced state power, but also forced nations to dramatically increase their revenue flow.

Gunpowder revolutionized warfare at a much more rapid pace than the introduction of bronze or iron weapons in ancient China or Greece. As matchlock yielded to **flintlock**, which in turn was surpassed by percussion muskets, individual soldiers could fire more rapidly and at longer range. Cannons evolved at the same time, while spin-off technologies like explosive shells, rifling, and multi-shot weapons further sped the race to have the most dangerous weapons on earth.

And woe betide the general whose nation could not afford or made light of the new systems. This spelled disaster for Shah Ismail I at Chaldiran (1514). His *Qizilbash* troopers had defeated numerous Iranian opponents and crushed the same Uzbeks who chased Babur to India. Uninterested in matchlock muskets or cannon, Ismail and his men attacked with traditional weapons and were mowed down by Ottoman cannon plus the massed volleys of Janissary musketeers.

China faced a similar problem during the **First Opium War** (1839–1840) with Great Britain. Consider the appropriately named *HMS **Nemesis***, a British iron-hulled steamer armed with rifled cannon that fired explosive shells. It wreaked havoc, destroying Chinese warships, bombarding ports, and as China's naval technology was far behind that of England, *Nemesis* suffered no significant damage in return. Half a century later, at **Omdurman** in the Sudan, an Anglo-Egyptian army armed with repeating rifles, breach-loading artillery, and machine guns crushed the Mahdi's *Ansar* (warriors) in another lopsided victory that demonstrated the value of advanced technology.

Neither the Iranians in 1514, Chinese in 1839, nor the Sudanese in 1898 were cowards or saddled with incompetent leaders. Rather, they were dramatically outclassed in military technology. They could not compete in a traditional set-piece battle, and their state structure did not allow for embracing asymmetrical warfare as practiced by twenty-first-century forces like Afghanistan's *Taliban*.

So, is warfare driven by technological change? Were there revolutionary moments, where Mehmet's bombards or Yi's turtle ships changed the course of history? Or were these more evolutionary than revolutionary?

These are questions have been hotly debated by historians since the 1950s. Michael Roberts (1908–1966) and Geoffrey Parker would answer yes, while Jeremy Black argues very much to the contrary. Other critics see a Eurocentric focus as obscuring similar developments in the non-Western world. Readers are encouraged to dig deeper, read more, and remember that history is both art and science, meaning this debate may prove more lasting than the walls of Constantinople.

War and Society in the Sixteenth Century

This military technology paradigm became obvious in the 1500s. Europeans, and to a lesser extent the Ottoman and Chinese empires, used advanced weapons systems to expand their territories.

The former, especially Atlantic rim states with a maritime tradition, exploited these advantages to the fullest.

While Spain captured the greatest rewards in the long term, neighboring Portugal expanded trading posts along the coast of Africa in the early 1500s after **Vasco da Gama** circumvented the continent to gain access to the many desirable products of the Indian subcontinent. Some of these formed the basis for future colonies like Angola, Guinea, or Mozambique—parts of the Portuguese Empire until the 1970s. Traveling there in the 1500s was possible due to new ship designs like the **carrack**. Weighing upward of 1,000 tons and carrying three masts with a multitude of sails, these were hardy designs that could travel across oceans.

As they did so, Portuguese sailors established outposts, which created tensions with Arab city-states on the Swahili coast, plus Mamluk Egypt, Safavid Iran, and numerous polities in the Indian subcontinent. As carracks traveled further eastward, they infringed on the trade monopolies of Muslim rulers located in the modern nations of Malaysia and Indonesia. The resulting violence was partially religious. Portugal was a Catholic state whose kings maintained a crusading tradition, and the various Muslim leaders, whether *Sunni* or *Shia*, were equally ready to respond with calls for *jihad* (religious struggle). Still, the most significant motivation was trade routes and local resources.

Spanish **conquistadors** held similar views during their invasion of the New World. They fought for "gold, glory, and God," but modern readers can safely assume that gold was their primary motivation. **Hernán Cortés** (1485–1547) started this trend when he landed on the coast of modern Mexico and marched toward the capital of the Aztec Empire. The Spaniards brought horses, metal armor, cannon, and matchlock muskets—all tremendously more lethal than the stone-tipped weapons and **linen** armor of Aztec warriors, but not enough to explain how 3,000 *conquistadors* could defeat their far more numerous opponents.

Aztec rule was heavy handed, and numerous native leaders were poised to rebel. Spain's advantage was not just gunpowder, but also diplomacy; Cortés portrayed his superior troops as the spearhead of an alliance that would overthrow the hated Aztec suzerainty over central Mexico. Thousands of local men subjugated to Aztec misrule joined his banner. It was the additional manpower, plus superior military technology and smallpox, that allowed Cortés to capture Tenochtitlan in 1521. Francisco Pizarro (1471–1541) also benefited from local political disputes during his conquest of the Inca Empire.

As New World gold and silver flowed back to Spain in quantities sufficient to inflate prices across the world, the conquistadors' success spurred others to seek riches through imperial adventures. Gold was the first choice, but Canadian furs helped expand the French economy, while the Dutch sought to dominate spice. In 1621 they landed troops on the Banda Islands, killed or enslaved most of the inhabitants, and half a century later, traded Manhattan to Great Britain to get Banda back and maintain a monopoly on the production and sale of nutmeg.

Other imperialists were less successful. Toyotomi Hideyoshi (1537–1598) fought brilliant campaigns that unified Japan under his rule. He sought to expand Japanese influence onto mainland Asia and organized several expeditions to take control of Korea. His soldiers were veterans, armed with excellent traditional and modern weapons, but they ran into a superior strategist—a self-taught admiral, Yi Sun-sin (1545–1598).

With no previous naval experience, Yi ordered the construction of large ships called *Geobuk-seon*, protected by iron armor and armed with a mix of cannon and catapults. He also secured the services of experienced pilots who knew the Korean coast. Taking advantage of tides and shallows, he lured several Japanese flotillas into disastrous defeats. At the Noryang Straits in 1598, Yi directed a smaller but technologically superior Chinese-Korean fleet that destroyed or captured 40 percent of Japan's **armada**. Yi's death at the moment of victory, caused by a musket bullet, guaranteed his place in Korea's historical pantheon would be like Horatio Nelson's in Great Britain.

Superior naval technology helped Portugal dominate trading centers on the coast of Eastern Africa, plus southern India, and among the "spice islands" of modern Indonesia. Portuguese carracks, each powered by wind hitting a complex set of canvas sails, started arriving in the Red Sea during the 1500s. Armed with ship-killing cannon, these were more than enough to overpower local naval units sailing in dhows or galleys.

Portuguese ships were faster, more robust, and could damage or sink enemy vessels outside the range at which they could shoot back. Thus, if faced with overwhelming force, the Portuguese could retreat, but more likely they would devastate an enemy flotilla while suffering little damage in return. The next step was to land troops, seize key ports like Hormuz (1515) or Macau (1557), then fortify the city, leave a garrison behind, and have a position that gave them dominance over local products and trade routes.

If given enough time, European invaders also gained advantage from superior military engineering. Starting in the late 1400s, fortress construction started to consider the impact of gunpowder weapons. Walls became thicker and lower, with purpose-designed platforms for defending artillery, all protected by deep ditches. Cannon were placed to provide enfilade fire, allowing them to strike at more vulnerable flanks, which guaranteed a better chance to cause casualties among attacking enemies.

The *Trace Italienne* Fortress

This system rapidly evolved as a response to the French invasion of Italy in 1494. Armed with heavy bombards, French armies destroyed traditional castles or captured cities, not in months, according to eyewitness Francesco Guicciardini, "but in days or hours." With French armies moving up and down the peninsula until 1559, locals responded with the low thick walls plus enfiladed fire patterns and dubbed this the *trace Italienne*.

These new defenses were expensive; indeed, the city of Sienna went bankrupt in 1544 after tearing down old walls and replacing them with those that met the *trace Italienne* standards. Cost was not simply that of labor and materials but also the need for skilled workers, and above all, a well-trained military engineer, who often left a lieutenant behind to supervise maintenance and direct the defense of the new system during war. Within a century, men like France's **Sébastien de Vauban** (1633–1707) became highly sought-after experts who straddled the globe with their star-shaped fortifications.

Despite the heavy costs, these new fortifications greatly enhanced defenders' chances to survive a siege. Malta in 1565 is a good example. Another formidable Ottoman army descended on this island, complete with significant naval assets and plenty of artillery. The outnumbered defenders effectively used their *trace Italienne* system to hold out until reinforcements arrived, and the Ottomans retreated. For African, Asian, or New World enemies, who did not possess modern siege artillery, a European new-model fortress was formidable.

Force Projection via Naval Power

These European bases, like Vera Cruz in Mexico or Mombasa in East Africa, could also serve as jumping-off points for further expansion. Most of South and Central America was conquered by Spain in this manner, establishing a long presence which planted Spanish language and culture so strongly, these regions are now dubbed Latin America.

Portugal used bases in Africa and India to alter the balance of power in the Horn of Africa. Under Francisco de Almeida (1450–1510), the Portuguese secured a great victory over the combined navy of several Muslim powers off Diu, India, in 1509. This emboldened them to intervene in a conflict between Christian Ethiopia and Muslim Somalia. The latter, under Imam **Axmad Ibraahim** (1506–1543) had hired Ottoman matchlock gunners like Babur and used these to great advantage. Axmad Ibraahim (aka Ahmad ibn Ibrahim) was a gifted and charismatic commander who parlayed his skills and technology to repeatedly defeat the Ethiopians. Portugal, viewing all Muslim states as potential enemies, sent troops, muskets, and gunpowder to the Ethiopians. These negated the Somali tech advantage, providing a morale boost to the Ethiopians. At Wayna Daga in 1543, Somali invaders were decisively defeated by an Ethiopian-Portuguese army.

Spain was far less successful using naval power to influence events close to home. Already fighting a religious war against the Ottoman Empire, Philip II (1527–1598) diverted attention from this struggle by attacking Protestant Christians in the Low Countries. This resulted in rebellion, fueled by the "Sea Beggars"—Protestant corsairs who not only captured Spanish merchant shipping but freed coastal towns from Philip's authority. Their actions encouraged more revolutionaries, which guaranteed a long struggle with Spain.

Despite the vast treasure fleets bringing New World gold and silver to Spain, even Philip II faced limitations on what was possible for a sixteenth-century monarch attempting to fight a global war. This became clear after he simultaneously attempted to continue his campaign in the Low Countries and overthrow Elizabeth I (1533–1603) of England in 1588.

Philip sent his *Armada* to conquer Britain. It was a mix of massive galleons, improved carracks, galleys, and galleasses, the latter combining sail and oar power for movement. The officers and crews of this fleet were trained for close combat and boarding, where sailors and marines would jump onto an enemy ship and fight hand-to-hand until it surrendered. Spanish sailors had done well using these techniques against their Ottoman counterparts in the Mediterranean.

The British fleet was more focused on maneuvers and long-range artillery fire. The officers and men from these ships were highly skilled and had the advantage of fighting on familiar waters. Toss in bad weather that impacted more on the Spaniards, plus fire-ships—crewless vessels filled with combustibles, set afire, then cut loose in hopes a favorable wind would carry these toward a Spanish ship—and the combination spelled disaster, with only a small remnant of the *Armada* returning to Spain.

Russia was more successful. Employing Cossack proxies, tsarist agents used rivers to reach deep into Siberia. Leading men armed with muskets and small cannon, the near legendary Yermak Timofeyevich (d. 1545) became a Russian *conquistador*. His example encouraged Russians to see their east as Americans once viewed the west. As in Mexico, a combination of sound leadership, smallpox, and gunpowder weapons greatly increased Russian chances for victory. By 1645, Cossack *ostrogs* (forts) stood on the Amur River, occupying territory claimed by China.

Trends in Warfare During the Sixteenth Century

Several key points reflect changes in warfare during the 1500s. Although many traditional weapons still had a place on the battlefield, their singular employment often led to disaster, like the Iranian cavalry at Chaldiran. This was also clear in Europe, where once-vaunted Swiss mercenaries suffered repeated defeats during the French invasion of the Italys. Previously, blocks of Swiss infantry, armed mainly with long pikes or halberds, could charge home with great success against enemy infantry or stand their ground against even heavily armored knights. At Marignano (1515), Bicocca (1522), and the Sesia River (1524), artillery and musket fire decimated Swiss columns.

Pikes—spears from 14–18 feet long—still had a place on the battlefield, but only if used in combination with muskets. The latter could fire only twice a minute and were not especially accurate. Their efficacy came from mass firing along with protection by pike-wielding comrades, whose presence kept horsemen from charging home while the musketeers were reloading their weapons. Spaniards were the first to recognize the benefit of this combined arms approach. Their *tercio* was a unit of roughly 3,000 soldiers, with roughly one-third armed with muskets, another third with pikes, and a final third with swords and bucklers (small shields).

Infantrymen, armed with long pikes and matchlocks, were a potent force on the battlefield. Mounted soldiers, cavalry, were required to scout, attack the flanks of enemy forces, and most important, chase down a retreating army to guarantee a decisive victory. Both cavalry and infantry were supported by gunpowder artillery, used to blast opponents on a battlefield or knock holes in the walls of the *trace Italienne* fortress.

On the high seas, carracks, and later galleons, were large oceangoing ships propelled by sophisticated square and lateen sails. With highly trained officers and crew, these vessels could transport soldiers, artillery, and cargo. They provided access to the entire globe and were vital for the support of European imperialism in the sixteenth century.

Above all else, this century showed martial power required increased flow of revenues into state coffers. Whether carracks and their crews, artillery, or *trace Italienne* forts, there were a myriad of costs involved in equipping, training, and maintaining state-of-the-art military machines. Great powers not only possessed potent armies and navies but expanded bureaucracies, enhanced fiscal systems, and more central authority. While these factors have been part of history since the first civilizations, the institutional growth of government advanced more rapidly during the 1500s.

Increased militarization had its critics. Dutch scholar **Hugo Grotius** (1583–1645), who once escaped prison hidden in a large bookcase, reflects this. Disgusted with the eighty years of war between Holland and Spain followed by the **Thirty Years' War** in the Germanys, Grotius authored *De Jure Belli ac Pacis* (On the Law of War and Peace) in 1625. He argued for rules regarding warfare to limit the destructive power of generals and their armies.

War and Society in the Seventeenth Century

Massive conflicts like the Manchu invasion of China (1644–1683) or central Europe's Thirty Years' War (1618–1648) focus our attention for war's impact on the seventeenth century. The former provided the last case of northern invaders wresting the "Mandate of Heaven" from an established dynasty. The latter devastated the Germanys to levels unmatched until the Second World War.

Manchu leaders had spent the previous 20 years preparing a potent military machine, one that copied many ideas from their southern enemies. Both Manchu and Chinese forces featured a mix of traditional weapons—lances, swords, bows, etc.—plus muskets, artillery, and rockets. Manchu generals benefited from divisions within the Chinese government, plus a long tradition that belittled military service.

The Thirty Years' War was an equally intense struggle, fought mainly in the Germanys and Bohemia. Part political and part religious, it pitted Catholics versus Protestants and produced horrible atrocities like the **Sack of Magdeburg** (1631), where 20,000 civilians were murdered and most of the town burned. On the battlefield, from diseases spread by marching armies or through famine due to requisitioned food, by war's end, many German states counted losses of one-quarter to one-third of their populations.

Hard men who joined the armies of both sides fought with pikes and muskets, as well as an assortment of bladed weapons. Many of these men were mercenaries, like Carlo Fantom (d. 1643), who was satisfied fighting for any side if they provided him with cash and "handsome women." For the Germans, the problem was these men were often paid very late, and their hostility over the arrears could be vented on local civilians.

A few soldiers of fortune had a very different experience. **Albrecht von Wallenstein** (1583–1634), a Bohemian nobleman serving with the Catholic forces, became one of the wealthiest men in Europe from his ability to organize mercenary armies. His political skill sets were less acute and conspiring with the enemy led to Von Wallenstein's assassination.

On German battlefields during the Thirty Years' War, Swedish generals introduced new tactics which set standards for all to copy. Under their brilliant king **Gustav II Adolf** (1594–1632), the Swedes repeatedly defeated pro-Catholic Imperialists and established themselves as a European power. These innovations were so important that military historians consider this the beginning of modern warfare.

Sweden's success had Dutch antecedents. Maurice of Orange (1567–1625) was first a general, then *stadtholder*, or chief executive of the Netherlands. A key leader during the long war with Spain, Maurice created a very effective military machine. He stressed training officers and men via drill, attention to logistics, and **volley fire**. The latter called for simultaneous discharge of muskets so that the volume of fire made up for the inaccuracy of individual smooth-bore barrels.

Other innovative ideas came from the Commonwealth of Poland and Lithuania, where cavalry tactics had reached their apogee. Being on the receiving end of these, like the disaster at Kircholm in 1605, the Swedes became graduates of the school of hard knocks. Young King Gustav learned to be a much better cavalry commander in this environment but also took a pistol shot in his back that prevented him from wearing bullet-proof armor, leading to his death at the Battle of Lützen (1632).

Swedish innovation took Maurice as a starting point, added lessons learned against the Poles, and then some of their own ideas. These focused on every branch of their army. Infantry regiments were paired together in brigades, allowing mid-level officers more striking power. Muskets were standardized, making it easier to resupply ammunition. Also, the number of firearms in relation to pikes increased, and Swedish musketeers made use of volley fire, where several ranks stood close together and simultaneously fired. If timed correctly, this could produce a wall of lead bullets so dense, the normally inaccurate smooth-bore musket became quite lethal. Swedish musketeers were also mixed with cavalry, allowing for a similar volley fire against enemy mounted troops.

Swedish horsemen benefited from regimental guns, small mobile artillery pulled by teams of horses, which could fire more rapidly for carrying premeasured gunpowder charges. Using the additional firepower support from their artillery and infantry, Swedish cavalry were also trained to press the attack with cold steel. Their Imperial counterparts were more likely to attempt a *caracole*, which called for riders to advance within pistol range, discharge highly inaccurate pistols, then race back, reload, and repeat the procedure. The latter rarely produced results against the new Swedish system.

Sweden's military prowess was very clear at the **Battle of Breitenfeld** (1631). Gustav, fighting with the Protestant side of the Thirty Years' War, had marched to the aid of his Saxon allies. He joined them at a crossroads northwest of Dresden. There he met the Imperialist Army under Johann Tserclaes (1559–1632), which represented the Catholics.

Both armies were about the same size. The Imperialists had well-trained infantry veterans who employed the *tercio* formation. Their mounted arm were crack troopers, mostly heavily armored on large horses. Artillery were traditional heavy guns, handicapped by civilian contractors who wisely removed their oxen or horses from the field, but in doing so ensured the guns were nearly impossible to move. Tserclaes, the Imperialist commander, had never lost a battle; he and his men were confident of success.

This seemed a good bet when a cavalry charge swept most of the Saxon troops off the battlefield. There followed a serious of unpleasant surprises. First, the better-trained Swedish infantrymen, deployed in lines, were more mobile. They formed new positions quickly, covering holes left by the Saxon retreat. Next, with better muskets and volley fire, they sent hails of lead shot that caused considerable casualties and halted the *tercios*. Gustav then took his own cavalry, covered by regimental guns and attached musketeer units, to rout Imperial cavalry on his left flank. He followed this by capturing the Imperial artillery, and because many of his soldiers were cross-trained, was able to point the newly acquired guns on the Imperialist *tercios* and cause more casualties. By this point, Tserclaes veterans had enough. They broke formation and fled the field, leaving gear behind as they attempted to escape Swedish horsemen bent on killing as many as possible.

Nearly 14,000 Imperialist were killed or captured, almost half the original force. All their artillery was abandoned, and these plus other supplies now added to the Swedish inventory. This remarkable victory encouraged numerous German princes to cast their lot with the Protestant forces; even Catholic France, a political enemy of the Imperialists, was now ready to provide much-needed gold to finance Sweden's war machine.

While Sweden provided a prototype for the new model of warfare, soldiers in Africa, Asia, and the Middle East also learned how to benefit from the gunpowder revolution. A good example introduces us to the pirate **Koxinga** (Zheng Sen, 1624–1662), dynastic change in China, and European imperialists on the island of Taiwan.

Northern invaders, Manchu people, overthrew China's **Ming Dynasty** between 1644–1683. Significant numbers of Ming loyalists explain the nearly 40 years needed to secure a Manchu triumph and the establishment of China's last dynasty, the Qing. One of these loyalists was Koxinga, whose father had directed powerful naval forces to bedevil the land-focused Manchu commanders. Using island bases, Ming loyalists were secure from retribution but needed more resources to continue the struggle.

Taiwan (Formosa), a large island over 100 miles from the coast of China, was targeted by Koxinga in 1659. He marshaled an army, complete with gunpowder artillery, to strike at the current rulers of Taiwan—the Dutch. A celebrated siege of Fort Zeelandia resulted, lasting 11 months in 1661–1662.

The Dutch had a well-designed fortress, albeit one with limited supplies of fresh water. The Chinese laid siege, digging trenches to provide cover for infantry, while placing cannon to knock down sections of the wall. These tactics were not especially dissimilar to how a fortress in Europe was attacked. Koxinga took Fort Zeelandia, although he died of malaria a few months after his triumph. His heirs made peace with the Qing, and Taiwan became part of the Chinese, rather than the Dutch, Empire.

A similar triumph for local forces took place in the Persian Gulf 40 years earlier. Hormuz Island was captured by the Portuguese in 1515. They strengthened the fortifications and used the very strategically placed Hormuz to levy tolls of all ships entering or leaving the Persian Gulf.

Iran's Shah Abbas I (r. 1588–1629) allied with England's nascent East India Company to retake Hormuz in 1622. British ships, Iranian soldiers, plus modern artillery were enough to drive the Portuguese from their stronghold.

Idris Alawma (1580–1617) presented another example of the far spread of gunpowder technology. Emperor of Borno, a part of modern Nigeria, his military comprised armored cavalry, Berber camel riders, plus infantry armed with traditional bladed weapons and bows. He supplemented these troops with Ottoman mercenaries who provided training for local musketeers. Borno imported significant numbers of firearms from Tunis and Morocco, and the added firepower played a significant role in Idris Alawma's many victories over neighboring states.

Gunpowder technology clearly offered advantages across the world. It would be a mistake, however, to assume that cannons blasting away were the sole reason for victory. There were plenty of them at the 1683 siege of Vienna. An Ottoman army skillfully employed artillery plus saps—zigzag trenches—that allowed soldiers to approach Vienna's walls under cover. Both sides tunneled under the other's positions to plant explosive charges, but by 8 September, Ottoman forces held the upper hand and were preparing for an assault into the city.

Four days later, a relief army under the command of Jan III Sobieski (r.1674–1696) arrived with a large cavalry component. As elected king of the Commonwealth of Poland and Lithuania, Sobieski brought some of Europe's best horsemen to this battle. The famous *Hussaria*, noted for their eagle-winged armor, combined with German dragoons and even Tatars (Polish Muslims), who fought pro-Ottoman Tatars on this day. They created one of the largest cavalry charges in history, which swept the Ottomans from the field.

Vienna proved a defeat from which the Ottomans never completely recovered. From this point onward, Austrian and Russian armies would press against Ottoman holdings in the Balkans. This was a decisive victory won by very old-fashioned soldiers—technology is important, but it does not guarantee success.

Atlantic Revolutions

As discussed in "Gender and Sexuality: Women's Rights in the Atlantic World," women like Adams, Sáenz, Wollstonecraft, De Gouges, Fatiman, and Nanny embraced, each in their own society and culture, the spirit of the Atlantic Revolutions. In the Atlantic World system between the seventeenth and nineteenth centuries, ideals of reason, ration, freedom, equality, and the pursuit of happiness, plus more romantic impulses of revolution and **nationalism**, combined to create the ages of **Enlightenment** (ca. 1600–1800) and Revolution (ca. 1775–1848), spurring the building of nation-states and reflections on human sovereignty on both sides of the ocean.

This section focuses on the Age of Revolutions specifically in the Atlantic world, including revolutions in England, France, and Haiti and the Americas. While in Eurocentric historical accounts the French are most often credited with pushing revolutionary Enlightenment ideals in politics to the tipping point—challenging traditional ancient regime systems to begin to develop modern democracies—other nations, colonies, and individuals in the Atlantic World participated in and spread the words of liberty, fraternity, and equality.

The traditional timeframe given to the Age of Revolution has been 1789 (French Revolution) to 1848 (across Europe). A Eurocentric chronology has been challenged by scholars who focus less on specific revolutions but rather on an age of revolutions in which global order was challenged—a complex combination of rebellions that stretched from the late seventeenth through the mid-nineteenth centuries, at minimum.

In the Atlantic World, a series of revolutions occurred with connections to new ideas about government, politics, and the roles ordinary citizens should play. This timeline includes standard dates for the American, French, and Haitian revolutions and includes the seventeenth-century English Glorious Revolution. The timeline helps reveal how revolutions spread across the Atlantic and were tied to ideas of national sovereignty and colonial reactions to empires and imperialism.

Timeline of Atlantic Revolutions

1688–1689	Glorious Revolution (England)
1775–1783	American (US) Revolution
1787–1799	French Revolution
1791–1804	Haitian Revolution
1810–1823	Venezuelan War of Independence

The Glorious Revolution

Traditionally, historians viewed England's Revolution of 1688–1689 as un-revolutionary. This was in part because it was regarded as a relatively short and bloodless skirmish among political elites. The Glorious Revolution is now interpreted as one of the first modern revolutions with consequences in England, Europe, and the colonies. Domestically, the Glorious Revolution catalyzed modern English foreign policy, religious culture, and political economy. It served as an early model for modern revolutions surrounding conflicting ideas about shifting economic and political systems which, in hindsight, historians mark as shifts from early modern to modern eras in world history.

The Glorious Revolution, like revolutions that followed it, was rooted in conflicts of ideas about modernization: in England, King James II and revolutionaries fought to determine how England would develop socially, politically, and economically. While historians have focused on the Glorious Revolution's impact on creating a constitutional monarchy, an important domestic change, the Revolution should also be remembered for its place in Atlantic World and modern revolutionary history.

The American Revolution

The American Revolution, despite traditional emphases on its central importance in US history, was also a crucial moment in Atlantic World and global history. Many historians consider it the first true Atlantic Revolution, related to the spread of European Enlightenment ideals, although this textbook argues it had a precursor: the Glorious Revolution, which occurred nearly a century earlier. Regardless, the American Revolution marks a turning point in the Atlantic World in which colonists, and despite the Revolution's identity as a "revolution from above," enslaved African Americans, challenged the power of the British Empire, demanded freedoms from tyranny, and elevated concerns about the Atlantic slave trade.[11] The American Revolution inspired other groups across the Atlantic to challenge traditional power structures and European imperialism.

The American Revolution, also known as the US War of Independence (1775–1783), followed years of conflict between American colonists and the British. In the wake of the **Seven Years' War** (1756–1763), also known as the French and Indian War, the British increased taxes to bolster the British Empire's economy as well as limit global trade in colonial ports. The **Tea Act** (1773), for example, which was issued to shore up the fortunes of the **British East India Company**, created resentment among American colonists. The **Boston Tea Party** of December 16, 1773, when colonists dumped hundreds of chests of British East India Company tea into the harbor, was a direct result of British attempts to monopolize the global tea trade.

What started as a civil war between British colonists in North America and British powers became a rebellion against the British Empire itself and took on additional global interactions as the French and Spanish became involved by supporting American revolutionaries. This support was not so much idealistic but economic, as Spain and France continued the power struggles among empires that characterized much of Atlantic World history.

By 1783, the British cut their losses and surrendered to the American forces. Britain then turned its attention to other areas of its vast empire, including India and Australia. American colonists reshaped their colonies and governments, in a complex series of discussions revising earlier agreements, into the US Constitution, ratified in 1788, which turned former British colonies into the

---

11 Aaron Spencer Fogleman, "The transformation of the Atlantic World, 1776–1867," *Atlantic Studies*, 6: 1, 2009, 5–28. DOI: 10.1080/14788810802696261

United States of America. The American Revolution, however, not only helped reshape North America but inspired others to seek freedom, liberty, and justice along idealistic and economic lines across the Atlantic World and beyond.

The French Revolution

While the traditional date given for the outbreak of the French Revolution is 1789, tensions emerged earlier. Global geopolitical and internal pressures, including the financial crisis in the 1780s tied to French involvement in the Seven Years' War (1756–1763) and the American Revolution, sparked revolutionary actions in France.

King Louis XVI moved to increase taxation to build revenues, invoking the **Estates General** (representatives of clergy, nobility, and commoners) by royal command. Similar to English revolutionaries, the **Third Estate** (French representatives of commoners) rebelled. The result: a civil conflict with serious domestic and global effects. One of many notable effects in both France and in the Atlantic World as a result of the French Revolution was the spread of ideas about national sovereignty and human rights to Asia, Africa, and the French colonies.

The French **National Assembly**'s (the body created by the revolutionaries from the Third Estate) key proclamation for human liberties, "Declaration of the Rights of Man and Citizen" (1789), spread to other groups of disenfranchised peoples within and outside France. Once the Third Estate in France rebelled, other members of the French population raised their own voices: in 1792, peasants and workers rebelled against the upper classes and called for wider-ranging reforms. Others—such as women and colonial French colonists and **subjects** of color—also began to demand political and social equality on a par with the Third Estate.

The widespread demand for reform coupled with existing and new internal problems created unmitigated social, political, and economic turmoil. A series of attempts to regain order and push through reform was unsuccessful until Napoleon Bonaparte rose through the ranks to crown himself emperor. This ironic turn of events—the reinstatement of an absolute ruler—was tempered with Napoleon's revolutionary reforms, including the **Napoleonic Code**. Although not the first revolution of the Revolutionary Age nor the last, the French Revolution served as catalyst to allow a "cultural-ideological" world consciousness to align with economic and political realities in a way the English Glorious Revolution did not.

Yet the French Revolution—like many of its fellow White Atlantic Revolutionary Age movements—was rife with irony. Although the French Revolution is given credit for inspiring nationalist and revolutionary movements the world over, its Francocentric ideals not only promoted French interests over the rights and needs of non-French peoples around the world but were limited originally to certain classes of White, male, French citizens.

The Haitian Revolution

If **self-government** was possible in England and France, why not in other parts of the Atlantic World? If liberty, fraternity, and equality were good for White middle- and upper-class men, then why not for women, the working classes, and people of color? Ideas and ideals from Paris spread to the rising middle classes in European colonial lands through economic trade, print culture, and the transmission of ideas. As enlightenment and revolutionary ideas spread, more groups of people were attracted to them and began to demand those rights for themselves as well.[12]

Although the Haitian Revolution occurred after the French, the two revolutions were tied not just by French revolutionary influences in Saint-Domingue but because colonial politics and policies had contributed to tensions in France. The revolution in the French Empire's metropole was closely watched by French citizens and subjects in the Caribbean. Although the French Revolution itself was more complex than a battle between the people and the monarchy, the Haitian Revolution added new layers to the aims of revolutionary thought as it addressed competing claims between social and racial classes. Racial systems in the Caribbean were complex, with differences shaded not only by parentage (White, Black, native, "mixed-race") but between free and enslaved peoples of color and free people of color and Whites, and made even more complex by social standing—official, planter, worker, enslaved. Thus, the Haitian Revolution served as an emancipation and colonial rebellion, and although its successes were not always assured, the revolution ultimately resulted in the creation of Haiti—and the end of French rule and slavery in what had been Saint-Domingue.

The Haitian Revolution is marked as the second successful revolution in the Americas against a European empire (the American being the first.) These revolutions were only the beginning of American revolts against colonial rule. The Spanish Empire faced a series of revolutions in the early nineteenth century, akin to the American and other colonial revolutions in the Atlantic World. Tensions between priorities of the metropole—in this case Spain—and its colonies, particularly the social, economic, and political classes of *Criollos* (South American–born colonists with Spanish ancestry) sparked dissent and rebellion in Spanish America. The Venezuelan Revolution (or Venezuelan War of Independence) was the earliest but just one of many South American regions to demand and gain **independence** from Spain. Much like other Atlantic Revolutions, the causes for rebellion in South America were complex: tensions in Europe threatened Spanish power, as did colonial tensions between and among colonial citizens and subjects. The spread of Enlightenment ideals, models of other successful colonial rebellions, and the rising economic and political power of middle-class White men all led to a series of skirmishes eventually leading to Venezuela's Declaration of Independence in 1811. This revolution, like many in South America, was led in part by Simón Bolívar, Manuela Sáenz's lover.

Conclusion

Atlantic Revolutions were important events in the Age of Revolutions, and an examination of revolutions in England, the Americas, France, and Haiti reveals how modern revolutionary ideas spread back and forth across the Atlantic World. These revolutions, although occurring in different places and cultures, reveal that diverse groups within the Atlantic world, including White commoners, people of color, and women, embraced Enlightenment ideals. They fought to bring to their societies what became in French a tripartite motto: *liberté, égalité, fraternité.*

---

12 Julius Sherrard Scott and Marcus Rediker, *The Common Wind: Afro-American Currents in the Age of the Haitian Revolution* (London; New York: Verso, 2018).

Chapter Summary

The history of the Atlantic World was traditionally told as a story related to "the rise of the West" and European exploration and colonization of the Americas, with discussion of the disturbing history of the Atlantic Slave Trade. Additional interpretations of the Atlantic World as a multicultural space reveal that indigenous peoples and enslaved African peoples, and others who traveled, lived, or colonized in the Atlantic World, made significant contributions to the culture, industry, social, and political development of the Atlantic World after 1500. These processes shaped not only the peoples and modern nations in Atlantic rim lands and islands but contributed significantly to modern global history.

Discussion Questions

1. Write a definition of the Atlantic World, keeping in mind its diverse histories.
2. What are some of the pros and cons of the Columbian Exchange?
3. How did Europeans, Africans, and indigenous peoples contribute individually to the making of the Atlantic World?
4. How did agriculture and botany contribute to Atlantic World science and culture?
5. How did women contribute to Atlantic revolutions?
6. Explain how and why race, class, and gender, as well as intersections of these identities, shaped societies in the Atlantic World.
7. How did the Atlantic World shape the contemporary world?

References

Using the Sources

Beyond the primary sources provided in this chapter, students will benefit from analyzing maps and images provided and additional readings and materials cited below. Students and instructors may find film and literary adaptations particularly helpful in the classroom or as additional assignments. References and suggested supplementary sources are provided.

Primary Sources

Barclay, A. 1827. *A Practical View of the Present State of Slavery in the West Indies; Or, an Examination of Mr. Stephen's "Slavery of the British West India Colonies": Containing More Particularly an Account of the Actual Condition of the Negroes in Jamaica.* London: Smith, Elder & Co.

Chandler, Julia D. 1905. "Food and Cookery in Jamaica." *The Boston Cooking School Magazine of Culinary Science and Domestic Economics (1897–1914)* 9, no. 7: 372.

De Gouges, Olympe. 1791. "Declaration of the Rights of Woman."

Equiano, Olaudah. 1789. *The Interesting Narrative of the Life of Olaudah Equiano, or Gustavus Vassa, the African. Slavery and Anti-Slavery: A Transnational Archive. Part 2: Slave Trade in the Atlantic World.* London: Printed for and Sold by the Author [and 12 Others]. https://www.gutenberg.org/files/15399/15399-h/15399-h.htm

Gabb, William M. 1873. "On the Topography and Geology of Santo Domingo." *Transactions of the American Philosophical Society* 15, no. 1: 49–259.

Madden, R. R., M.D. 1835. "Life in Jamaica." *Atkinson's Casket (1831–1839)*, no. 12: 687.

Wollstonecraft, Mary. 1792. "A Vindication of the Rights of Woman."

Secondary Sources

Andrade, Tonio. 2011. *Lost Colony: The Untold Story of China's First Great Victory Over the West*. Princeton: Princeton University Press.

Armitage, David, and Michael J. Braddick, eds. 2009. *The British Atlantic World, 1500–1800*. New York: Palgrave Macmillan.

Armstrong, Terence E. 1975. *Yermak's Campaign in Siberia: A Selection of Documents*. London: Hakluyt Society.

Bailyn, Bernard. 2005. *Atlantic History: Concept and Contours*. Cambridge, MA: Harvard University Press.

Berry, Mary Elizabeth. 1982. *Hideyoshi*. Cambridge. MA: Harvard University Press.

Black, Jeremy. 2008 *War and the World: Military Power and the Fate of Continents, 1450–2000*. New Haven, CT: Yale University Press.

Chamoiseau, Patrick. 1998. *Texaco*. Translated by Rose-Myriam Réjouis and Val Vinokurov. 1st Vintage International ed. New York: Vintage International.

Chandler, Julia D. 1905. "Food and Cookery in Jamaica." *The Boston Cooking School Magazine of Culinary Science and Domestic Economics (1897–1914)* 9, no. 7: 348.

Chase, Kenneth. 2003. *Firearms: A Global History to 1700*. Cambridge, NY: Cambridge University Press.

Cronon, William, and John Demos. 2003. *Changes in the Land: Indians, Colonists, and the Ecology of New England*. New York: Hill and Wang.

Crosby, Alfred W. 1972. *The Columbian Exchange: Biological and Cultural Consequences of 1492*. Contributions in American Studies; No. 2. Westport, CT: Greenwood Press.

———. 2004. *Ecological Imperialism: The Biological Expansion of Europe, 900–1900*. Studies in Environment and History. Cambridge, NY: Cambridge University Press.

Dominique, Lyndon J., ed. 2007. *The Woman of Colour: A Tale*. Peterborough, Canada: Broadview.

Elgood, Robert. 1995. *Firearms of the Islamic World: In the Tared Rajab Museum, Kuwait*. I. B. Tauris.

Fogleman, Aaron Spencer. 2009. "The Transformation of the Atlantic World, 1776–1867." *Atlantic Studies* 6, no. 1: 5–28.

Gibson, Carrie. 2014. *Empire's Crossroads: A History of the Caribbean from Columbus to the Present Day*. London: Macmillan.

Gilroy, Paul. 1993. *Black Atlantic: Modernity and Double Consciousness*. New York: Verso.

Goucher, Candice. 2014. *Congotay! Congotay! A Global History of Caribbean Food*. London: Taylor & Francis.

Gray, Richard. 1971. "Portuguese Musketeers on the Zambezi." *Journal of African History*, Vol. 12, No. 4: 531–33.

Greene, Jack P., and Philip D. Morgan, eds. 2009. *Atlantic History: A Critical Appraisal*. New York: Oxford University Press.

Hall, Bert. 1997. *Weapons and Warfare in Renaissance Europe: Gunpowder, Technology, and Tactics*. Baltimore: Johns Hopkins University Press.

Kaba, Lansiné. 1981. "Archers, Musketeers, and Mosquitoes: The Moroccan Invasion of the Sudan and the Songhay Resistance (1591–1612)." *Journal of African History*, Vol. 22: 457–75.

Kea, R. A. 1971. "Firearms and Warfare on the Gold and Slave Coasts from the Sixteenth to the Nineteenth Centuries." *Journal of African History*, Vol. 12, No. 2: 185–213.

Kean, Sam. April 4, 2019. "Historians Expose Early Scientists' Debt to the Slave Trade." *Science*. https://www.sciencemag.org/news/2019/04/historians-expose-early-scientists-debt-slave-trade

Lange, Dierk. 1987. *A Sudanic Chronicle: The Borno Expeditions of Idrīs Alauma'to'*. Wiesbaden, Germany.

Lorge, Peter A. 2008. *The Asian Military Revolution: From Gunpowder to the Bomb* (Cambridge University Press.

Lunde, Paul. July-August 2005. "The Coming of the Portuguese," in *Saudi Aramco World*. http://www.saudiaramcoworld.com/issue/200504/the.coming.of.the.portuguese.htm

Mintz, Sidney W. 1986. *Sweetness and Power: The Place of Sugar in Modern History*. New York: Penguin Books.

Newman, Brooke N. 2010. "Gender, Sexuality and the Formation of Racial Identities in the Eighteenth-Century Anglo-Caribbean World." *Gender & History* 22, no. 3: 585–602.

O'Neill, Peter D., and Lloyd David, eds. 2009. *The Black and Green Atlantic: Cross-Currents of the African and Irish Diasporas*. New York: Palgrave Macmillan.

Parker, Geoffrey. May 1988. "Why the Armada Failed." *History Today*, Vol. 38: 26–33.

———. 1996. *The Military Revolution: Military Innovation and the Rise of the West 1500–1800*. Cambridge University Press.

———. 1997. *The Thirty Years' War*. New York: Routledge.

———. 2007. "The Limits to Revolutions in Military Affairs: Maurice of Nassau, the Battle of Nieuwpoort (1600), and the Legacy." *Journal of Military History*, Vol. 71, No.2: 331–72.

Pincus, Steve. 2009. 1688: The First Modern Revolution. New Haven: Yale University Press.

Roberts, Michael. 1968. *Sweden as a Great Power, 1611–1697*. London: St. Martin's Press.

Schiebinger, Londa L. 2004. *Plants and Empire: Colonial Bioprospecting in the Atlantic World*. Cambridge, MA: Harvard University Press.

Scott, Julius Sherrard, and Marcus Rediker. 2018. *The Common Wind: Afro-American Currents in the Age of the Haitian Revolution*. London; New York: Verso.

Shannon, Timothy J. 2004. *Atlantic Lives: A Comparative Approach to Early America*. New York: Pearson/Longman.

Swope, Kenneth. 2014. *The Military Collapse of China's Ming Dynasty*. New York: Routledge.

Thornton, John. 1998. *Africa and Africans in the Making of the Atlantic World, 1400–1800*. New York: Cambridge University Press.

Thornton, John Kelly. 1999. *Warfare in Atlantic Africa, 1500–1800*. New York: Routledge.

Turnbull, Stephen. 2002. *Samurai Invasion: Japan's Korean War, 1592–1598*. London: Cassell & Co.

Walvin, James. 1997. *Fruits of Empire: Exotic Produce and British Taste, 1660–1800*. New York: New York University Press.

Weaver, Jace. 2014. *Red Atlantic: American Indigenes and the Making of the Modern World, 1000–1927*. Chapel Hill: University of North Carolina Press.

Wheatcroft, Andrew. 2010. *The Enemy at the Gate: Habsburgs, Ottomans, and the Battle for Europe*. New York: Basic Books.

Williams, Eric. 1994. *Capitalism and Slavery.* Translated by Rose-Myrian Réjouis. Chapel Hill: University of North Carolina Press.

Wilson, Peter H. 2011. *Europe's Tragedy: A History of the Thirty Years' War.* Cambridge, MA: Harvard University Press.

Documentary Films

America Before Columbus. 2009. Directed by Cristina Trebbi. National Geographic. TV Movie.

Égalité for All: Toussaint Louverture and the Haitian Revolution. 2009. Directed by Noland Walker. PBS Home Video. TV Movie.

Credits

Fig. 1.1: Source: https://commons.wikimedia.org/wiki/File:Carte_antilles_1843.jpg.

Fig. 1.2: Copyright © Jbermudez (CC BY-SA 2.5) at https://commons.wikimedia.org/wiki/File:Caguana_Ceremonial_Ball_Courts_Site_-_Utuado_Puerto_Rico.jpg.

Fig. 1.3: Source: https://www.loc.gov/resource/g4900m.gar00006/?sp=1.

Fig. 1.4: Adapted from: Source: https://pixabay.com/en/world-map-earth-global-continents-146505/

Fig. 1.5: Source: http://www.kingscollections.org/exhibitions/specialcollections/caribbean/.

Fig. 1.6: Source: https://commons.wikimedia.org/wiki/File:Casta_painting_all.jpg.

Fig. 1.7: Source: https://commons.wikimedia.org/wiki/File:Agostino_Brunias_-_Linen_Market,_Dominica_-_Google_Art_Project.jpg.

Fig. 1.8: Source: https://commons.wikimedia.org/wiki/File:Manuela_S%C3%A1enz.jpg

Empires and Imperialism

Introduction to Chapter Themes

This chapter focuses on the themes of empire and imperialism. These are truly global themes in both time and place. This chapter, however, focuses on the role of European empires after 1500 as specific examples of empires and imperialism in that era and the global interactions of imperialists, colonists, **intermediaries**, imperial citizens, and subjects or subalterns.[1] Instead of focusing on a traditional reading of the "rise of the West" and the European **Age of Imperialism**, this chapter puts the story of European empires into a broader lens of the global processes of empires and imperialism after 1500, with continued emphases on cultural and ecological imperialism.[2] The chapter examines the themes of this textbook: Geography and Environment; Material Culture; Science and Technology; Gender and Sexuality; and War, Peace, and Diplomacy.

Student Learning Objectives

After reading this chapter students should be able to describe and discuss:

- The complexities in scholarly definitions of empire and imperialism.
- How the concepts of empire and imperialism are global through time and place.
- How Europeans established themselves on a world stage as imperial powers
- How imperialists, colonists, intermediaries, imperial citizens, and subjects all played active roles in creating, building, maintaining, and dissolving empires.

---

1 This chapter will use both subject and subaltern to refer to groups of people holding the lowest political, social, and economic ranking in an imperial setting. The difference between the two terms is described as a difference in agency—subjects are often depicted as having little agency in a colonial setting, while subalterns, in postcolonial studies, while historically subject to a dominant power, also served as protagonists in colonial settings.

2 Chapter 1, "Atlantic World," discusses Alfred Crosby's argument for Ecological Imperialism. This chapter continues that theme, but with reference to John Bellamy Foster and Brett Clark's development of this theme to include its biological, capitalist, and imperialist connections. Thus, this chapter will refer to ecological imperialism using lower-case letters to differentiate from Crosby's text of the same name.

Timeline of Selected Dates

1415	Portuguese capture Ceuta (Puerto Rico)
1488	Bartolomeu Dias enters Indian Ocean
1493	Christopher Columbus introduces sugarcane to the Caribbean
1494	Spain and Portugal sign Treaty of Tordesillas
1522	Ferdinand Magellan and crew circumnavigate the globe
1565	Spain begins colonization of the Philippines
1585	Richard Hakluyt publishes *Inducements to the Liking of the Voyage Intended towards Virginia*
1865	Thomas J. Barratt begins marketing British soap to global audiences
1884–1885	Berlin Conference divides Africa among European powers
1898–1902	United States annexes Hawaii, Puerto Rico, and the Philippines
1945–1960	Decolonization processes begin in Asia and Africa

A World History of Empire and Imperialism

Recent scholarship has pointed to the long-term and continued importance of empire and imperialism in world history. Despite a nineteenth- and twentieth-century focus on the rise and global importance of nation-states, historians have returned to examining how the longer history of empire and imperialism shaped world history. Scholars continue to debate definitions of empire and imperialism and their defining characteristics, which may include political, cultural, economic, legal, and ethnic dominance of one country or region over other countries or regions. Despite the prominence of European empires since 1500, Europeans do not represent the world history of empires and imperialism. Significant empires existed in the Americas and Afro-Eurasia before 1500, and empires and imperialism have existed globally for millennia. In addition, recent scholarship on empires and imperialism notes that they are extremely complex, may have positive and negative characteristics, and while often using or maintaining exploitive tactics of rule, have also been more flexible and innovative than many scholars once thought. This has suggested scholars hold a deeper appreciation for the complex motives and actions of imperialists, intermediaries, and subalterns of empires.

Defining empire and imperialism is difficult as their meanings change through time and place. Basic definitions of empire suggest an empire consists of a variety of places and peoples under the authority of a single ruler. A simple definition of imperialism suggests it is the policy by which this authority is imposed or spread. Thus, each empire must be understood by apprehending which places and peoples are within that empire; who the ruler is; what kind of authority is used; and how that authority is imposed or spread. More recent understanding of empires and imperialisms argue that the actions and perspectives of imperialists, colonists, intermediaries, and subalterns must also be considered to fully understand an empire and its imperialism. World historians provide some notable common characteristics of empires in world history:

- A charismatic leader and a large and strong military were critical to empire building
- Empires generally introduced new political and administrative institutions, but also adapted to existing institutions and local elites

- Empires spent energy and resources to control production and trade within their realms
- The comparative study of empires reveals that peoples widely separated by time and place independently created common forms of political and social organization that may be labeled empires

Although this scholarship suggests a more global and historical approach to empires and imperialism that highlights their similarities, there are also notable shifts in the history of empires and imperialism. Clear markers are in the shifting methods of modern empires—those after 1500—from earlier empires. These differences include resource management, civilizing missions, economic systems, and significantly, treatment of what is called "**the other**": subalterns of a race, ethnicity, class, or religion who differ from those in power. Another shift is related to the interplay of empire and imperialism to nation-states and nationalism. These characteristics may be applied to European empires after 1500.

Empires and Imperialism Before 1500

European imperialism between 1500 and 1900 transformed the world. Although scholars disagree on specific periodization of changes during these centuries, most agree that a "rise of the West" and Europe's subsequent use of **imperial methods** to build overseas empires in these centuries also marked a fundamental shift in the longer history of empire and imperialism. After 1500, world systems shifted, and Europeans played a more significant role in global affairs than they had previously, including displacing power wielded in earlier world systems and in creating a global network of European empires. European empires and imperialism, however, were connected to historical and world events, trends, and global complexities. In fact, without global innovations, global communities, and global resources, European—and world—history after 1500 might look very different today.

The period between the early fifteenth and seventeenth centuries has often been referred to as the European **Age of Discovery.** European acts of discovery or exploration led to European colonization and empire building around the world. An introduction to European empires and imperialism in the early modern and modern eras must examine how, when, where, and why Europeans began their Age of Discovery and exploration. In world history, scholars recognize that the specific European Age of Discovery does not encompass human history of discovery and exploration as many peoples and cultures have their own significant periods—past, present, and future—of discovery, exploration, and empire building. The Chinese, for example, had noted sailors, explorers, and cartographers. In the early fifteenth century, the Ming Dynasty's explorer **Zheng He** led fleets of Chinese ships into the Indian Ocean and Arabian Sea, contacting peoples living in the Indian subcontinent and on the coast of Africa (Figure 2.1).

Why did China support this extensive effort? The newly created Ming Dynasty (1368–1644) had chased Mongol conquerors out of China and was building prestige to continue "the mandate of Heaven." This concept held that subjects owed loyalty to a dynasty if it provided prosperity and protection from violence. The Yongle Emperor, third of the Ming dynasts, was a usurper who came to power killing many political rivals, and constantly worried about his status.

He viewed impressive accomplishments as the way to increase prestige. As a result, Yongle ordered construction of Nanjing's famous Porcelain Pagoda, a dramatic expansion of the Grand

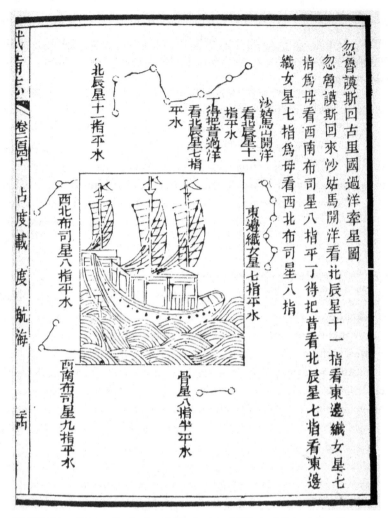

FIGURE 2.1 Chinese Navigational Chart, circa 1600, depicting stellar diagrams, based on Zheng He's navigators' work.

Canal, and established the Forbidden City, an imperial headquarters in Beijing. He also directed an aggressive foreign policy with Chinese armies advancing into Mongolia and Vietnam.

Yongle also favored imperial eunuchs, as their inability to produce children made it more likely they would remain loyal rather than promote family interests. Zheng He, a Muslim eunuch, had been part of Yongle's household since he was a teenager. Zheng's devotion and considerable talents allowed for increasing responsibilities. When Yongle became emperor in 1402, Zheng was promoted to Grand Director of Imperial Servants.

The Ming navy was already large, and Yongle favored an expansive foreign policy. These connected Zheng to a major undertaking. He was directed to build more ships and take them on voyages across Southeast Asia, the coast of East Africa, and the Persian Gulf. This began nearly three decades of visits by Ming treasure fleets to these regions.

These fleets were designed to promote trade, eliminate piracy, and establish the superiority of China. Seven expeditions sailed between 1405–1433, commanded by Zheng or one of his subordinates. Chinese sailors had visited these spots before, but never on this scale. Zheng commanded 25,000–28,000 sailors and soldiers on each voyage. Modern experts debate the size of his ships, but all agree they were especially large for this time and probably had a tremendous impact on locals when they appeared on the horizon.

Zheng's primary goal was bringing other Asian states into a tributary relationship with China. This was usually enacted via diplomacy, trading of gifts, or promise of trade. There were also cases of violence, where Chinese marines helped place a more compliant leader in power. Pirates, the enemies of all mariners, obtained no respite, and entire fleets were destroyed by Zheng's armadas.

Zheng returned from his last voyage in 1424. The Yongle Emperor was dead, and the new emperor had more pressing agendas. Historians are not certain on Zheng's career after this point, with conflicting primary sources indicating he died about this time or continued to serve the dynasty in different projects.

Why did China end this maritime venture? Disasters on the Mongolian frontier, palace politics, and the high cost of Ming treasure fleets were major factors. Imperial attention—and spending—were now focused on soldiers and fortifications to defend Beijing; it was not possible to find funding for these projects and naval ventures. Although Chinese armadas never returned, Southeast Asia's maritime history was shaped by Zheng's remarkable voyages. He is remembered in the People's Republic of China on 11 July, "Maritime Day," and by the Republic of China, where his name is bestowed on a naval vessel.

Primary Source 1

China's Zheng He and Portugal's Vasco da Gama in Calicut

This excerpt, from George Phillips's article which summarizes his translation of the memoirs of Mahuan, a Chinese Muslim fluent in Arabic who served as Zheng He's translator in the early fifteenth century, reveals Chinese experiences in Calicut [Ku-li] (in southwestern India) in 1409. Phillips notes the area was known for both its raw and finished silk and cotton textiles which area merchants exchanged for gold currency.

> This seaport, of which Mahuan gives us a most lengthy account, is described as a great emporium of trade frequented by merchants from all quarters.
>
> [In] Calicut, much pepper is grown on the hills. Cocoanuts are extensively cultivated, many farmers owning a thousand trees; those having a plantation of three thousand are looked upon as wealthy proprietors. The king ... like his brother ... is a sincere follower of Buddha, and as such does not eat beef; his overseer, being a Muhammadan, [Muslim] does not eat pork. ... The king at his devotions prostrates himself before an image of Buddha every morning ...
>
> Many of the king's subjects are Muhammadans, and there are twenty or thirty mosques in the kingdom, to which the people resort every seventh day for worship.

Selections from George Phillips, "Mahuan's Account of Cochin, Calicult, and Aden," *The Journal of the Royal Asiatic Society of Great Britain and Ireland*, pp. 345-347. 1896.

On this day, during the morning, the people being at the mosques, no business whatever is transacted; and in the after part of the day, the services being over, business is resumed.

When a ship arrives from China, the king's overseer with a Chitti [merchant hired by king to conduct his transactions] make an invoice of the goods, and a day is settled for valuing the cargo. On the day appointed the silk goods ... are first inspected and valued, which when decided on, all present join hands whereupon the broker says, "The price of your goods is now fixed, and cannot in any way be altered."

The price to be paid for pearls and precious stones is arranged by the [king's merchant], and the value of Chinese goods taken in exchange for them is that previously fixed by the broker in the way above stated.

They have no abacus on which to make their calculations, but in its place they use their toes and fingers, and what is very wonderful, they are never wrong in their calculations.

Geo. Phillips, "Mahuan's Account of Cochin, Calicut, and Aden," *The Journal of the Royal Asiatic Society of Great Britain and Ireland* (Apr. 1896), pp. 345–47.

Primary Source 2

This excerpt, from "The Geographical Discoveries: Vasco da Gama" in Oliver J. Thatcher, ed., The Library of Original Sources, *reveals the memoirs of Vasco da Gama's 1498 experiences in Calicut (Calecut), now called Kozhikode, in southwestern India on the Malabar Coast.*

[Vasco da Gama and his crew] set sail July 8, 1497 ... and reached Calicut ... May 20, 1498. The Moors [African Muslims of Berber and Arab descent with preexisting trade relationshipsin Calicut] instigated the zamorin (ruler) [the text refers to the zamorin as king] against [them], and [Da Gama] was forced to return with bare discovery. ... Da Gama was sent on a mission of vengeance in 1502. He bombarded Calicut and returned with great spoil.

1498. Calecut. [Arrival.] That night (May 20) we anchored two leagues from the city of Calecut, and we did so because our pilot mistook *Capua*, a town at that place, for Calecut. Still further there is another town called *Pandarani*. We anchored about a league and a half from the shore. After we were at anchor, four boats (*almadias*) approached us from the land, who asked of what nation we were. We told them, and they then pointed out Calecut to us.

On the following day (May 21) these same boats came again alongside, when the captain-major sent one of the convicts to Calecut, and those with whom he went took him to two Moors from Tunis, who could speak Castilian and Genoese.

Selections from Vasco da Gama, "Round Africa to India," *The Library of Original Sources: 9th to 16th Century, ed. Oliver J. Thatcher. 1915.*

The first greeting that he received was in these words: "May the Devil take thee! What brought you hither?" They asked what he sought so far away from home, and he told them that we came in search of Christians and of spices.

[*A description of Calecut*] The city of Calecut is inhabited by Christians. [The first voyagers to India mistook the Buddhists for Christians.] They are of tawny complexion. Some of them have big beards and long hair, whilst others clip their hair short or shave the head, merely allowing a tuft to remain on the crown as a sign that they are Christians. They also wear moustaches. They pierce the ears and wear much gold in them. They go naked down to the waist, covering their lower extremities with very fine cotton stuffs. But it is only the most respectable who do this, for the others manage as best they are able.

The women of this country, as a rule, are ugly and of small stature. They wear many jewels of gold round the neck, numerous bracelets on their arms, and rings set with precious stones on their toes. All these people are well-disposed and apparently of mild temper. At first sight they seem covetous and ignorant.

[*Presents for the King.*] On Tuesday [May 29] the captain got ready the following things to be sent to the king, viz., twelve pieces of *lambel*, four scarlet hoods, six hats, four strings of coral, a case containing six wash-hand basins, a case of sugar, two casks of oil, and two of honey. And as it is the custom not to send anything to the king without the knowledge of the Moor, his factor, and of the *bale*, the captain informed them of his intention. They came, and when they saw the present they laughed at it, saying that it was not a thing to offer to a king, that the poorest merchant from Mecca, or any other part of India, gave more, and that if he wanted to make a present it should be in gold, as the king would not accept such things. When the captain heard this he grew sad, and said that he had brought no gold, that, moreover, he was no merchant, but an ambassador; that he gave of that which he had, which was his own [private gift] and not the [Portuguese] king's …

The king [t]hen asked what kind of merchandise was to be found in his country. The captain-major said there was much corn, [grain], cloth, iron, bronze, and many other things. The king asked whether he had any merchandise with him. The captain replied that he had a little of each sort, as samples, and that if permitted to return to the ships he would order it to be landed, and that meantime four or five men would remain at the lodgings assigned them.

On the following day, Saturday, June 2, in the morning, these gentlemen [i.e., the *bale* and others] came back and this time they "wore better faces." They told the captain that as he had informed the king that he intended to land his merchandise, he should now give orders to have this done, as it was the custom of the country that every ship on its arrival should at once land the merchandise it brought, as also the crews, and that the vendors should not return on board until the whole of it had been sold. The captain consented … They said this was well, and that immediately after the arrival of the merchandise he would be permitted to return to his ship. The captain-major at once wrote to his brother to send him certain things, and he did so at once. On their receipt the captain was allowed to go on board, two men remaining behind with the things that had been landed.

At this we rejoiced greatly, and rendered thanks to God for having extricated us from the hands of people who had no more sense than beasts, for we knew well that once the captain was on board those who had been landed would have nothing to fear. When the captain reached his ship he ordered that no more merchandise should be sent.

Discussion Question

1. Compare the two sources. What might these excerpts tell you about the Chinese versus European experiences in the fifteenth century and familiarity with the Indian Ocean World?

Europeans' exploration, as illustrated by Da Gama's recollections, was specific to European experiences. As historians have argued, the centuries before significant European engagement with American and Afro-Eurasian world systems were marked by significant economic, cultural, and political world system and exchanges outside of Europe. This included networks of trade across land and water routes in, for example, Eurasia (the **Silk Roads**), Africa (the "**Land of Gold,**") (Figure 2.2), the Americas (**turquoise trade**), the **Indian Ocean system**, and an extensive river network in North America centered in **Cahokia** located in modern-day Illinois, among others.

Events, including the expansions of the complex Islamic world systems into parts of modern-day Europe, contact with peoples, goods, and systems in Mediterranean world systems from the start of the Crusades in 1095, and European exploration by travelers such as **Marco Polo** in the late thirteenth century, had introduced Europeans to economic, cultural, and political systems across Afro-Eurasia. By the fifteenth century, Europeans encountered these networks located in Afro-Eurasia. Because of local European conditions—including a dearth of natural resources and desire for finished goods—Europeans became increasingly interested in expanding their global connections in the fifteenth century. Although these contacts had been made between Europeans and other regions, it took technological triumphs over northern Atlantic Ocean currents for Europeans to make notable advances in global discovery and exploration. With the added benefit of global **conjunctures**, European entry into existing world systems led to the "rise of the West" and an age of European empires and imperialism.

Entry of Europeans into World Systems

It was not until the late fifteenth century that Europeans' participation in exploration resulted in significant engagement with global world systems. Until the late fifteenth century, Europeans—northern Europeans in particular—had been relatively isolated compared to other groups across Afro-Eurasia.

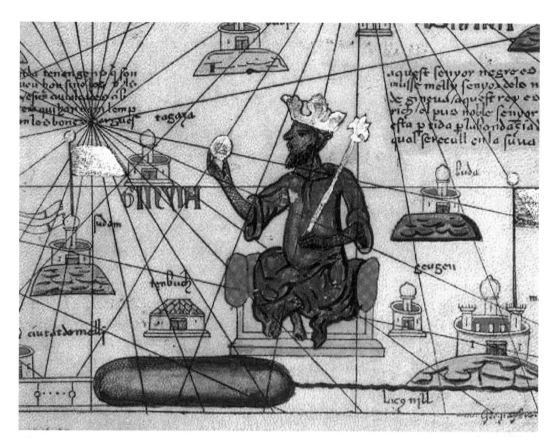

FIGURE 2.2   Mansa Musa I, fourteenth century ruler of Mali, holding a large gold nugget, depicting the wealth of West Africa as the "Land of Gold."

A range of European countries played significant roles in European imperialism after 1500, including Spain's and Portugal's experiences in the Americas; France's role in the Caribbean; the British creation of a global empire; and Belgium's notorious exploitation of the African Congo. The United States' path to local and global imperialism, highlighted by colonization of the Americas and events like the 1898 **Spanish-American War**, reveals how early European imperialism morphed into a more broadly Western imperialism that played a significant role in the making of the modern world. The following sections will offer an introduction to some of these events and then turn to specific chapter themes (Geography and Environment; Material Culture; Science and Technology; Gender and Sexuality; War, Peace, and Diplomacy) with a focus on the British Empire and its imperialism and interactions with colonists, intermediaries, and subalterns in its vast global spheres of influence.

Spain and Portugal

For all its historical complexities, the story of Spain's and Portugal's colonies in the Americas may be marked with Christopher Columbus's arrival on Hispaniola (modern-day Haiti and the Dominican Republic) in 1492. A curious fact that has been left out of contemporary Western historical memory is that **Ferdinand II** and **Isabella I** did not unite Castile and Aragon to form

Spain until 1492 when they drove the last of Muslim power from the **Iberian Peninsula**. The origins of the Spanish empire, then, can be said to parallel the making of Spain, as a nation itself and are tied to a more complex Afro-Eurasian history. This history includes the reshaping of the Iberian Peninsula after centuries of Muslim rule, including molding the region's diverse population into a culturally Spanish and Christian nation. The formation of Spanish nationalism paralleled Ferdinand's and Isabella's attempts to enter existing world markets and compete with other rising European powers—Portugal will serve as a prime example of Spanish rivalry in this chapter. An ultimately lucky outcome of these events was Christopher Columbus's arrival into the Americas (including the Caribbean), islands and continents he was not expecting to find during his daring attempt to reach Asian markets by sailing west. Columbus's arrival into the Americas would have unforeseen global consequences for Spain and the rest of the world.

In the years surrounding Columbus's journeys across the Atlantic, Portuguese-sponsored sailors such as **Bartolomeu Dias** and Vasco da Gama had already sailed off the coast of the Iberian Peninsula trying to reach existing world systems. Dias successfully reached the Cape of Good Hope on the southern tip of Africa in 1488; Da Gama reached Calicut, a city in the Indian subcontinent in 1498. Spain and Portugal's fierce competition for trading routes, encouraged by Columbus's successful journey to and from the Americas, led to an audacious attempt to divide these trading routes and regions between the Spanish and the Portuguese through agreements such as the **Treaty of Tordesillas** in 1494 (Figure 2.3).

Primary Source 3

In 1494 Spain and Portugal signed the Treaty of Tordesillas, an agreement meant to preclude conflicts over the landmasses brought to their attention by Christopher Columbus and subsequent other European travelers. This treaty was sanctioned by the Spanish-born Pope Alexander VI; it set a line of demarcation about 300 miles west of the Cape Verde Islands. Spain was given rights to lands west of the demarcation line (an agreed-upon geopolitical border), while Portugal laid claim to those on the east, with the exception of any land already claimed by another Christian power.

Excerpt of Treaty between Spain and Portugal concluded at Tordesillas; June 7, 1494
Frances Gardiner Davenport, Charles Oscar Paullin, trans.

> [I.] That, whereas a certain controversy exists between the said lords, their constituents, as to what lands, of all those discovered in the ocean sea up to the present day, the date of this treaty, pertain to each one of the said parts respectively; therefore, for the sake of peace and concord, and for the preservation of the relationship and love of the said King of Portugal for the said King and Queen of Castile, Aragon, etc., it being the pleasure of their Highnesses, they, their said representatives, acting in their name and by virtue of their powers herein described, covenanted and agreed that a boundary or straight line be

Selection from Frances Gardiner Davenport and Charles Oscar Paullin, "Treaty Between Spain and Portugal Concluded at Tordesillas, June 7, 1494," *European Treaties Bearing on the History of the United States and Its Dependencies*, pp. 95. 1917.

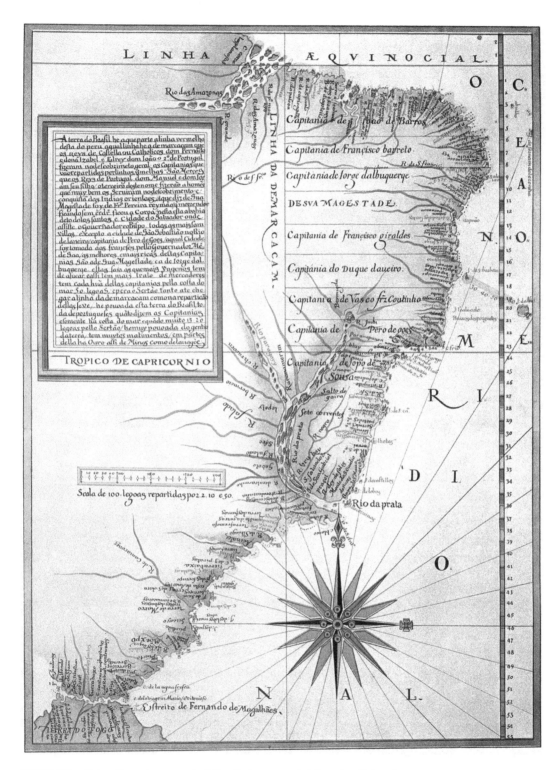

FIGURE 2.3   Sixteenth-century map depicting Portuguese administrative divisions (capitanias) and the line of demarcation set by the Treaty of Tordesillas.

determined and drawn north and south, from pole to pole, on the said ocean sea, from the Arctic to the Antarctic pole. This boundary or line shall be drawn straight, as aforesaid, at a distance of three hundred and seventy leagues west of the Cape Verde Islands, being calculated by degrees, or by any other manner as may be considered the best and readiest, provided the distance shall be no greater than abovesaid. And all lands, both islands and mainlands, found and discovered already, or to be found and discovered hereafter, by the said King of Portugal and by his vessels on this side of the said line and bound determined as above, toward the east, in either north or south latitude, on the eastern side of the said bound provided the said bound is not crossed, shall belong to, and remain in the possession of, and pertain forever to, the said King of Portugal and his successors. And all other lands, both islands and mainlands, found or to be found hereafter, discovered or to be discovered hereafter, which have been discovered or shall be discovered by the said King and Queen of Castile, Aragon, etc., and by their vessels, on the western side of the said bound, determined as above, after having passed the said bound toward the west, in either its north or south latitude, shall belong to, and remain in the possession of, and pertain forever to, the said King and Queen of Castile, Leon, etc., and to their successors.

Frances Gardiner Davenport, Charles Oscar Paullin, trans., *European Treaties Bearing on the History of the United States and Its Dependencies*, Carnegie Institution of Washington Publication. Papers of the Department of Historical Research; No. 254. (Washington, DC: Carnegie Institution of Washington, 1917), 84–100.

Discussion Questions

1. What are the specific details of the agreement between Spain and Portugal in this portion of the Treaty of Tordesillas?
2. How might other countries around the world feel about this agreement?
3. How might the indigenous leaders and rulers of the lands under this agreement feel about the treaty?
4. How does the Treaty of Tordesillas connect to themes of empire and imperialism?

Geography and Environment

A series of so-called Spanish and Portuguese discoveries, continued competition, and subsequent treaty agreements to divide up what the Spanish and Portuguese saw as unclaimed territories led to the rise of Spanish and Portuguese colonies in the Americas. By the 1550s, Spain, for example, controlled most of South and Central America. It should be noted, however, that Spain's reach in this period was even more global, as Charles V and his son controlled not only the Spanish Empire in the Americas but also vast European holdings as Holy Roman Emperor. This was truly a global empire, built using methods of cultural imperialism, such as language and religion; historical imagination; warfare; and the spread of European flora and fauna, including diseases, in what historian Alfred Crosby coined the Columbian Exchange.

Timeline of Portuguese Voyages

Although travel from the country we now know as Portugal has a much longer world history that includes the diverse population of the Iberian Peninsula, credit for Portuguese voyages beginning in the fifteenth century are usually connected to the energy and interests of Portuguese prince Henrique o Navegador (Henry the Navigator), son of Portuguese king John I. Henry's interest and patronage are also given credit for helping spur the European Age of Discovery.

1488	Bartolomeu Dias sails around the Cape of Good Hope and enters the Indian Ocean
1492	First exploration of the Indian Ocean
1494	Treaty of Tordesillas between Portugal and Spain
1495	João Fernandes and Pedro Barcelos sail to Greenland
1498	Vasco da Gama leads the first fleet around Africa to India, arriving in Calicut
1498	Duarte Pacheco Pereira sails into the South Atlantic and explores the South Atlantic American coastline
1500	Attempting to reach India, Pedro Álvares Cabral sails to what would become Brazil
1500	Gaspar Corte-Real sails to Newfoundland
1500	Diogo Dias sails to what is known today as Madagascar
1502	Looking for his brother, Gaspar, Miguel Corte-Real sails to North America
1505	Lourenço de Almeida becomes the first Portuguese to sail to what is known today as Sri Lanka
1509	Diogo Lopes de Sequeira sails the Bay of Bengal and reaches Malacca
1511	Duarte Fernandes becomes the first European to visit what is known today as Thailand
1513	Jorge Alvares brings the first European trading ship to the Chinese coast
1517	Portugal sends diplomats to the Ming Dynasty (China) to open relations between the two powers
1519–1521	Ferdinand Magellan begins the first known circumnavigation of the globe across the Atlantic and then across the Pacific Ocean. Magellan died in the Philippines, and Juan Sebastián Elcano finished the journey in his stead

The successes of the Portuguese and the Spanish motivated other Europeans to investigate what was, for Europeans, a new world. By the sixteenth century, the French had also entered the Americas. While the French presence in North America was significant, the French also established colonies in South America and created a significant Caribbean empire, including gaining possession of Saint-Domingue, a western section of Hispaniola, in 1697. Saint-Domingue (modern-day Haiti) became a wildly successful sugar colony worked by slaves for the French. French presence in the Caribbean was extensive, including other islands such as Guadeloupe and Martinique, which remain under French influence.

While Spain, France, and Portugal and other European powers successfully established colonies in the Americas and elsewhere following Columbus's arrival to that landmass, European empire and imperialism after 1500 became a global experience, eventually reaching every continent, including Antarctica, where the French and the British made territorial claims. The British Empire has since 1500 established territorial claims on all seven continents, although some were more informal and shorter-lived than others (Figure 2.4). At its height, the British Empire held influence over one-fifth of the global population and one-quarter of its land. British imperialism, some scholars argue, began with English interests in Ireland as a testing ground for colonization and then spread to the Americas, Asia, Africa and Oceania. British imperialism varied in its formality and methods but included economic, political, military, cultural, and ecological imperialism. The British Empire will serve as the go-to empire for discussing key chapter themes.

While European sailors and travelers such as the **Vikings** and Marco Polo had traveled outside the boundaries of European world systems before the fifteenth century, extensive European exploration had been limited by geography and ocean currents, particularly in northern Europe. Travel by land outside of Europe involved long distances and difficult terrain. While parts of the

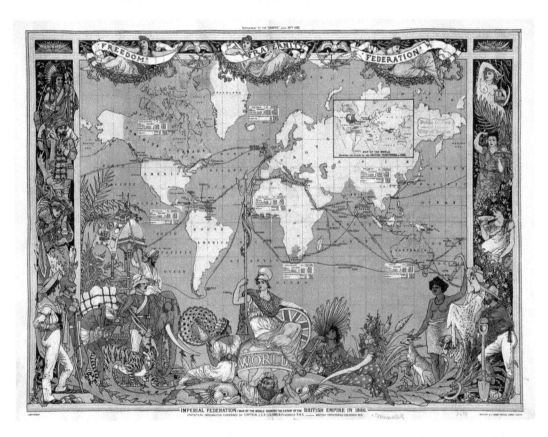

FIGURE 2.4   Imperial Federation, Map of the World Showing the Extent of the British Empire in 1886 (leveled).

Atlantic coast were previously traveled and a few hardy sailors had sailed to Atlantic islands, journeys deeper into the ocean were limited by maritime technology, lack of knowledge about Atlantic currents and winds, and continued suspicions of the Atlantic as a "Green Sea of Darkness," a name given to it by medieval Arab sailors.

Atlantic World

These limitations in Atlantic travel would be overcome, after centuries of relative inactivity, in a surprisingly short period of time. By 1488, Bartolomeu Dias had entered the Indian Ocean system by sailing around the Horn of Africa. Christopher Columbus had successfully sailed from Spain to the Americas by 1492. By the late sixteenth century, a new global system had developed in the decades after Ferdinand Magellan's journey to circumnavigate the globe finished in 1522 by what was left of his crew. Historians identify several catalysts for Europeans' seemingly sudden interest in world systems outside their own and their increasing abilities to reach them across water routes: These include renewed curiosity about the world; desire to find and share Christianity; economic issues (resources and demographics); perceived threats from Muslim powers in the Iberian Peninsula; and historical memory and imagination.

Ecological Exchange and Conquest

Environmental problems in Europe, such as overfishing, deforestation, and lack of resources for growing populations, drove the need for Europeans to find new resources. Although most familiar with goods and trade from Asia, Europeans' accidental arrival in the Americas (including the Caribbean) provided them not only with luxury goods like silver, but seemingly endless supplies of resources, including fish, lumber, land, and new crops—maize and potatoes, for example—that allowed Europeans to add new crops to their traditional fields of wheat, oats, and rye. The vast geography of the Americas was conducive as well to the transplant of European agricultural resources, including flora and fauna. Geography and environment and their manipulation by humans on both sides of the Atlantic led to the watershed Columbian Exchange and ecological imperialism.

A Global World System

European maritime advancements and entry in new world systems were complemented, in terms of considering the centuries after 1500 as a "rise of the West," by relative declines of traditional powers in existing world systems. A primary example is Ferdinand and Isabella's defeat in 1492 of centuries-long Muslim power in the Iberian Peninsula. Global recessions, the spread and aftermath of the bubonic plague, and rebellions, such as the Ming in China, also had global effects that, in part, allowed Europeans to enter—and in some cases redirect—existing world systems. Decline, however, does not always equate collapse, and despite increasingly significant European involvement in an emerging global world system, China, and regions such as the Indian Ocean, continued (and continue) to play important roles in world history.

Conclusion

By the nineteenth century, European empires had spread across the globe, where they remade geographic and environmental spaces to suit their own needs. Historians often note advances

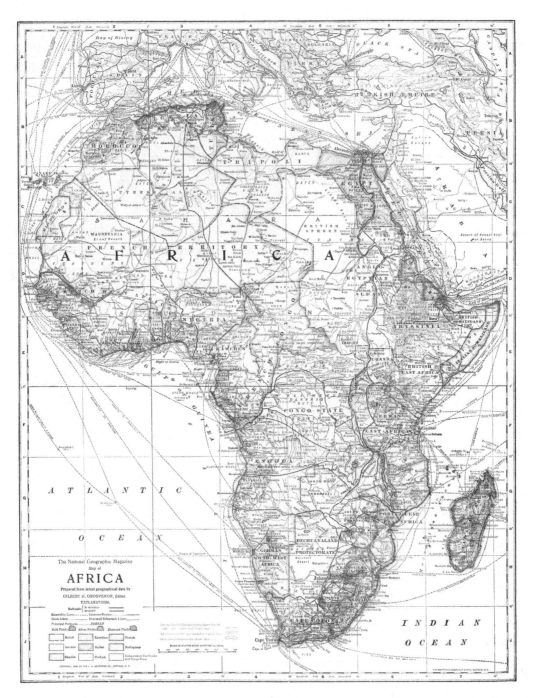

FIGURE 2.5   Map of Africa, 1909, showing European colonies and independent territories, trade commodities, and railroads.

made in the sixteenth and seventeenth centuries in controlling new lands and resources as the markers that led to the European Age of Imperialism in the late nineteenth and early twentieth centuries (Figure 2.5). There is a deeper global story, however, to the main theme of this chapter, empires and imperialism after 1500, that can continue to link ecological imperialism to material culture.

Material Culture

Although scholars have identified common characteristics of empire and imperialism that can be broadly applied to world history, specific characteristics and methods changed over time and place. As interest in cultural history has grown, so, too, has an interest in how empires were built and spread by culture. This section will examine how material culture—physical objects that can be touched or seen, including spaces, resources, and commodities—were used to claim, build, and maintain empires and imperialism.

The British Empire's use of material culture in their imperial methods took many forms, but two fascinating approaches were reshaping environments and ecologies of colonized territories and the use of commercial commodities such as soap as material culture used to promote a civilizing mission on intermediaries and imperial subjects and citizens. Ecological imperialism included establishing native European flora and fauna in places such as the Americas. The establishment of new ecosystems demanded importation of European material culture, such as boundary fences to delineate property ownership and keep transplanted flora and fauna protected. The British mission of demarcating land usage was a civilizing mission of the landscape itself.

Traditional European use of flora and fauna developed over centuries of domestication of plants, animals, and landscapes. British reliance on grains and domesticated Afro-Eurasian animals—sheep, pigs, horses, and cows—had long been established by the sixteenth century. With this agricultural history came firmly established practices of land use. Scholars have noted British interest in finding and using new lands to ease the tensions of growing populations and diminishing resources in the British Isles. For example, growing populations, the demand for fish to feed those populations, better ship technology, and the abundance of fish populations in the western Atlantic were significant catalysts for British (and other European) fishermen and colonists. **Richard Hakluyt** the elder, for example, noted the wealth of sea life in North America in his 1585 *Inducements to the Liking of the Voyage Intended towards Virginia*.[3] He also noted the fertile lands available for cultivation.

Although British colonists took time to understand and successfully cultivate North American flora and fauna, their greatest successes in the long run was reshaping the land for European domesticated plants and animals. By the seventeenth century, the New England colonies were aptly named as they re-formed what the British saw as untamed land into a facsimile of English countryside. Scholars have noted the British use of clearing forests for fields and the use of fences to demarcate and protect their newfound agricultural spaces. The clearing of North American landscapes served a variety of purposes: fields were used both to grow European grains and graze European livestock introduced to the Americas—wheat and beef still dominate American landscapes. Forests yielded timber necessary to replenish dwindling supplies of wood in Eurasia and

---

3   Peter C. Mancall has an excellent version of Hakluyt's inducement in *Envisioning America: English Plans for the Colonization of North America* (Boston: Bedford/St. Martin's, 2017).

to build ships as well as fences to extend and protect the emerging British Empire in the Americas. Unintentional transplants such as weeds, pests, and diseases came on board ships carrying colonists, enslaved peoples, grains, and livestock and reshaped environmental systems and native populations, as well. Indeed, scholars agree that diseases such as smallpox played significant roles in creating what looked to Europeans as unclaimed spaces as indigenous populations were devastated by Afro-Eurasian diseases.

Ecological exchange was a two-sided coin: As Afro-Eurasian animals, crops, and people came to the Americas, so did American flora and fauna spread across the globe. Significant American domesticates such as corn, potatoes, and chocolate became staples of world cuisines. This exchange influenced cultures and cuisines worldwide.

Potatoes were the unsung hero of the Columbian Exchange and successes of Europeans and the "rise of the West." Scholars such as Alfred Crosby argue that the potato, still one of the key global food commodities, played a role in the rise of European populations and power after 1500.[4] The potato was easily grown, made an excellent border crop, and was highly nutritious. As many Europeans had predicted, potatoes became widely popular and supplemented the diets of people across the globe. The potato, for example, became the catalyst for the rapid rise and fall of Irish populations in the eighteenth and nineteenth centuries. Perhaps ironically, the spread of the potato from South America to Europe was a catalyst in sending Irish immigrants to the Americas. The impact of the potato on world history—and European imperialism—has been overshadowed, however, by plantation crops such as sugar, cotton, and tea. All these crops and the wealth they produced for Europeans either in extra calories or emerging capitalism were tied to European entry into existing world systems and European successes through ecological imperialism.

This did not stop at the farm or plantation gate. Indigenous raw materials, technologies, and labor were used to create luxury commodities in European metropoles—goods such as sweetened chocolates, finished cotton fabrics, and in the case of palm kernel and other tropical oils, soap, that were then sold back to indigenous peoples in colonies.

"Cleanliness" as Material Culture: The Civilizing Mission of Soap

Although historians disagree on the exact origins of soap, the product has a long world history, with some of the oldest evidence of soap making in the **Fertile Crescent,** where the skill to make and use a mixture of animal fats and wood ashes to clean cooking utensils has been dated to some six thousand years ago. Other peoples around the world also developed methods for cleaning their goods and their bodies, although earliest uses of soap were tied to cleaning tools and goods rather than the human body. Personal hygiene, however, also has a deep and varied world history.

While the British soap industry was prominent from at least the thirteenth century, the expense of goods such as tallow for soap limited its use to the wealthy. The business of soap making and its association with beauty industries were given a boost during the **Industrial Revolution**. New markets, new goods, and new technologies allowed people around the world to engage in new world systems. New goods included ingredients used in hygiene products like soap.

---

4   Crosby, *Columbian Exchange.*

The use of tropical oils has a long history in places like West Africa. Palms, for example, have myriad uses in foodways and medicinal products. Europeans had been introduced to tropical oils such as coconut by at least the thirteenth century, and the use of palm oil by slavers to cosmetically improve the physical bodies of slaves devasted by the **Middle Passage** is well documented. As the uses of tropical oils like palm oil and palm kernel oil were spread out of Africa into the Americas and Europe, it was a natural progression for these oils to be used in luxury goods such as soap. In the seventeenth and eighteenth centuries, British soap makers made use of newly available ingredients, and industrial advances allowed for mass production. British soap makers not only used palm oils but invested in or owned palm plantations in Africa and Oceania.

By the eighteenth and nineteenth centuries, British soaps had become global commodities. British entry into world systems and the success of British colonization efforts in places like Africa and Asia gave them new markets in which to flex their economic power. Selling soap, however, was not just a practice in making money, but a commodity that honed British marketing through advertisements and served as material culture that helped shape the British civilizing mission abroad. British soap advertisements of the nineteenth century have become infamous for their promotion of a racist civilizing mission and racial stereotypes (Figure 2.6).

Soap advertising, such as the campaigns by Pears, reveals the links between material culture, industrialization, and imperial projects. Early soap advertisements directed at European and colonial consumers suggested the superiority of the British Empire and White Anglo-Christian culture.

FIGURE 2.6   Pears' soap advertisement, 1884.

Conclusion

Material culture played a significant role in Europe's colonial enterprises and imperial methods. World historians today agree that the impact of cultural imperialism is a leading factor in the making of modern and contemporary world culture. They tend to disagree, however, if cultural imperialism had overwhelming negative or positive effects on global empires, imperialism, citizens and subalterns. A middle ground between seeing European (and Western) empires and imperialism as both progressive and regressive allows historians to focus on the processes rather than the outcomes—while power dynamics were not equal, culture was transmitted among imperialists, colonists, citizens, and subalterns: all participated in one way or another, and these interactions helped shape the modern world. The reshaping of world systems was evolutionary rather than revolutionary because world systems are built on existing technological, economic, cultural, and social systems. European-shaped world systems often devolved into global systems rife with inequalities, particularly in imperial settings. British use of African tropical oils for a global soap market is a case study in these processes and inequalities with specific ties to the rise of **industrialism** and capitalism and the hardening of real and perceived differences between societies and cultures based on race, ethnicity, and religion under the guise of imperial civilizing missions.

Science and Technology

In the modern world, it is easy to forget that products used daily have staggeringly complex world histories. The development and expansion of agriculture to provide foods and beverages, for example, is one of the oldest scientific and technological feats performed by humankind. Global agricultural practices shifted radically again under the European Age of Imperialism in part due to the European entry into new continents and their adaption and adoption of new flora and fauna. In fact, many scholars argue that the Industrial Revolution itself might have been shaped very differently without the Columbian Exchange of goods, peoples, and foodways and that industrialized agriculture performed on plantations were the seedlings for the growth of industrialization, capitalism, and the power and wealth of sectors of some empires. The science and technology of agriculture was a key facet of the European age of empires after 1500 and the science and technology that fueled advances, such as railways that cut across metropoles and colonized spaces.

Agro-Industrialization in Europe and the Caribbean

In a modern Eurocentric historical reading, the practice of agriculture modernized in the years following European agrarian revolutions in the mid- to late eighteenth century.[5] A combination of factors led to four significant advancements in British agricultural practices in the sixteenth through eighteenth centuries: improvements in livestock breeding; **enclosure**; adoption and improvements in growing new and traditional crops; and the work of a small group of men, including **Jethro Tull**, inventor of the **seed drill**. These shifts led to more intensive, higher-yield agriculture, which allowed a decrease in the number of British farmers and a subsequent increase in industrial and service workers to work the burgeoning machine that was the British Industrial Revolution.

In a broader perspective, however, the agricultural revolution in Britain and its concurrent rise in industry was not an **island story** but a world history. British good fortune in agriculture and industry after 1500 was built in part by use of raw agricultural and botanical materials taken from the Americas, India, China, and Africa and the labor of slaves and indentured servants. British and European entry into modern agro-science and technology relied on these materials and labor. Thus, the science and technology of existing world agricultural practices, including the domestication and processing by indigenous peoples of the potato (South America), sugar (New Guinea), tobacco (Americas), coffee (Africa), tea (China), and cacao (South America), allowed European empires, imperialists, and colonists, supported by indigenous and African labor, to capitalize on the Columbian Exchange through ecological imperialism leading to European industrialization, capitalism, and global power.

Slavery, the plantation system, and biopiracy in this light can be considered part and parcel of the agricultural revolutions after 1500, and tied as well to European empires and imperialism, as many colonial systems depended on plantation economies and the labor of enslaved peoples.

---

5   Agricultural revolutions around the world have taken place since Neolithic times some 12,000 years ago.

In turn, these new agricultural systems in metropoles and colonies allowed the British to focus on specialized tasks in science and technology that helped Britain not only to be the first of the modern industrialized countries (although many world historians argue that industrialization had global precursors) but to become the world's leading empire. Again, however, the British benefited from not only local resources and ingenuity, but global resources and ingenuity. Sugar provides an illuminating example.

Sugar

Growing and refining sugar for human consumption in its most processed form—white sugar granules—is a labor-intensive and complex system that is based on historical agricultural and industrialized processing systems. The growth and development of successful sugar plantations, such as those in the Caribbean, were based on existing sugar agricultural practices from the origins of sugarcane cultivation in New Guinea circa 8000 BCE to its adoption and refinement in Islamic practices. Spread by medieval Islamic empires to Europe, Europeans slowly but surely became addicted to sugar's sweet taste and the wealth growing, processing, and selling sugar brought to their economies. Through a centuries-long process, sugar agriculture and production spread west from New Guinea to the Mediterranean, then off the Atlantic coastline, and finally, by the fifteenth century, was introduced into the Americas. Existing technology and intensive labor systems traveled with sugar crops—specifically sugarcane—and came to an agro-industrial height in the Caribbean, where the Portuguese, Spanish, Dutch, French, and British experimented with perfecting the agriculture and production of sugar. **Steam engines** replaced horse power in sugar mills, although slaves continued to perform heavy and dangerous manual labor.

Sugar refinement changed little for centuries, but the nineteenth century saw significant contributions to sugar production in early techniques in the field of chemical engineering. In 1813, the English scientist Edward Charles Howard patented his vacuum evaporation method, which allowed lower temperatures in the crystallization process, leading to an improved finished sugar. Howard's vacuum pan became extremely successful, and his methods were further improved by **Norbert Rillieux**, son of a Louisiana slave and her common-law husband, a Louisiana sugar plantation owner. Rillieux's advances allowed production of top-quality sugar at a reduced price. Ironically, improved sugar refinement technology did not improve but rather worsened the plight of sugar plantation slaves who fed the demand for more raw sugar with their sweat.

The discovery and subsequent commercial, scientific, and consumptive history of what Europeans saw first as exotic luxury products and later as commonplace goods also inspired a European interest in pure, rather than applied, sciences of agriculture, botany, and chemical engineering to increase their use and production of other commercial and industrial goods. Chemical engineering played a role in producing goods like synthetic rubber (natural rubber supplies proved difficult to maintain and control) and new methods of extracting and transporting colonial (native) resources. An interest in the economic, political, and sociocultural use, spread, and control of markets and goods (of empire and nation) helped spur the need for faster communications and transportation systems. The development of railroads served these needs, and the reshaping of European nations and their colonies abroad through railways is another piece of the material and technological world history of European empires. African colonies serve as prime examples of landscapes reshaped by the spread of European advances in transportation—trains and railways.

Empires of Rail

African regions had been recognized as one of the last great frontiers for Europeans in the nineteenth century, with vast lands, resources, markets, and peoples not yet under European influence. Resources like rubber, minerals such as gold, geopolitical access to the Indian Ocean and subcontinent, agricultural opportunities, and a native labor force drew Europeans to colonize Africa. While many European colonies were built using a variety of imperial methods, the advent of the European Industrial Revolution meant that goods, people, information, and imperialism could rapidly spread across the African continent.

A second European Age of Imperialism, sometimes called **New Imperialism** or the **Scramble for Africa**, began in the late nineteenth century and ended in the devastation of **World War I**. This period is marked by the **Berlin Conference**, held in Germany in 1884–1885. The conference, also known as the Congo or West Africa Conference, set agreements between Western powers— led by France, Germany, Great Britain, and Portugal, but including Austria-Hungary, Belgium, Denmark, Italy, the Netherlands, Russia, Spain, Sweden-Norway, the Ottoman Empire, and the United States. Although Africa had already been colonized by Europeans before the conference, the Berlin agreement formalized European control of parts of Africa and set borders that divided the land by European geopolitics, rather than by traditional African land use or population. This act was akin to the Treaty of Tordesillas (1494) in that European powers arbitrarily divided up land, people, and resources by their own designs and for their own benefit. The railway allowed the "Scramble for Africa" to proceed quickly and was a method of imperialism that had long-lasting effects on European colonization and control in Africa and had significant effects on indigenous African populations, African environments and ecosystems, and political, social, and economic history in Africa.

Africans, it should come as no surprise, found the Berlin treaty an affront to their own sovereignty. Notably, **Menelik II** of Ethiopia (**Abyssinia**) refused European entry into his lands. Menelik II defeated Italian troops in the Battle of Adwa (1896) after Italy tried to push its claims in Ethiopian lands, and negotiated a treaty with Great Britain allowing him to protect his subjects, borders, and resources. Menelik II is recognized as a skilled leader and politician who not only maintained his Ethiopian empire during the Scramble for Africa but expanded its borders while repelling European influence within Ethiopia. At the same time, Menelik II recognized the benefits European technology, such as trains and railroads, could have for Ethiopians and other African peoples.

While moving goods by wagons on wooden rails stemmed from sixteenth-century German innovations, in the heady years of British industrialization, iron rails and the steam engine were developed to help move goods even faster. Thomas Newcomen and **James Watt** developed the steam engine between 1712 and 1781, and in 1804, Richard Trevithick created the first steam locomotive. Within a decade, steam locomotion had become commercially viable. The technology and railways spread quickly both because of the relative amazing speed and efficiency of steam locomotion and by understanding of their use in military, political, and economic expansion.

The British Empire began building rail in India in the mid-nineteenth century and by the 1880s had constructed thousands of miles of track between major cities. In Africa, the British built the Uganda Express, the French constructed the Dakar–Niger Railway, and Germany developed the Usambara Railway. African leaders such as Menelik II, although wary of British and French imperial aims after successfully repelling Italian colonization efforts in 1896, made concessions for the building of a railroad to link Addis Ababa, Ethiopia, and Djibouti, which helped support Ethiopian power in Africa and against European imperialism.

Conclusion

Agricultural and botanical advances during the Age of European Empires are important facets of the Industrial Revolution and the science and technology that drove it. England is recognized as the first country to develop a modern industrial revolution, but that revolution was built not just by White British peoples but by the knowledge, labor, and resources borrowed—and sometimes stolen—from indigenous and African peoples. Advancements in science and technology allowed Europeans to harness new sources of energy and improve travel and communication symbolized by the construction of railways in domestic and colonial spheres. In Africa, Menelik II of Ethiopia was able to withstand and successfully assimilate European technologies such as railroads; however, for the most part, rail building in Africa by Europeans served European economic interests. It also opened African lands to White colonists and allowed them to enter, colonize, and dominate African peoples and landscapes. Karen Blixen, writing as Isak Dinesen, revealed her experiences in Kenya, including running a coffee plantation using native African labor and resources; she recorded her experiences of travel by rail during her time in Africa.[6] Railways allowed Europeans to travel through and experience Africa in the comfort of Europeanized private train cars. Many scholars note that European women's travel into colonial spaces by rail not only increased and cemented European colonies but opened a frontier for reaffirming and challenging European cultural, social, and racial mores of sex and gender.

Gender and Sexuality

In the Metropole: England

In London in 1854, Arthur Munby, a middle-class civil servant, met Hannah Cullwick, a working-class house servant, and engaged in a sexualized relationship with her that crossed what had been regarded—in traditional interpretations, at least—the norms of English Victorian society. Munby and Cullwick's history was carefully documented in Munby's diaries and through photographs that when made public revealed negotiations between class, gender, sex, and race that now are understood to have shaped Victorian life—even if often closeted—at home and abroad. Several scholars, including Anne McClintock, have shown how these interactions, which included not only cross-dressing but racial sexualized fantasies by Europeans, overturn the stereotypes of Victorian prudery to a Victorian era of fissure, friction, and challenge to gender and sexual

---

6   Isak Dinesen, *Out of Africa* (New York: Random House, 1992).

stereotypes often tied to imperial encounters and imagination.[7] Ironically, supposed European gender and sexual norms and the European **frontier mentality** also played a role in the oppression, often violent, of indigenous subjects who were considered uncivilized because of differences in how they negotiated sex and gender in their own societies and cultures. The story of Arthur Munby and Hannah Cullwick illustrates how domestic relationships mirrored the reality of gender and sexual issues played out abroad. The intersection of race, class, gender, and sex occurred in European metropoles and colonies.

Some of the most evocative and accessible sources of European experiences with reaffirming and challenging sexuality and gender come through in autobiographical and auto-fictional recollections. Authors, including Isak Dinesen, E. M. Forster, and George Orwell, had firsthand experiences in colonial spaces which they later wrote about in novelized forms. Dinesen's and Forster's works, *Out of Africa* and *A Passage to India*, were also popularized as feature films that reveal visual contemporary interpretations of many of the themes of empire and imperialism discussed in this chapter, including excellent illustrations of issues surrounding gender and sexuality.

It is important to remember that the terms *sexuality, sexual orientation, gender,* and *gender identity* have related but separate meanings, as well as to understand that people's understanding and expression of these terms change over time, place, and culture. Scholars have noted that exploration and renegotiation of culturally specific gender and sexual norms played a critical role in metropole and colony and that gender and sex were often closely tied to issues of race and class at home and abroad. In the colonies, an imbalance between European male and European female populations sometimes led to sexual encounters between European men and prostitutes, indigenous women, and other men. The arrival of European women into European colonies might counter these experiences by encouraging European male-female relationships including marriage but did not necessarily re-create traditional European social norms of marriage and family. Orwell's novel *Burmese Days,* based at least in part on his experiences as a colonial officer in Burma, reflects this history, as do the biographical and fictionalized accounts of Dinesen and Forster's Adela Quested. In both works, female and male characters negotiate encounters with gender and sex—including miscegenation—in the colonies, juxtaposed against the supposed social norms of gender, sex, race, and class in Europe.

Although culturally Europeans may have carried with them gender and sexual norms, scholars note that experiences in the colonies, where political and social restraints were diminished (like US historical interpretations of the "Wild West") often reflected or affected gender and sexual tensions in European societies, reshaping gender and sexual cultures abroad and in metropoles.

In Colonial Settings

One of the most notorious sexually promiscuous colonial settlements that gained popular and salacious interest was Happy Valley in Kenya, where the aristocratic community (the so-called Happy Valley set) engaged in adultery, cross-dressing, wife-swapping parties, alcohol, and drugs, as well as, in its most infamous popular story recounted in books, film, and newspapers, the

---

7 Anne McClintock, *Imperial Leather: Race, Gender, and Sexuality in the Colonial Contest* (New York: Routledge, 1995).

mysterious murder of playboy and serial adulterer Josslyn Hay, Earl of Erroll. Although some of the coverage of Happy Valley has been more prurient than strictly factual, reporting on the Happy Valley set reveals not only the frontier mentality of European colonists toward sex and gender, but the continued metropolitan fascination, whether outraged or titillated, of free-spirited White colonial settlements abroad and the sexual encounters among European colonists and between European and indigenous peoples.

Orwell's *Burmese Days* and Forster's *A Passage to India* examine issues of miscegenation, sex, marriage, and friendship between men and women and White colonists and indigenous colonial subalterns. In *Burmese Days*, protagonist Flory's mistress is a Burmese woman, but then he throws her out to please the White woman he hopes to marry to secure their White colonial statuses. Forster explores the biases and tensions of friendship or equality between the English and Indian populations and the tensions of sex, marriage, and (feared) miscegenation among his protagonists Adela, Ronny, and Aziz and their communities.

Conclusion

Despite stereotypes of European—specifically British Victorian—prudishness, scholars have come to recognize that gender and sexuality played important roles in European metropoles and colonies. This included a frontier mentality in the colonies, where White men engaged in sexual relationships outside of perceived norms. Specific examples include relations with women of color and the tensions of miscegenation. While White men tended to control sexual and gender norms and relationships in the metropoles and colonies, White women also played a role in renegotiating sex and gender in colonial spaces. Experimentation and shifts in European norms in the colonies often sparked changes in the metropoles.

War, Peace, and Diplomacy

Global Warfare in the Eighteenth Century

Military affairs in the 1700s saw refinements of technology combined with new battle formations. They also called into question the role of military forces and state building. In nations like Sweden, Prussia, or France, armies and navies dramatically increased. **Louis XIV** (r. 1643–1715) provided a model for growth. The "Sun King," who very much subscribed to the "divine right of kings," saw a large French army as not only a protector of the state but a guarantor of his power. For this very reason, the United Kingdom and the Commonwealth of Poland and Lithuania maintained small armies to limit royal authority.

While some armies still had pikemen, most infantry employed flintlock muskets, which could become pike-like by attaching a bayonet. Although flintlocks were more reliable than the earlier matchlocks, they retained smooth-bore barrels, like a modern shotgun, and were inaccurate beyond 100 yards. Colonel George Hanger (1751–1824) claimed that soldiers aiming muskets at targets 200 yards away "may as well aim at the moon."

Officers compensated for the flintlock's inaccuracy by firing massed volleys. This required soldiers to stand close to one another and hold their fire until the enemy was very close. At that point, they unleashed a volley of shots, and with so many pointing their muskets in the same direction, inaccuracy abated. Victory often went to soldiers who could reload quickly while standing firm as comrades fell from enemy shots.

Packed in dense blocks while wearing their very noticeable white, red, or green uniforms, the infantrymen were also targeted by artillery. Firing 3- to 12-pound iron balls at ranges far beyond that of a musket, artillery was more mobile than before, and although most ammunition was solid and did not explode, cannon balls bounced toward a line of infantry with the ability to kill or maim multiple soldiers. If they broke under fire and fled the field, enemy cavalry, armed with lances, sabers, or pistols, were ready to chase them down.

Keeping soldiers on the battlefield under such conditions required drill and discipline. Learning to march at the start of a military career today teaches discipline, but in the 1700s, it also instructed soldiers on basic maneuvers necessary to win battles. Throughout the eighteenth century, generals debated the efficacy of sending infantry to battle in a dense column, which provides mass, or lines, which present smaller targets and allow more muskets to fire.

Warfare outside of Europe influenced the debate on, for example, the four conflicts between Britain and France to dominate North America. Called the French and Indian Wars in America, these were often spinoffs from larger wars in Europe fought between 1688–1763. Followed by the American Revolution a decade later, all emphasized the value of **light infantry**.

These soldiers carried less gear, were better trained, and most often picked men who were much less likely to desert than regular line infantry. Light infantry fought in loose order, were employed as scouts and skirmishers, and usually were better marksmen. Some were armed with rifled muskets, where the barrel contained internal grooves that spun a bullet being fired, making it easier to hit targets. By the 1790s, all major armies fielded light infantry.

Light infantry could also be tasked with keeping watch over line troops. Most armies practiced harsh discipline, mainly because serving as a soldier was very unpopular. Unlike elite units, line soldiers obtained little pay, poor food, and many chances of death, from the battlefield or disease. The navy was no better, for as Dr. Samuel Johnson put it, "No man will be a sailor who has contrivance enough to get himself into jail; for being in a ship is being in a jail, with the chance of being drowned."

Modern readers probably know someone who wore yellow ribbons to "support the troops" in early-twenty-first century America. That would be a rare individual in the 1700s. Most soldiers came from the lowest levels of society; in many cases, they had been "pressed" into service and were constantly watched in barracks or camp for fear of desertion. Soldiers were viewed as the scum of the earth.

Governments knew this and even used the popular image of soldiers as a coercive tool. Wanting to convert or chase Protestants from France, Louis XIV had authorized "dragonnades," where his mounted infantry, dragoons, were given the right to live in the homes of French Huguenots. When Parliament passed the **Quartering Act** (1774), this was to punish truculent colonists in North America. They dubbed it one of the "Intolerable Acts" and feared degenerate soldiers might be placed in their homes. The Third Amendment to the United States Constitution is a direct result of the Quartering Act.

Distaste for lowly privates did not extend to army leaders, who could often be both generalissimo and head of state. With few checks on their authority, they could start wars with long-term consequences. An example was the Great Northern War (1700–1719), which provides lessons on the difference between good and great generals. The conflict started when a cabal of monarchs attempted to gain advantages over 18-year-old King **Karl XII** (r. 1697–1718) of Sweden.

Karl proved a brilliant tactician who defeated one enemy after another. His success was ephemeral, as his foes possessed greater resources, and in the case of Russian Tsar Pyotr I (r. 1682–1725), could learn from their mistakes. This combination brought Sweden low after disaster at Poltava (1709), where, lured deep into the Ukraine, Karl lost most of his army. Fighting for ten more years, the Swedish monarch died in battle but not before Sweden lost so much, it was no longer a great power.

An Iranian version of Karl provided a similar lesson. **Nader Shah** (r. 1736–1747), who admired Genghis Kan and Amir Timur, led Iranian armies to victories in Iraq, Central Asia, and the Indian subcontinent. He smashed through the Khyber Pass, capturing Delhi, capital of India's Mughal Empire. Allowing his troops to loot and murder at will, Nader gathered enough treasure to provide Iranians with a three-year tax holiday.

Returning home, he fought more battles, which, combined with his deadly paranoia, alienated so many subjects; his own officers murdered the shah in 1747. Within a year, his empire collapsed. Nader and Karl were good generals. Good generals win battles; great generals win wars.

Frederick II of Prussia (r. 1740–1786) was a great general. Inheriting a militarized state from his father, he employed it to wrest valuable territories from Austria. Frederick not only mastered battlefields but understood coalition warfare and always had a powerful ally. With the best-drilled army in Europe, his Prussian soldiers regularly defeated Austrian, French, and Russian counterparts.

He was highly aggressive, constantly seeking ways to fix enemy forces in place, then take advantage of his superbly drilled soldiers to rapidly combine the force necessary to crush one part of his opponents' line. At Rossbach (1757), Frederick masked his intentions so that less-disciplined enemies were unable to respond to a powerful flank attack. Two years later at Kunersdorf, he failed to reconnoiter Russian positions and sent his men into an unwinnable battle. Frederick described Russian failure to follow up their victory as a "miracle," learned from his error, and went on to triumph. Unlike Karl XII or Nader Shah, Frederick used military supremacy to make his country more powerful via lasting change.

Under Frederick, Prussia became a model of excellence. His former enemies copied some Prussian ideas and sought to make their militaries more efficient. French generals fared poorly against Frederick but could claim they played an important role in assisting rebellious English colonists to establish the United States of America in the 1780s.

American rebels significantly benefited from money and military support provided by France and Spain. These nations had large fleets and military engineers—vital force multipliers when conducting siege warfare. Yorktown and Pensacola both capitulated in 1781 due to European trained engineers who advanced their artillery to successfully bombard British defenders, while supporting navies prevented escape.

The French army took lessons from their defeats by Frederick and success in America. These resulted in new military formations and improved artillery. Jean-Baptiste de Gribeauval (1715–1789) redesigned the cannons, howitzers, and mortars employed by France. His **Gribeauval system** called for uniform designs to allow for easier maintenance while reducing the weight of each gun and carriage, so that they were more maneuverable on the battlefield.

Employing these cannons, along with soldiers on foot and horseback in a "combined arms" approach, was a sound tactic. Each group contributed unique values, and wise generals understood they were more powerful as a team. Commanders like Frederick were very good at mixing different types of soldiers to create victory.

The French made combined arms tactics more flexible with their use of divisions and corps. These were large bodies of troops from all three branches, directed by a subordinate commander. The combination of divisions, corps, and Gribeauval artillery dramatically improved the strength of French armies, which was made very clear under Napoleon Bonaparte's leadership in the 1790s.

Selim III (r. 1789–1807), Padishah of the Ottoman Empire, also sought to improve his armed forces. Disturbed by Russia's successful annexation of the Crimea, he also witnessed the start of the French Revolution. Transformation was in the air, and Selim saw a need for drastic changes at home. He pushed a multipronged agenda called *Niẓām-ı Cedīd* (new organization), which sought to change Ottoman educational, economic, political, and military norms.

Ottoman soldiers were asked to turn in their additional swords, pistols, daggers, and flamboyant uniforms. In exchange, they obtained European-style garments, a musket, and bayonet. *Niẓām-ı Cedīd* reformers argued the status quo had produced few victories over the last century, and for the Empire to remain a great power, it had to adopt English, French, or Prussian ways of war.

The new organization was not just about weapons and uniforms, but also about tactics. Officers unwilling to learn new drills had no place in the reforming army and navy of Selim III. They joined forces hostile to change and combined with the distraction of a foreign war in 1806, staged a coup overthrowing the sultan.

The counterrevolutionary victory halted Ottoman military reforms for almost two decades. Other parts of the world also witnessed quashed revolutions. Pontiac (d. 1769), a leader of the Odawa people, attempted to form a confederation for fighting British expansion in North America, but failed. José Noguera (1738–1781), who claimed Inca royal descent and declared himself Túpac Amaru II, played a similar role in Peru. Both indigenous revolutions failed; Spain and Britain were too powerful.

Another New World revolution was very successful and featured the largest slave uprising since the Zanj Revolt in southern Iraq during the Abbasid Caliphate. Centered in the French colony of Saint-Domingue, it was a brutal conflict with atrocities provided by both sides. Rebel forces benefited from a self-thought strategist, General Toussaint Louverture (1743–1803), who organized effective militias to dominate the island and proved an adroit diplomat in dealing with the British.

Louverture's efforts were enhanced by a simultaneous revolution taking place in France. From 1789–1815, France went from monarchy to republic to empire, and back to monarchy. The revolutionaries called for "liberty, equality, and fraternity," but like American revolutionary leaders who declared "all men are created equal," slaves were a different matter. To secure their liberty, ex-slaves of Saint-Domingue had to defeat French regulars and create the New World's second republic—Haiti.

Their success came from hard fighting, simultaneous involvement of the French in multiple wars, plus tropical diseases like **yellow fever**, for which Europeans had no acquired immunity. Possibly a third of the troops sent to crush the revolution died this way. It took a century for military medicine to determine how to combat yellow fever and reduce it virulence.

Primary Source 4

Following the lead of the United States and France, Toussaint Louverture offered Haiti, which would become a former French colony (Saint-Domingue), a constitution to legitimize the gains of the Haitian Revolution and the ideals of the revolutionary age. This constitution did not last, as Louverture was deported to France, where he died in the French prison Fort de Joux in 1803. He did not live to see official Haitian independence in 1804.

Constitution of 1801

The representatives of the colony of Saint-Domingue, gathered in Central Assembly, have arrested and established the constitutional bases of the regime of the French colony of Saint-Domingue as follows:

...

Of the Territory

Art. 1. – Saint-Domingue in its entire expanse, and Samana, La Tortue, La Gonave, Les Cayemites, L'Ile-a-Vache, La Saone and other adjacent islands form the territory of a single colony, which is part of the French Empire, but ruled under particular laws.

...

Of the Inhabitants

Art. 3. – There cannot exist slaves on this territory, servitude is therein forever abolished. All men are born, live and die free and French.

Art. 4. – All men, regardless of color, are eligible to all employment.

Art. 5. – There shall exist no distinction other than those based on virtue and talent, and other superiority afforded by law in the exercise of a public function.
    The law is the same for all whether in punishment or in protection.

...

Of Men in Society

Art. 12. – The Constitution guarantees freedom and individual security. No one shall be arrested unless a formally expressed mandate, issued from a functionary to whom the law grants the right to order arrest and detention in a publicly designated location.

Toussaint Louverture, "Haitian Constitution of 1801," 1801.

Art. 13. – Property is sacred and inviolable. All people, either by himself, or by his representatives, has the free right to dispose and to administer property that is recognized as belonging to him. Anyone who attempts to deny this right shall become guilty of crime towards society and responsible towards the person troubled in his property.

...

Of Cultures and Commerce

...

Art. 16. – Each cultivator and each worker is a member of the family and shares in parts of the revenues.

...

Art. 18. – Commerce in the colony consists uniquely of exchange goods produced on its territory; consequently, the introduction of goods similar in nature is and shall remain prohibited.

...

Of the Legislation and Legislative Authority

Art 19. – The colonial regime is determined by laws proposed by the Governor and rendered by a gathering of inhabitants, who shall meet at fixed periods at the central seat of the colony under the title Central Assembly of Saint-Domingue.

...

Of the Government

Art. 27. – The administrative direction of the government shall be entrusted to a Governor who corresponds directly with the government of the Metropole, on all matters relative to the interests of the colony.

Art. 28. – The Constitution nominates the citizen Toussaint-Louverture, Chief General of the army of Saint-Domingue, and, in consideration for important services rendered to the colony, in the most critical circumstances of the revolution, and upon the wishes of the grateful inhabitants, he is entrusted the direction thereof for the remainder of his glorious life.

Art. 29. – In the future, each governor shall be nominated for five years, and shall continue every five years for reasons of his good administration.

Art. 30. – In order to strengthen the tranquility that the colony owes to steadfastness, activity, indefatigable zeal and rare virtues of the General Toussaint-Louverture, and in sign of the unlimited trust of the inhabitants of Saint-Domingue, the Constitution attribute exclusively to this general the right to designate the citizen who, in the unfortunate event of the general's death, shall immediately replace him. This choice shall remain secret; it shall be cosigned under sealed envelope and to be opened only by the Central Assembly, in presence of all active generals and chief commanders of departments of the army of Saint-Domingue.

...

Art. 31. – The citizen that shall be chosen by the Governor Toussaint-Louverture to take the direction of the government upon his death, shall swear in front of the Central Assembly to execute the Constitution of Saint-Domingue and to remain attached to the French government, and shall be immediately installed in his functions; all shall be in presence of active generals and chief commanders of departments of the army of Saint-Domingue, who all, individually and without delay, shall swear obedience to the orders of the new Governors Saint-Domingue.

...

Art. 77. – The Chief General Toussaint-Louverture is and shall remain charged with sending the present Constitution to be sanctioned by the French government ...

...

Signed: Toussaint-Louverture

Discussion Question

1. How does the Haitian Constitution attempt to uphold the ideals of "liberty, equality, and fraternity?" Give some specific examples and explain why they are important.

Global Warfare, Empires, and Imperialism

Warfare in imperial history is long-reaching and complex. Many argue that imperialism itself is rooted in violence and exploitation, and thus separating it from these characteristics is pointless. A direct connection can be made between European empires and global warfare in the Seven Years' War (1756–1763), fought in battles on several continents, and these conflicts, collectively, are linked to the twentieth-century World Wars. Winston Churchill, prime minister of England during **World War II**, famously connected the eighteenth-century conflicts to later wars by calling the Seven Years' War "the first world war" in his *A History of English-Speaking Peoples*. This great war of empires was a notable conflict in the history of European and global warfare, leading to a twentieth century of violence that Europeans found astonishing and post-colonialists found a logical outcome of imperial violence.

Although the Seven Years' War has been regarded as either a European war of religion or an American (French and Indian Wars) conflict, its history is global and complex. Great Britain, Prussia, Portugal, and allies fought on several fronts against France, Spain, Austria, Russia, Sweden, and allies. These fronts included colonial spaces in the West Indies, Africa, and India. Participants included indigenous peoples around the world living under European dominance or those interested in the outcome of battles for their own sakes. Indigenous peoples, for example, fought on the North American fronts of the Seven Years' War—the French and Indian Wars. The outcome of these battles cemented British power in North America at the expense of their rival France. Different groups of North American indigenous peoples sided with the British or the French, or, in the case of the Iroquois, attempted to avoid the conflict except for their own economic interests.

Despite British success and the 1763 Peace of Paris, signed by Britain, France, Spain, and Portugal, the tensions of these wars festered, and hot spots helped spark the American Revolution, the French Revolution, and the Napoleonic Wars. Threads of the Seven Years' War can then be connected to global conflicts that played out in the nineteenth, twentieth, and, arguably, the twenty-first century.

As a key result of the Seven Years' War, the British Empire began its path to global domination, expanding its reach to Africa. Although attempts were made in the Berlin Conference to divide the continent through diplomacy, tensions and conflicts among Europeans and between Europeans and Africans emerged that continued the course of modern global conflicts. An illustrative example is the Boer or **South African War.**

South African War

By the nineteenth century, South African populations and settlements included native Africans and Dutch (Boer) and British colonists, as well as smaller populations of peoples from around the world. Conflicts of national identity emerged between African, Dutch, and British internal claims to land, power, and sovereignty, as well as global pressures of increasing **globalization** and industrialization.

These conflicts often led to violent clashes, including what many identify as the first war of the twentieth century—the South African or Boer War from 1899–1902. This conflict is illustrative of the changing culture of war from traditional nineteenth century to the modern industrialized warfare of the twentieth and twenty-first centuries. The conflict is also another episode of the clash of imperialism and nationalism around the globe as the Dutch (Boer) colonized South Africa and fought against the encroaching power of the British Empire. The British not only feared a loss of prestige if they lost to what they regarded as ragtag groups of farmers but to a loss in a colonial space to less sophisticated European and African populations.

Because the war was fought between an imperial army and Dutch farmers and civilians, it saw the use of **guerrilla warfare**, where British troops reacted in kind to Dutch farmers' methods rather than in a traditional British military fashion. At the same time, advancement in military technologies meant that British soldiers were subjected to constant shelling and forced to retreat to unsanitary dugouts (precursors to World War I trench warfare) and suffered from anxiety, boredom, and disease as much as (if not more) from actual casualties. This experience was a foreshadowing of the shell shock and disillusionment of World War I, as well as a humiliating experience for British troops who not only outnumbered the Dutch in South Africa, but who were supposed to represent the greatest global power at the time. The South African War added to British doubts about their continued abilities to rule as an empire. This clash between European claims within a colonial space was also a harbinger of the World Wars to come.

World War I

In 1914, localized national conflicts, as well as imperialistic international conflicts, flared into global war in what is known as the **July Crisis**. The catalysts of World War I continue to be debated among historians, but from a world history perspective, the causes of the war are best looked at broadly. These included continued tensions and skirmishes between empires, empire-states, and burgeoning nationalism, which led to disruption of authority systems. Unresolved disputes and a web-like alliance system between European powers (and hence European colonies), as well as indications that Europe's balance of power was crumbling, led to miscalculations and misunderstandings between political and military leaders within nation-states and among countries that played a role in the complex European alliance system. Many of the tensions leading up to 1914 can be traced backward through time to long-standing imperial tensions, including the traditional marking point for the outbreak of World War I: the June 28, 1914, assassination of **Archduke Franz Ferdinand** by Serbian nationalist **Gavrilo Princip**.

Ferdinand served as heir apparent for the Austro-Hungarian Empire, which comprised parts of Poland, Italy, Austria, Hungary, and the former Czechoslovakia. In 1908, the Austro-Hungarian Empire annexed Bosnia in the Balkans, a historical hotbed of ethnic, religious, and nationalist struggles. Annexation of Bosnia clashed with Serbian plans to create a southern Slavic state, and when Archduke Ferdinand toured the region in June 1914, the **Black Hand**, a radical nationalist group to which Princip belonged, planned his assassination. After an initial bungled attempt, Princip shot and killed the archduke and his wife, Sophie, Duchess von Hohenberg. Within months, this dispute spread to encompass Europe and concurrent conflicts in Asia and the Middle East.

Yet, World War I affected populations outside of Eurasia as European nations with overseas colonies often brought their colonists and subalterns into the conflict as troops, support troops, and workers to provide services and resources—for examples, oil and rubber—to the Eurasian fronts of the war. Britain and France sought influence in Middle Eastern geopolitical holdings, and these as well as internal tensions brought the Ottoman Empire into the war on the side of Germany.

Although World War I's cease-fire was initiated by a series of armistices and the signing of treaties, including the **Treaty of Versailles** (between the **Allied Powers** and Germany) and the **Treaty of Sèvres** (France and Britain with the Ottoman Empire), tensions between nations, states, and empires continued in the interwar period. Although Western accounts traditionally mark the outbreak of World War II with Hitler's 1939 invasion of Poland, that account glosses over global imperial ambitions, such as those by Japan and Italy in Asia and Africa, as those two nations attempted to follow Western models of empire building.

World War II: Marco Polo Bridge Incident and the Invasion of Ethiopia

By 1931, Japan, like the rest of the world, faced the **Great Depression,** leading to internal political and social unrest in which nationalist and militarist forces flourished. Japan had already signaled its imperialist aims in Manchuria and its interests in expanding its influence in Asia, especially in China. In the summer of 1937, the **Marco Polo Bridge Incident** gave Japan an excuse to expand their aggression against China. Global historians mark this as not only the beginning of the Pacific Theater of World War II but the first action of World War II. It was also an act of empire building.

The **Italo-Ethiopian War**, 1935–1936, was another contributing factor to the outbreak of World War II. In 1935, Italy, with a stated goal of building its own empire, invaded Ethiopia. Ethiopia was not only one of the last remaining areas of Africa to have successfully resisted earlier European (including Italian) imperialism but served Italian geopolitical needs as a region rich with fertile land and minerals. Ethiopian troops clashed with Italian forces and appealed to the **League of Nations** for protection against Italian imperialist aims. League intervention was slow and ineffective, and Italian forces under **Benito Mussolini** finally conquered Ethiopia.

North African Campaign and Colonial Troops

The aftermath of Italy's invasion led to the North African front of World War II. With the need for military resources such as oil, Europeans sought to protect their interests in colonies or **protectorates**, which led to a **North African Campaign**. This campaign was a series of battles fought for control of Northern Africa, with British goals for continued influence and management of the **Suez Canal**. The Suez Canal had crucial geopolitical and economic importance as a conduit for trade and travel between Africa and Asia, access to oil reserves, and a centerpiece of British imperial power in the region.

Although traditionally couched as battles between the main European Allied and **Axis** powers, the location of this front, as well as the use of colonial troops, is a key example of how the World Wars were intimately tied to empire and imperial citizens and subalterns. African, Indian, and Caribbean troops of color served on a variety of World War II fronts as military support and even as combatants. British African troops gathered from groups across the African continent served a crucial role in helping defeat not only Germany and Italy in North Africa, but on other fronts as well.

British Commonwealth White troops from New Zealand and Australia also served in North African (and other) campaigns, as did **Maori** soldiers from New Zealand. The 28th or Maori Battalion (Figure 2.7), some 16,000 volunteer troops from the indigenous New Zealand population, served with distinction in North Africa and battalion soldiers, including **Te Moananui-a-Kiwa Ngārimu,** were awarded the Victoria Cross given to Commonwealth troops for bravery and gallantry in action.

Unfortunately, this recognition of colonial troops, especially those of color, did not settle issues of race relations in the metropoles or the colonies. Colonial troops of color, disillusioned after their service in World War I and

FIGURE 2.7   Maori soldiers in North Africa, July, 1941.

World War II, embraced the goals of freedom and popular sovereignty and fought their own battles against racism, imperialism, and degradation, leading to successful decolonization movements after World War II across Asia and Africa.

Conclusion

Some scholars have noted that like World War I, where tactics like those of the South African War made their way to Europe, World War II showed how the European dehumanization of fellow Europeans mirrored European dehumanization of indigenous peoples in colonial spaces. The horrors of the World Wars caused people around the world to question the sophistication and civilization of the modern world—especially the civilization lauded by **the West**. This questioning led to initiatives to create global international relations and humanitarian action, including decolonization efforts, in part because of the recognition that Western imperialism had gone beyond the pale, and peace treaties, including those of the World Wars that embraced the ideal of **self-determination**, had not been fully realized on a global scale. In the wake of World War II, despite the formation of the **United Nations**, decolonization—and an end to the geopolitics of empire and imperialism on the world stage—was still an aspiration, not a completed project. Although waves of decolonization did occur in the late twentieth century, scholars argue that remnants, at least, of empires and imperialism linger in the contemporary world. From questions over the role of the United States and the Soviet Union during the Cold War to contemporary meanings of globalization, and, as United Nations' secretary-general Ban Ki-moon has noted, the continued existence of non-self-governing territories in the twenty-first century suggests that decolonization is not yet complete. It is also not certain that the history of empires and imperialism has ended.

Chapter Summary

The history of empires and imperialism after 1500 was traditionally told as a story related to the "rise of the West." Global scholarship has turned this narrative on its head to reveal that European empires and imperialism after 1500 were rooted in historical and geographical complexities and that imperialists, colonists, and subalterns all played important roles in empire building, the culture of imperialism, and decolonization efforts. While the rise of European empires and the spread of European methods of imperialism left an indelible stamp on the world after 1500, empire and imperialism are conjunctures with global causes and effects, including modern warfare, globalization, and continued global inequities and racism.

Discussion Questions

1. How did imperialists, colonists, intermediaries, and imperial citizens and subalterns shape empires and imperialism?
2. As related to empire and imperialism after 1500, how did these groups participate in:
   a. Material culture
   b. Science and technology

    c.   Gender and sexuality

    d.   War, peace, and diplomacy

5.   How did the science of agriculture contribute to European imperial power and industrialization?

6.   How did race intersect with gender and sexuality in metropoles and colonies?

7.   Explain why the World Wars were not just global but imperial conflicts.

8.   Analyze the Pears' Soap advertisement in Figure 2.6. What messages does the advertisement give to consumers? How do these messages relate to empire and imperialism and their themes and methods? It may be useful to examine additional Pears' Soap advertisements, which are widely available on the internet.

9.   Watch *Out of Africa* (Sydney Pollack, 1985) or *A Passage to India* (David Lean, 1984) and discuss in class how the films depict the intersections and negotiations of gender, sexuality, and race in European colonies.

References

Using the Sources

Beyond the primary sources provided in this chapter, students will benefit from analyzing maps and images provided and additional readings and materials cited below. Students and instructors may find film and literary adaptations particularly helpful in the classroom or as additional assignments. A list of suggested supplementary sources is provided.

Primary Sources

Césaire, Aimé. 1972. "Discourse on Colonialism." *Monthly Review Press*, 1–31.

Davenport, Frances G., Charles Oscar Paullin, and Carnegie Institution of Washington, Issuing Body. 1917. *European Treaties Bearing on the History of the United States and Its Dependencies*. Carnegie Institution of Washington Publication. Papers of the Department of Historical Research; No. 254. Washington, DC: Carnegie Institution of Washington.

Halsall, Paul, ed. "Internet History Sourcebooks Project." Fordham University. Accessed April 20, 2018. https://sourcebooks.fordham.edu/index.asp

Louverture, Toussaint. "Haitian Constitution of 1801 (English): Constitution of 1801." Translated by Charmant Theodore. *The Louverture Project, Haitian Constitution of 1801 (English)*. http://thelouvertureproject.org/index.php?title=Haitian_Constitution_of_1801_(English)

Mancall, Peter C., ed. 2017. *Envisioning America: English Plans for the Colonization of North America*. Boston: Bedford/St. Martin's.

Phillips, Geo. 1896. "Mahuan's Account of Cochin, Calicut, and Aden." *Journal of the Royal Asiatic Society of Great Britain and Ireland*, 341–51.

Thatcher, Oliver J. 1915. *The Library of Original Sources: Ideas That Have Influenced Civilization, in the Original Documents*. Milwaukee, WI: University Research Extension, 1915.

Film

America Before Columbus. Directed by Cristina Trebbi. National Geographic, 2009. TV Movie.

The Battle of Algiers. Directed by Gillo Poolyntecorvo. Criterion Collection, 2013. DVD.

Breaker Morant. Directed by Bruce Beresford. New World Pictures, 1997. DVD.

The Kitchen Toto. Directed by Harry Hook. Warner Home Video, 1995. VHS.

Out of Africa. Directed by Sydney Pollack. Universal Pictures Home Entertainment, 2000. DVD.

A Passage to India. Directed by David Lean. 1984. Sony Pictures Home Entertainment, 2001. DVD.

Wah-wah. Directed by Richard E. Grant. Roadside Attractions, 2005.

The War of the World. Directed by Adrian Pennick. PBS Home Video, 2006. DVD.

Secondary Sources

Adkins, Lesley, and Roy Adkins. 2017. *Gibraltar: The Greatest Siege in British History.* New York: Hachette.

Burbank, Jane, and Frederick Cooper. 2011. *Empires in World History: Power and the Politics of Difference.* Princeton, NJ: Princeton University Press.

Clark, Brett, and John Bellamy Foster. 2009. *Ecological Imperialism: The Curse of Capitalism.* Merlin Press.

Cooper, Frederick, and Ann Laura Stoler, eds. 1997. *Tensions of Empire: Colonial Cultures in a Bourgeois World.* Berkeley: University of California Press.

Cronon, William. 2003. *Changes in the Land: Indians, Colonists, and the Ecology of New England.* New York: Hill and Wang.

Crosby, Alfred W. 2003. *The Columbian Exchange: Biological and Cultural Consequences of 1492.* Westport, CT: Praeger Publishers.

———. 2004. *Ecological Imperialism: The Biological Expansion of Europe, 900–1900.* Cambridge: Cambridge University Press.

Dash, Mike. 2012. "The Blazing Career and Mysterious Death of 'The Swedish Meteor,'" in Smithsonian. Accessed online September 12, 2018.

Dreyer, Edward L. 2007. *Zheng He: China and the Oceans in the Early Ming Dynasty, 1405–1433.* New York: Pearson Longman.

Englund, Peter. 2003. *The Battle that Shook Europe: Poltava and the Birth of the Russian Empire.* London: I. B. Tauris.

McClintock, Anne. 1995. *Imperial Leather: Race, Gender, and Sexuality in the Colonial Contest.* New York: Routledge.

McNeill, J. R. 2010. *Mosquito Empires: Ecology and War in the Greater Caribbean, 1620–1914.* New York: Cambridge University Press.

Middleton, Richard. 2007. *Pontiac's War: Its Causes, Course and Consequences.* New York: Routledge.

Mintz, Sidney W. 1986. *Sweetness and Power: The Place of Sugar in Modern History.* New York: Penguin Group.

Ross, Steven T. 1996. *From Flintlock to Rifle: Infantry Tactics, 1740–1866.* London: Taylor & Francis.

Walker, Charles F. 2014. *The Tupac Amaru Rebellion.* The Belknap Press of Harvard University Press.

Walvin, James. 1997. *Fruits of Empire: Exotic Produce and British Taste, 1660–1800.* New York: New York University Press.

Williams, Eric. 1994. *Capitalism and Slavery.* Translated by Rose-Myriam Réjouis. Chapel Hill: University of North Carolina Press.

Yaycioglu, Ali. 2016. *Partners of the Empire: The Crisis of the Ottoman Order in the Age of Revolutions.* Stanford, CA: Stanford University Press.

Fiction

Achebe, Chinua. 1958. *Things Fall Apart.*

Chamoiseau, Patrick. 1998. *Texaco.* Translated by Rose-Myriam Réjouis and Val Vinokurov. New York: Vintage Books.

Dinesen, Isak. 1937. *Out of Africa.*

Forster, E. M. 1924. *A Passage to India.*

Orwell, George. 1974. *Burmese Days.* New York: Houghton Mifflin.

Singh, Khushwant. 1956. *Train to Pakistan.*

Credits

Chapter 3

The Global Industrial Revolution

Introduction to Chapter Themes

Even in academic and economic circles, confusion still exists about the meaning of industrialization, the period and place of its inception, and its subsequent global impact. As a concept, industrialization is much older than the more recently coined but widespread term *globalization*. To complicate the issue, the word "revolution" has been added to the term *industrialization*. It was British economic historian Arnold Toynbee who popularized the expression "Industrial Revolution" through his lectures at Oxford University during the early 1880s, which, in 1884, resulted in the publication of his book *The Industrial Revolution*, whose theme was Britain's transformation from a hand- or manual-based to a mechanical-based economy during the mid-eighteenth and the late nineteenth centuries. Historically, the concept of revolution, especially political revolution, has been applied to the unexpected rapid and substantive change of widespread impact, often, but not always, achieved through violence. The current chapter focuses on two global phenomena: namely, industrialization and its globalization from the eighteenth century to the present era and the economic, social, political, and environmental impact on the world of the time as well as on our own, following the themes the textbook addresses, that is, geography and environment; material culture; science and technology; gender and sexuality; and war, peace, and diplomacy.

It would be inaccurate to conclude that the Industrial Revolution was not intricately related to the prevailing economic conditions prior to its start. The state of commerce prior to 1760 or so, which some historians have called the period of the **Commercial Revolution**, gave impetus to the new developments beginning around 1300 up to 1700, to the extent that, without it, the Industrial Revolution would not have occurred at the time it did. The new economic activity marked a drastic and almost sudden break with the past, leaping from the essentially static, localized exchange of goods and often non-profitable enterprises to the innovations of the period we call the Industrial Revolution. The *Encyclopaedia Britannica* (2018) describes this period as one that experienced increased commerce that had begun during the Middle Ages, spurred by the New World explorations initiated by the Portuguese, the Spaniards, and the British, specifically characterized by the creation of chartered companies, mercantilism (an economic system where the state is directly involved in the economic sector at the expense of the other nations), a money economy, increased specialization, banking, the bourse (stock exchange), and a "futures market."

The preceding general innovations, precursors of the Industrial Revolution, are succinctly identified by Edward Burns and Philip Ralph as follows: monopolization of the Mediterranean trade by Italy and the resulting commercial relations between the Italian cities and the merchants of the Hanseatic League in Northern Europe; the massive increase in coin minting for commercial transactions; continuous availability of surplus capital from trade, banking, and mining; increased demand for raw materials that resulted in more taxable income; and desire for goods from the Far East, especially China, whose attraction increased after Marco Polo's voyage during the thirteenth century. There were, in fact, several technological advances before the commonly accepted beginning period of the Industrial Revolution. These included the pendulum clock, the spinning wheel, iron and brass forging through the melting and shaping process, techniques for glass blowing, artistic fine woodwork, the air pump, the thermometer, and navigation instruments, including the compass. Socially and economically, an incipient but fast-growing capitalist class needed to invest its wealth, which accelerated the pace and scope of technological development.

Starting with improved transportation from the use of coal, the core of the Industrial Revolution spread to iron and steel manufacturing techniques and the successful tapping into sources of energy leading to the malleation (shaping) of metals, the invention of the steam engine, the use of electricity and petroleum, and during the second Industrial Revolution, the development of an internal combustion in automobiles, the steam-propelled railroad, the spinning jenny for textiles, and the power loom that led to higher output, using less manual or mechanical energy, the airplane in 1903, the telegraph in 1884, and the radio in 1895. All these innovations were tied to new scientific methods that made production faster and higher in volume in a shorter time.

Student Learning Objectives

After reading this chapter students should be able to describe and discuss:

- The differences between an agrarian economic system and the Industrial Revolution
- Concepts and factors that led to the impact of the Industrial Revolution in transportation, communication, and the globalizing trends that have continued to the present day
- The negative and positive consequences of the Industrial Revolution in the non-Western developing world
- The Industrial Revolution and the most recent technological developments, which some have called the third Industrial Revolution, especially those related to cyber learning and communication

Timeline of Selected Dates

1712	Thomas Newcomen invents first productive steam engine
1764/5	James Hargreaves invents the spinning jenny
1776	Adam Smith publishes *The Wealth of Nations*
1782	James Watt patents the double-acting engine

1788	First modern coins struck by steam presses at Soho Mint
1793	Eli Whitney invents the cotton gin
1801	Richard Trevithick patents the "steam carriage," leading to steam-powered locomotion
1802	Marc Brunel perfects the pulley block machine
1825	**Stockton & Darlington Railway** begins the first freight and passenger service railway
1828	James Beaumont Neilson improves on hot blast system for making pig iron
1844	Samuel Morse sends first telegraph message
1870	Start of the Second Industrial Revolution

Geography and Environment

The perennial question posed by scholars and non-scholars alike is why England, known now as the "cradle of industry," and later the rest of (western) Europe, were the earliest beneficiaries of the first and second Industrial Revolutions that began in the late 1700s. Several factors are said to have accounted for the geographic origins of this economic transformation. For England, one should first note its insular location, surrounded by water resources, such as the long River Thames and the harbors along the Atlantic Ocean and the English Channel. These seem to have played a major role in the process, as they are said to have propelled the inventions of the **water pump** and the steam engine, which from the start had an unexpected impact on economic production and life changes, most specifically in transportation, including the use of steam as the locomotive energy, for both short- and long-distance travel.

Origins of the Industrial Revolution

Experts note that the impact of the abundant natural resources in Europe, particularly England, needed to sustain the ongoing new "revolutionary" changes, including coal and iron deposits that later led to an improved water pump and the steam engine. These latter advancements allowed the inundated coal mines to dry and created a relatively comfortable working environment. As a result, many former coal sites of the various new factories and plants, sources of textile establishments, particularly **wool**, gained their hold from the presence of the available vast herds of sheep and other resources. The **merino sheep** especially enriched and increased the availability and quality of good cloth for the rich and the poor, and local and imported **silk**, flax, and linen in such places as Manchester.

The Industrial Revolution appears now to have started in specific small places such as Birmingham, England, a town that, because of the presence of numerous crafts became the center of lucrative economic activity. Indeed, Birmingham was known as the Center of the British *artisanats* of metal works, and an attractive site for skilled laborers and entrepreneurs, that later became the "first location of modern industry," followed by Yorkshire, with its woolen specialization and production; Flanders in Belgium for its linen craft; Lyon, France, as the silk capital; Siegerland and Silesia, Germany, for metalwork and linen; and other parts of France that later grew to become the center of cotton, linen, silk, and wool, or the textile hub of western Europe.

The industrial developments in Europe were transplanted or transported to North America by the pilgrims and other European emigrants. Here, the original industrial activities consisted mainly of shoemaking, nail forging, and textiles production for which some cities became famous. Besides their textiles, Philadelphia and New York were also renowned for food production and cotton mills, as well as silk weaving and reeling.

Prevailing Cottage Crafts

Prior to the Industrial Revolution, small localities both in Europe and North America specialized in beer brewery, tailoring, carpentry, cobbling, plumbing, and iron smelting, using coal, saw and paper mills, hammer and nail forging, and glassworks, some of which required water power even prior to 1750. Economically at the time, the busiest and most productive *artisanat* workshops were owned by powerful merchants, who controlled the markets and distributed the raw materials needed in those cottage manufacturers employing the centuries-old traditional manufacturing techniques. In other words, until the eighteenth century, in most countries in Europe and in the cottages (small country houses), skilled work was done or manufactured or handmade, even though the word "manufacture" was later applied to mechanization. It is important to realize here that the word *manufacture* came from the Latin ablative case *manu* (by hand) and the verb *facere* (to do). When the two words are combined, they mean "building" or making something by hand, or *manufactura*. This has caused much confusion when *artisanat's* production, mainly handicraft work, no longer had its original meaning, as it began to be applied to machinery rather than to hand production.

Among the enabling resources available in the British Isles and most of Europe was grain, which fed the rapidly growing sheep herd and other needed animals of work, such as horses and cattle, as well as the growing population in the rapidly emerging cities and towns, particularly in what has been called the West Midlands, where the most important industrial changes began. As a result, the West Midlands have been called "Cottonopolis" for their high production of cotton at one point during the eighteenth century. It was in the West Midlands that the best known centers of manufacturing and population growth, including Birmingham, Coventry, and Wolverhampton, emerged. The growing need for the use of iron, especially in the form of steel, was greatly spurred by the shortage of wood and the deforestation of many regions of Britain.

No wonder the European nations that were similarly endowed with natural resources were able to catch up quickly after the revolution had begun to spread, as was the case with Belgium, Switzerland, parts of France, such as Lyon, Italy, and the Scandinavian countries, and eventually the German states and unified Germany itself after 1870. In these regions of Europe and in North America, the rail mode of transportation, for example, spread very fast: Belgium, 1834; France, 1842; Switzerland, 1847; Germany, the 1850s; and America, 1832. The use of rail was so critical to the concept of Manifest Destiny for Britain's former colonies in North America that by 1900, they had surpassed all Europe in manufacturing, accounting for 24 percent of the "global output." America, in fact, outpaced even India, which, by the dawn of the nineteenth century, had been the number one producer of cotton in the world. Of course, in America, the cheap labor of enslaved Africans and their descendants explains why the United States overtook England's cotton manufacturing lead.

The Textile Industry and the Industrial Revolution

With the advances in spinning and weaving and therefore in the use of technology in the textile industry, Great Britain is said to have been importing some 500,000 tons of cotton a year by 1860. British colonial expansion in Africa, Asia, and Australia and the exploration and exportation of their raw materials needed to feed the factories and the transportation system in Europe, did nothing but help to spread and improve the progress of the new revolution in commerce and technological innovation on the old continent. The discovery of oil and natural gas occurred much earlier than the Industrial Revolution in England and the rest of Europe, but the two were used only for simple lighting purposes, such as lamps, candelabra, lanterns, and similar small devices and not as they were later used during the mid-twentieth century for automobiles and all types of electrical needs. The fast-growing population in England (as was the case in other European cities and towns) created new markets to meet the people's old and new needs. As a result, by the mid-nineteenth century, around 1851, the majority of the population of England and Wales was living in urban centers and not in the countryside as it had been for centuries.

In contrast to England, Belgium, France, Spain, Russia, and most other European countries did not start their Industrial Revolution in earnest until the mid-nineteenth century. Asia, Japan, China, and Taiwan, whose industrialization will be further discussed in this chapter, did not begin a serious industrial effort until the mid-twentieth century. For China, one scholar notes that "industrialization and economic development did not start in earnest until the change of economic policies by the communist national government toward the end of the twentieth century."[1] In explaining the lack of the early industrialization of China, one author notes the fact that China never ventured outside its own sea surroundings like Britain did and that its vast iron ore deposits were located in the north and not in the south, the economic hub of the future giant nation.

England had another advantage: government policies. Since the Magna Carta of 1215, aristocrats, and latter middle-class subjects of the monarchy, had forced legal changes that enhanced property rights. Additionally, the British had higher literacy rates, making for a more educated talent pool. Finally, British monarchs were supportive of private industry.

The French philosopher Voltaire wrote about these benefits in his 1733 essays entitled *Letters on the English*. He argued Great Britain had a powerful economy because the political and legal system made successful business ventures more likely. Voltaire continued with a note that British businessmen were more important than their aristocrats noting that these merchants added "to the felicity of the world." He was not the only foreigner to share this view, as witnessed by Jews and Huguenots fleeing persecution on the continent, who established businesses in the United Kingdom.

With these advantages, the British Isles raced ahead of European neighbors. In some cases, like France, numerous wars, the 1789–1815 revolutionary era, and lack of raw materials slowed efforts to industrialize. Germanys and Italy, with their motley collection of city-states, principalities, and nations, were not unified until the 1860s–1870s, and with a myriad of tax laws, customs barriers, and competing legal systems, not conducive to allowing a complete embrace of the Industrial Revolution. When unified after the **Franco-Prussian War** (1870–1871), it was no surprise that

---

1   "Industrial Revolution," *Geography*, http://geography.name/industrial-revolution/

Alsace and Lorraine were detached from the defeated French, so that the vast iron deposits of these provinces would benefit Germany.

Conclusion

The Industrial Revolution is believed to have begun during the late 1700s in what has been called "the cradle of industry"—England, more specifically Northern England—in such cities as Birmingham and Manchester, from which it spread to the rest of Europe and to other parts of the world, including North America. The insular location of England, its abundant natural resources, such as sheep, coal, and iron deposits, used later for water pumping, the steam engine that propelled trains and ships, silk, flan, and linen accounted in part for the industrial origins in this part of Europe. The rapid economic development had started centuries earlier with crafts at family cottages, evolving into the **factory** system that became characterized by mass and fast production, further propelled later the development of **assembly lines** that slowly but steadily began employing a large number of women, men, and children. Coal and textile production activities became the first and most important manufacturing centers. The impact of the changes was spurred further by the growing number of people coming from many parts of the countryside, which gave rise to modern towns and cities. Yet, many employees lived in slums and poor housing provided by the employers, causing intolerable conditions socially, especially in the area of health, as was particularly the case with tuberculosis and other infectious diseases. These conditions improved over time, however, through sanitation programs and legal protection of workers' rights.

Material Culture

The Industrial Revolution: Resources, Production, and Human Dignity

Material culture, a focus and concept dear to anthropologists and rarely ever mentioned by historians, refers, according to the *Encyclopaedia Britannica*, to man-made aspects of culture, such as "tools, buildings, weapons, utensils, ornaments, art, monuments, written records, religious images and clothing" specific to a group of people or culture.[2] Some historians hold the view that the foundation of the Industrial Revolution was not the steam engine that spurred the production of coal or iron (the latter in the form of steel) but an effect of it. The real propeller of changes, they believe, was the demand for an effective source of power to manage the heavy machinery, already available to the textile industry. Indeed, say Burns and Ralph, "Watt's engine, at least, would have never become a reality if there had not been a demand for textile heavy machinery production power" and that the improvement of the steam engine was certainly a cause of the more rapid growth of industrialization, making possible the tremendous changes in transportation.[3] Self-taught engineer George Stephenson provided an example of this in 1821, when he took the idea of horse-powered rail cars and replaced animals with a steam engine. The reader must keep in mind,

---

2   "Material Culture," *Encyclopaedia Britannica*, https://www.britannica.com/topic/material-culture

3   Edward Burns and Philip Ralph, *World Civilizations* (New York: Norton, 5th ed., 1974), 798.

however, that rail cars had existed before George Stephenson's invention of the steam-powered locomotive in 1821. The problem was that they were first pulled by horses.

This British-led revolution produced change due to need. A demand for turning linen, cotton, or wool into cloth encouraged the invention of better looms and the spinning jenny. These in turn encouraged James Hargreaves's 1767 steam engine. Steam engines made it easier to transform iron into steel, allowing for the creation of large factories, and giving Britain a dominant position in this vital ingredient of the nineteenth century.

While industrial progress made Great Britain strong and created great wealth, like all revolutions, there were winners and losers. Large numbers of laborers did not benefit in the success side of the Industrial Revolution, while weak nations now faced even greater threat from aggressors, who could harness its military technology. Karl Marx, economic historian and founder of **communism**, argued the Industrial Revolution benefited the upper classes, which he labeled the bourgeoisie, while subjugating the working class, whom he called the "proletariat."

The Critical Role of Coal

The great abundance, need, and use of coal in England led to the mechanized use of energy and to the accelerated spread of the Industrial Revolution to other parts of Europe. Coal, plus iron, was the raw materials needed for any nation to embrace this revolution. Copious quantities at home or extracted from colonies were critical. Otherwise, a nation had to import coal and iron, often an expensive proposition. Mehmet Ali's Egypt provides an example of this dilemma. The Ottoman Empire's autonomous *Wali* (Governor) from 1805–1848 understood the tremendous economic and industrial advantages offered by factories and steam engines. Lacking significant sources in his realm, the only way he could support native factories was to create monopolies and tariff barriers against competition from European firms that could obtain inexpensive raw materials. Egypt's Industrial Revolution ended with the Treaty of Balta Liman (1838). This was an agreement between the Ottoman sultan, Mehmet Ali's nominal overlord, and Great Britain. For England, Balta Liman promised an end to tariff walls like those of Egypt; for the sultan, this reduced Mehmet Ali's independence. For Egypt, incapable of fighting the United Kingdom, Balta Liman marked the start of an economic collapse. Mehmet Ali's factories could not compete with their better-financed British counterparts.

For countries with access to inexpensive coal, it fueled urban growth and dramatically altered industrial activities. Furthermore, starting in the second half of the eighteenth century, canals and later railways made it cheaper to move greater amounts of coal for markets of scale. Also, steam-powered water pumps made it easier to dig deeper and exploit even more of the United Kingdom's coal reserves.

Coal was more efficient for heating a home and preserved local timber for construction. Most English homes were converting from wood to coal by the early nineteenth century. But revolutionary changes seldom come without costs, and conversion to coal was no exception. Burning coal smoke, pouring from household and factory chimneys, created considerable amounts of air pollution. Locals referred to "pea soup" when weather conditions kept coal smoke–laden clouds overhead, dramatically reducing visibility to the point one could not see the other side of a street during daylight hours. A most dramatic example of this occurred in 1952, when more than 10,000 Londoners died from respiratory illnesses induced by a week-long pea soup.

The Social and Material Impact of the Factory

Science and technology advanced **industrialism** and led to a factory system of labor using power-driven machinery, such as the water frame and automatic loom. The booming textile and iron industries lured many people from the countryside to urban centers to look for jobs and other new opportunities. Populations also increased: England's population, for example, rose from 4 million to 6 million between 1600 and 1700 and to 9 million at the end of the nineteenth century; in France, it reached 26 million in 1800, up from 17 million in 1700. Naturally, with such an increase in population, the markets also grew larger, and people demanded more products, thus fueling further the implicit and dire need for the Industrial Revolution and mass-produced goods in factories. Factory owners (usually men) worked to expand productivity and their earnings. Richard Arkwright, for example, a former barber and wigmaker, often called "the *father of the modern industrial factory system*," established the first textile factory powered by water in 1771.

Early factory workers often worked under dire conditions with long hours and low pay. Factory work was by nature so repetitive and monotonous, especially if it required long sitting time that it could interfere with the worker's attention and result in mistakes harmful to workers. Early worksites were not regulated by labor laws, and factories were notorious for the constant noise and accidents leading to a variety of worker injuries, including dismemberment and death. Even children worked long hours in dangerous conditions. Children were valued as laborers in mills and factories in part because they were "nimble and small" enough to climb under machinery if needed. Although children had long worked in home or **cottage industries**, the Industrial Revolution intensified child labor practices in the mines, factories, and the assembly lines.

As business continued to improve during the latter part of the twentieth century, the use of scientific knowledge and methods in management, reinforced by studies of the adverse impact of time, repetitiveness, and motion on the worker in the assembly line, replaced many hand-based tasks with a carefully controlled automation conveyor, which ran from one station of the production to the next. The same principles were soon globalized, resulting in a safer working environment, which by law had to be well lit, clean, well ventilated, healthy, spacious, and safe. Still, these regulations never solved the social and physical problems emanating from the working conditions in the factory.

Primary Source 1

By the 1830s, the social, material, and physical harm of factory labor was well recognized and the British government began to enact regulations, including the 1833 Factory Act. The 1833 act addressed child labor specifically and began the process of making factory work more humane for the youngest workers, although it did not solve all the problems as is made clear by this short description of new legislation published in the Ragged School Union Magazine. *The Ragged School movement aimed to provide free education to underserved children, as well as to offer other charitable acts to youth.*

The New Act on Juvenile Labour

Thinking that it will be serviceable to all who are interested in the physical well being of youth, we give the following epitome of the new Act for regulating the labour of juveniles in workshops. With the necessary modifications, it is based on the Factory Act promoted by Lord Shaftesbury above thirty years ago. By the new Act every branch of juvenile labour comes under Government supervision for the first time. We can only hope that the same beneficial results may spring from the new statute as has resulted from the operation of the Factory Act.

(1.) No child under the age of eight years shall be employed in any handicraft. (2.) No child shall be employed on any one day in any handicraft for a period of more than six and a half hours, and such employment shall take place between the hours of six in the morning and eight at night. (3.) No young person shall be employed in any handicraft during any period of twenty-four hours for more than twelve hours, with intervening periods for taking meals and rest amounting in the whole to not less than one hour and a half, and such employment shall take place only between the hours of five in the morning and nine at night. (4.) No young person shall be employed in any handicraft on Sunday, or after two o'clock on Saturday afternoon, except in cases where not more than five persons are employed in the same establishment, and where such employment consists in making articles to be sold by retail on the premises, or in repairing articles of a like nature to those sold by retail on the premises. (5.) No child under the age of eleven years shall be employed in grindings, in the metal trades, or in fustian-cutting. If any young person is employed in contravention of this Act, the following consequences shall ensue:—First, the occupier of the workshop in which such child is employed shall be liable to a penalty of not more than £3. Second, the parent of or the person deriving any direct benefit from the labour of, having the control over the child, shall be liable to a penalty of not more than 20s., unless it appears that the offence has been committed without the consent of that person. The next clause enacts that the owners of workshops where grinding is carried on shall, where necessary, provide fans for the protection of their *employés;* and in default shall be liable to a penalty of not more than £10 nor less than £3.

Clause 9 provides that if it appears to any justice of the peace that there is reasonable cause for believing that any of the provisions of this Act or of the Sanitary Act, 1866, are contravened in any workshop, it shall be lawful for such justice to empower the complainant to enter into such workshop at any time within forty-eight hours from the date of such order, and to examine such workshop. Any inspector of factories may, when any person is at work at any handicraft, enter any workshop and inspect the condition thereof, and examine, touching any matter within the provisions of this Act, or of the Sanitary Act, 1866, so far as relates to such workshop,

"The New Act on Juvenile Labour," *Ragged School Union Magazine,* 1867.

the persons therein, provided that he report to one of her Majesty's principal Secretaries of State the fact of such entry, and the condition of the workshop in his next half yearly report. All penalties under this Act may be recovered summarily, before two or more justices.

The following regulations are made (subject to the provisions hereinafter mentioned) respecting the education of children employed in workshops:—(1.) *Every child employed in a workshop shall attend school for at least ten hours* in every week during the whole of which he is so employed. (2.) In computing for the purpose of this section the time during which a child has attended school, there shall not be included any time during which such child has attended either—(*a*) In excess of three hours at any one time, or in excess of five hours on any one day; or (*b*) On Sundays; or (*c*) Before eight o'clock in the morning, or after six o'clock in the evening; provided that the non-attendance of any child at school shall be excused—(1.) For any time during which he is certified by the principal teacher of the school to have been prevented from attendance by sickness or other unavoidable cause. (2.) For any time during which the school is closed for the customary holidays, or for some other temporary cause. (3.) For any time during which there is no school which the child can attend within one mile from the workshop or residence of such child. The parent of every child employed in a workshop shall cause that child to attend school in a manner required by this Act. Every parent who willfully fails to act in conformity with this section shall he liable to a penalty of not more than 20s. for each offence.

The following schedule provides for temporary exceptions alluded to above:— During the first six calendar months next ensuing the day on which this Act is to come into operation, children of not less than eleven years of age may be employed for the same time, and subject to the same conditions, for and subject to which young persons may be employed under this Act. During the first thirty calendar months next ensuing the commencement of this Act, children of not less than twelve years of age may be employed for the same time, and subject to the same conditions, for and subject to which young persons may be employed under this Act. During the first twelve calendar months next ensuing the commencement of this Act, children, young persons, and women may be employed on Saturdays until half-past four o'clock in the afternoon. During the first thirty calendar months next ensuing the commencement of this Act, children may be employed in the manufacture of preserves from fruit in the same manner as they were employed therein before the passing of this Act. During the first thirty calendar months next ensuing the commencement of this Act, male young persons of not less than sixteen years of age may be employed in any workshop where the manufacture of machinery is carried on in the same manner as if they were male persons exceeding the age of eighteen years.

The New Act of Juvenile Labour

"The New Act on Juvenile Labour." *Ragged School Union Magazine*, Jan.1849-Dec.1875 (10, 1867), 233–35. https://alliance-primo.hosted.exlibrisgroup.com/permalink/f/lvbsh/TN_proquest3877003

Discussion Question

1. What were the benefits of the Industrial Revolution versus the misery and social injustice that came out of it?

Conclusion

As noted previously, the earliest and most critical sources for the revolutionized production of goods out of the factories and human exchange were coal, textiles, weaved wearing in the form of linen, wool, and silk, new machinery, and efficient use of timber in cities and towns. Incidentally, silk—another element of material culture introduced to England from France through the specialized work of persecuted Huguenots during the seventeenth century—became a critical need. This led to the emergence of the working class, which Karl Marx called the proletariat, and the middle class or the bourgeoisie, contributing to a continued decline of the aristocracy, which by the end of the nineteenth century had virtually disappeared from Europe. Exchanges and the spread of new knowledge from inventions and the use of the water pump, the steam that propelled locomotives forward, and several of the inventions associated with the first and second Industrial Revolutions provided impetus to the discovery of electricity, the telegraph, the telephone, and a faster transportation system, such as the automobile and the aircraft during the early twentieth century.

Science and Technology

Defining the Contextual Role of Science and Technology

The role and use of science in industrialization was the application of scientific principles and practices and the adoption of new technologies in many sectors of life, such as infrastructure; the art of war; use of plant leaves or roots for effective drugs manufacturing; transformation of natural products into synthetics; experimentation and repetition simulating war situations; use of better medical and public health medicines and treatments of disease; and a quantum leap from the "primitive" computers of the 1980s to the laptops, tablets, and cell phones we utilize today. In other words, industrialization through science and technology was the application of basic research and scientific findings to the solution of real human problems. Most scholars consider the post-1860 period as the time of the second or even the third Industrial Revolution as the world entered the mid-twentieth and twenty-first century industrialization.

If one accepts this distinction, the main features of the second Industrial Revolution were the introduction and expansion of the railroad, which revolutionized the transportation system by carrying goods, such as raw materials and people, faster from place to place, whereas the first Industrial Revolution introduced for the first time extensive mechanization of goods production.

That the railway locomotive was suddenly able to travel 15 miles an hour was a major feat in the development of the transportation system. Indeed, the first revolution primarily changed for the better the textile and iron industries, while the second focused on the advanced transportation and faster exploration of many natural resources producing synthetics (new chemicals), new plastics, alloys, light metals, new energy resources, such as oil and natural gas used in large scale, new machines, new tools, and eventually, computers, and further automation, different from the assembly line, thus contributing to a larger pool of ownership of the means of production; stock markets; larger insurance schemes; corporations; big businesses; and banks—all with government turning now to the needs of the citizen.

Timeline: Critical Inventions or Improvements of Earlier Inventions

1763–1775   Improvement of Thomas Newcomen's first practical steam engine by Scottish inventor James Watt

1830s–1840s   Improvement to a single-wire telegraph system by American Samuel Morse and friends

1839   The "vulcanization" of rubber introduced by Charles Goodyear

1846   First practical and fast-producing sewing machine by Elias Howe, American inventor

1870s   Creation of the effective steel industry by Scottish American Andrew Carnegie

1873   Oil refinery industry made more efficient by American entrepreneur John D. Rockefeller (Standard Oil Company)

1874   Modern commercial typewriter by American journalist Christopher Latham Sholes

1876   Modern telephone by Scottish inventor Alexander Graham Bell

1877/1879   Phonograph and incandescent electricity light invented by American Thomas Edison

1895   American financier J. P. Morgan (J.P. Morgan & Company helped build several business companies related to the railroad, the steel industry, and General Electric)

1913   **Henry Ford** perfects the assembly line from Frederic Taylor's model. Ford's work allows automobiles like the Model T to be more efficiently built.

FIGURE 3.1   Henry Ford with his Model T, 1921.

Industrialization and Globalization: Europe, Asia, Africa, and Latin America

In Germany, a "moderately backward country" in western Europe, the catch-up process was aided greatly by a comprehensive banking system in its effort to industrialize as fast as it could.[4] Germany had to organize the private sector, in contrast to England, where the private capitalist sector and its wealth made the country "the forerunner that … pioneered the Industrial Revolution," as well as of "individual entrepreneurs," who played the central role in the process. In Russia, a less developed country, it was the intervention of the state that facilitated a faster industrialization process. Indeed, in Europe, the aim of the latecomers was to catch up by using "the most technological dynamic industries of the day and leapfrog the forerunners in size of plants and enterprises" and not by mobilizing all potential sources of industrial advancement possible.[5] The secret was, therefore, strategic selection, following analysis and identification of the most realistic potential of a country's capabilities and resources following the examples proven successful in England and Wales, Belgium, and perhaps France, and North America, especially the United States.

In Asia, especially the Far East, Japan stood as a moderately backward country during the post–World War II period compared to the United States, with which it decided to compete. Here, the Japanese companies used the German strategy by "focusing on the most technologically dynamic industries of the day and by leapfrogging in plant size and investment," while specifically aiming at the iron and steel industry as in Germany during the nineteenth century, followed by

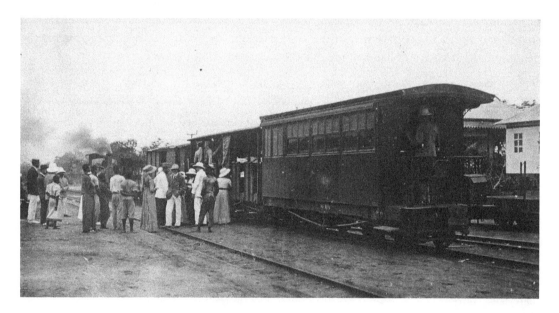

FIGURE 3.2   Steam Train on the Cape to Cairo Railway, ca. 1900–1915.

---

4   See Jang-Sup Shin, "The East Asian Industrialization in the Gerschenkronian Mirror: Catching-Up Strategies and Institutional Transition." (Singapore: National University of Singapore, Department of Economics, Working Paper No. 0208, 2002), 1–41.

5   This is an excellent discussion of the catching-up theme. I therefore use it generously throughout this section.

efforts in the semiconductor industry. Japan did the catch-up differently, even though it was not endowed with the raw materials needed on its own soil. Instead, it achieved its goal by focusing on the most advanced technology in the best factory layout and competing "internationally" or on a "global scale" through "bigger and bigger plants." The strategy was to accelerate "the economics of scale," underscored by the deep-water port projects Japan undertook on the seacoast. Thus, by 1977, Japan had the largest eight steel mills in the capitalist world, as it did likewise in the semi-conductor industry.

According to most economists, including Jang-Su Shin, this was done by using the *keiretsu* tradition and the state developmental model, since the military and the landlords' influence was gone. Here, one saw the role of the "developmental state," whereby the "Japanese state not only applied a variety of macroeconomic stimuli to its industries but also employed comprehensive industrial policies," with the *keiretsu* as the most critical conduit competition. As a result, the Japanese electronics industry overtook the United States during the 1950s. The *keiretsu* allowed an "interlocking shareholdings" system, internal resource transfers, loan guarantees, and other transactions in laissez-faire services. The *keiretsu* was, therefore, as critical as the German banks had been, even though the latter were the "de facto center of German capitalism" and led in capital lending and industrial reorganization, such as promoting cartel associations. In Japan, by contrast, "competing banks mostly backed competing large firms within the confines of individual *keiretsu*." The *keiretsu* is a group of enterprises, a manufacturing partnership that allows stable and long-term functioning of a goal or venture, which was a common economic model in Japan during the second half of the twentieth century, a truly "interlocking" business relationship reinforcing the bonds and the strength of shareholding. As *The Economist* (2009) notes:

> The American variety, however, was fundamentally different from the Japanese model. In Japan the keiretsu were regulated by specific laws, and they were structured is such a way that cooperation between them was almost compulsory. But outside Japan, the word keiretsu became attached to any loose network of alliances between more than two organizations.[6]

In Korea, the strategy was similar to that of Japan's, which focused on heavy and chemical industrialization programs during the 1970s, as was the case with the creation of "bigger and bigger plants." By locating them on the seacoast, following Japan's footsteps in the semiconductor industry, resulted by the end of the 1970s in the country having "…the largest textile plant, the largest plywood plant, the largest shipyard, the largest cement plant and the largest heavy machinery plant in the world," according to *The Economist*. However, Korea chose to rely heavily on imported materials. The critical force behind Korea's industrialization was the statebanks—chaebols "nexus." Chaebols were massive family-run enterprises, sometimes called business empires, comprising at times several powerful family conglomerates.

This was the Korean version of family-owned business groups to build the new industries, whereas in Japan, the bank system was paramount in financing new ventures. Still, Japan, Korea, Singapore, and Taiwan are said to have implemented "complementary strategies, which relied on

---

6 "Keiretsu," *The Economist*, 2009. https://www.economist.com/news/2009/10/16/keiretsu.

strengthening the involvement of 'multinational' companies" (MNCOs) investments by making available to them "complementary assets," such as "infrastructures, human capital, fiscal investment, and so on."[7] Among the four Asian countries included so far in the present discussion, Singapore seems to have used more than the other three: an internationalist industrialization policy from which came, almost necessarily, a rapid globalization process during the 1960s and thereafter. In contrast to Korea, both Taiwan and Singapore used the state "only in high-risk ventures" because in the former the local private sector was "severely" underdeveloped compared to the Asian industrial latecomers.

Notwithstanding the past challenges facing the Far East today, Japan, Korea, Singapore, and Taiwan managed to become the industrial giants of the region, with China, the latest to arrive on the scene, trying to first overcome its long emphasis on farming, communal villages, and equitable wealth distribution. Of course, it operated in a Communist ideological environment that could make it become an industrial capitalist system in orientation only through force, even if surrounded by people and private enterprises that had to compete with the global and their own industrialized capitalist systems. The attraction of the system employed by the neighbors was that the latter could show tangible results of wealth ownership and higher individual and national income or GDP that seemed to spur individual enterprise, creating a higher standard of living in the final analysis.

Similar, but less recorded, industrial achievements in Latin America should be briefly mentioned here. The transformation of sugar plantations, whose work was done manually in Cuba, can now be characterized as mechanized through boilers that have made this tiny island the world's largest producer of sugar. However, since labor was scarce here, every year Cuba had to import tens of thousands of Chinese laborers (*coolies*). The beef industry in Uruguay is also another achievement of a Latin American country. The railway system in the region is worth mentioning as well, as it began to spring up in this part of the world during the second half of the nineteenth century. Yet, the continuous lack of nationally based technological know-how did not help Latin America's dependency on the United States and Europe.

In Africa, even after it had been abolished during the latter part of the nineteenth century, slavery retarded the continent's transition to industrialization, notwithstanding the fact that several areas, such as Kush, Ghana, Mali, Songhay, Ethiopia, and Zimbabwe, had used iron, bronze, silver, copper, and gold many centuries prior to slavery. The 1884–1902 scramble for Africa, which divided the continent into over 50 small territories, settler- and non-settler colonies, and "protectorates" made the prospects of catching up in the globalizing industrialization race less likely. Historians, such as the late Walter Rodney, make a convincing argument that, at the time Africa's incipient industrialization was on its way toward a takeoff, conquest and **colonialism** that sought raw materials—gold, silver, iron, rubber, cocoa, coffee, sugar, palm oil, petroleum, cotton, diamonds, tea, tobacco, corn, sisal, and other natural resources such as wood and timber—made its industrial process either impossible or extremely difficult.

Europeans used Africa, as well, as an inexhaustible source of free human labor to build railroads, roads, government infrastructures, facilitate private White farmers' enterprises, and in *porterage* that linked one colonial region with another and the coast for easy export of raw materials to

---

7   Ibid.

European cities and towns. Europeans always have boasted their industrial achievements but forget to realize that their continent would not be what it is today without Africa's human and natural resources, which they robbed from its soil by force. Today, even though a few small industrial factories or warehouses that process beef and other meats or make cigarettes, matches, tobacco, sisal, corn flour, and tea can be seen on the continent, no country in Africa is able to build a new car with parts made in Africa by Africans, let alone a bicycle. Every automobile part must be imported either from the former colonizers or from Asian plants and manufacturers.

While the railroad transportation system, such as the rail, and oil refineries are now being built in Africa by the Chinese (who might be called the new economic colonizers), the roads are also built by such countries as Italy, China, and Portugal. All these new saviors of Africa have little interest in helping to industrialize the continent, making it self-sustaining when the sporadic projects are completed. Indeed, when things go wrong or specialized engineers are needed, Africa does not have the capabilities to repair much of what it imports: technician expatriates must be recalled to fix the system. In the process, there is no transfer of knowledge, and essential parts are not available! As a result, Africa continues to beg, advancing only at a snail's pace, when others, like China and countries in Latin America, are moving rapidly to the finish line.

According to some scholars and nationalists, if left alone, all societies would go through the same developmental stages, just like most of Europe has experienced. First of all, common would have been the primitive stage where everyone or small families fended for themselves, leading isolated and naturally selfish lives, preoccupied with raw survival and security—as all elements and the surrounding animal kingdom seemed to conspire to eliminate them from the earth. With experience, eventually things began to improve, and "social contracts" in various forms showed how working in harmony and organizing as a larger group would make life less miserable. Such thinking led to communal living, where property and responsibilities were shared and supplemented by hunting and herding.

This second lifestyle was followed by a period of social and economic control by individuals intent on exclusive ownership of land and other resources using force, if necessary, treating others as subjects, serfs, or slaves—a period that can be characterized as serfdom, servitude, and slavery. As the leadership narrowed with time, certain lifestyles and economic specialization for a better life emerged, giving place to the cottage or domestic industry that sprang up virtually all over the various continents, including Africa. Specialization eventually led to industrialization, capitalism, and globalization. For this stage to take place, conquest, slave labor, colonialism, and racism were all needed to secure raw materials that would ensure automation, mass production, and an easier life—unfortunately, in the hands of a few—introducing what Karl Marx called "exploitation of man by man."

Industrialism, as Marxists have claimed, would lead to **socialism,** where the downtrodden, tired of selfish capitalism, would revolt, forcing society into a new type of ownership and sharing while recognizing the dignity of every man and woman. This phase would result in a government system that would transition to a permanent period of complete material sharing, where the police state and class distinctions would disappear or become obsolete, ushering in a new era of perfect harmony and happiness called communism. Of course, this long trajectory toward nirvana was often disrupted by hegemonic military goals, continued selfishness, war, and conquest, trapping conquered societies and preventing them from enjoying the normal developmental stages.

Conclusion

As one looks at the development of our society, one cannot dispute that the Industrial Revolution accelerated production, making goods cheaper and available to more people, including the masses who had been left out of the predominantly feudal and agricultural system of Europe and other parts of the world.

Another major impact of the newly improved economic, transportation, and communication systems was the realization by society in general of the importance of basic and applied research and the use of technology, which gave rise to a spirit of experimentation and inspired all discoveries of the last 400 years, including the phonograph, the telegraph, and the telephone, as noted earlier; and later the oil refineries and the vastly improved ship and locomotive steam engines. As a result, by the end of the nineteenth century, the Industrial Revolution had reached all continents, including Africa (here through the imposed advent of colonialism), spurred by a new wave of transportation and developments in communication that contributed to what has been called globalization, where differences among nations based on culture and lifestyle began to get blurred, blended, and even abandoned. These rapid and massive developments tended to make the world more interdependent, and in a sense, smaller and smaller.

Gender and Sexuality

The Factory and Women's Social Status

One of the most salient outcomes of the Industrial Revolution was the changing role of women. In prior centuries, women either worked outside their expected marriage-confined responsibilities as farmers for their families, landlord servants in the period of serfdom in Europe, craft laborers in the cottage "industry," weavers in the manual textile business, or perhaps as nannies for rich families' households. As a result of industrialization, many women's domestic jobs were taken over by the new machines in the factories because of the heightened need of added human resources to fill the mass production goal. In addition, given that some women were unwilling to leave the home and that at times there were not enough men in the workplaces of the new towns and cities, relatively many of them abandoned the farm and the home and began their lives as employees of the new production system.

The need for an increased labor force led to the employment of minors, including girls, as young as 10 and 16 years of age. Receiving a meager salary, they were exploited by both the factory owners and the older male employees. Invariably, women and children were employed in menial and "monotonous" occupations, with the most lucrative and skilled responsibilities reserved for men. In other cases, the division of labor along gender and sex became more pronounced in the industrial setting than ever before in Europe and other parts of the world that had decided to fast-track the new economic model. In fact, the same occurred in such countries as Japan with the silk industry, where men and women worked together side by side to grow cash crops prior to the introduction of the factory system. From industrialization, it became more common for Japanese farmers to become wage earners. However, most jobs available were stratified along gender lines.

As was the case with China, Taiwan, Korea, and Singapore, silk, rice, cotton, tea, and other industrial commodities brought men and women together, a traditional taboo in most Asian towns and cities outside the home and the work fields. As a result, the division of labor became even sharper, and as always, women were relegated to the end of the stick in the assembly lines even as early as the **Meiji Restoration** in 1868, when these products ran 10 times faster in production at the end of the 1800s. Thus, according to one article, "When the Meiji period ended, with the death of the emperor in 1912, Japan had a highly centralized, bureaucratic government; a constitution establishing an elected parliament; a well-developed transport and communication system; a highly educated population free of feudal class restrictions; an established and rapidly growing industrial sector based on the latest technology; and a powerful army and navy."[8]

Thus, notes Wilde, by the end of the nineteenth century, "Women had come to dominate Japan's factory work force but not in increased pay," just as it still is in the rest of the world. In terms of salaries and supervisory responsibility, things have not changed much either: men continues to be the decision-makers in the factories, coal mines, and mechanized agriculture. Quite often, women had two jobs, one at the factory and the other in domestic business, as socially expected during the pre-Industrial Revolution era. Little accommodation was made to meet their needs in factories, which were most often unsanitary and dangerous. Studies in England show that, during the nineteenth century, males working in the factories received about 10 shillings per week, in contrast to two shillings among women whose main job in the mines, for example, was hauling "carts of coal up mine shafts" under inhuman conditions. As History Crunch Writers put it in "Role of Women in the Industrial Revolution," "The woman would have the cart fuel of coal attached to her waist by a strap and she would be expected to haul it through the narrow space."[9]

Philip Alder and Randall Pouwels have an interesting observation in their section on the Industrial Revolution and the roles and occupations of women:

> By the early nineteenth century, when factory work had become fairly common in Britain, young women also had the option of taking a job tending a machine. Entire families often staffed the earliest factories, but increasingly, young women and children replaced the male adults and family units in the unskilled jobs such as cotton spinning and mechanical weaving. The owners of the textile and shoe mills found that young women would work for lower wages than young men commanded and were more reliable. Many country girls preferred factory jobs—where they could be with their peers and have some freedom in their off hours—to going into domestic service with its many restrictions.[10]

---

8   Robert Wilde, "Coal Demand in the Industrial Revolution." THOUGHTCO., https://www.thoughtco.com/coal-in-the-industrial-revolution-1221634

9   History Crunch Writers, "Role of Women in the Industrial Revolution" (2016). .https://www.historycrunch.com/role-of-women-in-the-industrial-revolution.html#/

10   Philip Adler and Randal Pouwels, *History of Civilizations*, 7th ed. (Boston, MA: Cengage Learning, 2008), 445.

One might say, therefore, that the Industrial Revolution was harsh on women but that it also made them freer and better prepared for the struggle they would wage during the next centuries (1860–1920s) to gain their rights as human beings and citizens.

Conclusion

The Industrial Revolution altered the relations within the family structure, allowing women, men, and minors to leave the safety of the home and work in the various new factories. However, higher pay always favored men over women. Yet, even though women got the worse deal from the new economic system, the Industrial Revolution allowed them to assert a certain degree of independence and unwittingly prepared them for future battles on behalf of the human rights of all citizens, as was the case, of the right to vote in the United States during the 1920s. Their just cause has now been heralded globally through the work of the United Nations in the form of the Universal Declaration of the Human Rights of Women, resonating loudly in the most traditional continents such as Africa. The move toward the protection of women's rights has been propelled by the advances in transportation and communication initiated during the age of the Industrial Revolution, particularly with the advent of the second and third industrial stages.

War, Peace, and Diplomacy

Introduction: Overview of Global Warfare in the Nineteenth Century

Revolutions—whether political, industrial, military, or intellectual—dramatically altered warfare during the nineteenth century. France had gone full circle in the decade following the events of 1789, allowing a master of the battlefield, Napoléon Bonaparte, to follow in the footsteps of Julius Caesar. As first consul, or later emperor, he dominated the nation for 15 years. Bonaparte benefited from significant military reforms that had transformed the French armies since the 1780s. Gribeauval artillery, along with new ways to employ such new weapons as the cannon, allowed good tacticians to create "grand batteries," which massed firepower to blow holes in enemy lines. French victories at Austerlitz (1805) and Friedland (1807) came from the use of this tactic. It also helped Marshal Jean-de-Dieu Soult to gain an advantage over his Spanish opponents at Ocaña (1809), although in the end, traditional cavalry made this the worst defeat of a Spanish army on home soil.

With their self-contained combined-armed subgroupings resembling divisions or corps, the French had a more mobile and flexible system. These could march separately, moving faster as a result, making it easier to resupply while rapidly gathering and forming into one army for battle. Continental enemies, at first modeled on traditional eighteenth-century traditions, were hard pressed to counter French armies under aggressive leaders like Bonaparte.

It was a different matter on the high seas, where Britain's Horatio Nelson repeatedly demonstrated the value of highly trained crews under good officers. As Turkish historian Emir Yenner reminds us in *From Sail to Steam* (2010), sailing ships represented the most complicated industrial efforts of this time. Gathering the raw materials for construction the skilled artisans needed to complete, then train officers and men to operate a frigate or the much larger ship-of-the-line,

FIGURE 3.3   Robert Whitehead with a Test Torpedo.

required significant resources and organizational skills. These needs connect us to the life of Marc Isambard Brunel. A royalist who fled France during the "reign of terror," he put his mechanical skills to work for the United Kingdom. With the largest navy in the world, Britain needed vast quantities of a small but very important component—the **pulley block**. These made the management of large canvas sails much easier but needed constant replacement; they were made by hand in small batches and arrived in various degrees of quality.

Brunel created steam-powered machines to produce pulley blocks to a consistent standard. Although each ship-of-the-line needed 1,000 pulley blocks, Brunel's machines provided enough for the entire Royal Navy by 1807. His efforts introduce us to the Industrial Revolution, which started in the United Kingdom and then spread across the globe. With its factories and armies of workers, the Industrial Revolution changed the world just as much as any political revolution. Militaries used it to produce more sophisticated weapons, and like Brunel's machine-made pulley blocks, these were often less expensive per unit, maintained more consistent quality, and with interchangeable parts were easier to repair. The Industrial Revolution's factories spewed out breech-loading artillery, rifled muskets, and armored warships. It also established a race for technical superiority, which tremendously increased the cost of war, as rival generals and admirals lobbied their governments to purchase Gatling guns or Whitehead torpedoes (see Figure 3.3). The Ottoman Empire and Egypt, both lacking factories, went broke in the mid-nineteenth century after purchasing an imported weapons system. Emperor Menelik II of Ethiopia, on witnessing the firepower of a Maxim machine gun, argued it fired so rapidly, the cost of ammunition would bankrupt his treasury.

Menelik's dilemma connects us not just to the Industrial Revolution, but also to another powerful thread of the nineteenth century—imperialism. While the idea of conquering less powerful states is as old as human history, new factories with their steam engines provided powerful weapons like the Maxim gun Menelik could not afford. Marry technology with another nineteenth-century phenomenon, nationalism, and the result is a potent combination that allowed politicians and generals to support a more robust imperialism. Railroads, steamships, and the telegraph supplemented weapons systems, allowing industrialized nations to carve out large empires. It should not be surprising that Great Britain, where the Industrial Revolution began, used factories and wealth resulting from that move to create an empire on which "the sun never set."

Many other nations produced empires, and not all were centered in Europe. Northeast Africa witnessed the rise of Ethiopia during the mid- to late- nineteenth century. Local notables held control a century earlier during the "Era of the Princes." Then a trio of strong leaders restored

FIGURE 3.4   "We Hold A Vaster Empire than Has Been."

An 1898 Canadian Christmas Stamp Featuring a Map of the British Empire with British Holdings Marked in Red. The Text States: "We Hold a Vaster Empire than Has Been."

unity and made Ethiopia a regional power. A charismatic adventurer, Téwodros II (1818–1868) created a bandit army that grew powerful enough to end the "Era of the Princes." Although he ran afoul of Great Britain in 1867, shooting himself with the Colt revolver sent as a gift from Queen Victoria to avoid capture, Téwodros established a foundation for a new "King of Kings," Yohannes IV (1872–1889). Yohannes had assisted the British in their 1867 invasion and obtained a cache of modern weapons in exchange. He imported even more, building an army capable of defeating Egyptian invaders with their American mercenaries at Gundat (1875) and Gura (1876). Menelik II (1884–1913) completed the transformation begun by Téwodros, modernizing his government, continuing to import modern weapons for his soldiers then using them to defeat Italian imperialists at the battle of Adwa (1896).

The latter was atypical for Africa, as even after major setbacks like Isandlwana (1879), European invaders usually sent in reinforcements and defeated native forces. Adwa was a resounding defeat from which Italy could not quickly recover. Menelik was also a skilled negotiator who understood European rivalries, and using these divisions to his advantage, managed to parley Adwa into recognition of Ethiopia's independence by the major powers. Taking this a step further, Menelik embraced imperialism himself, expanding Ethiopia's southern boundaries and fighting Somali neighbors. What made the Ethiopian army different from other African militaries like those of the Zulu kingdom in South Africa or the Ashanti in Ghana? First, the Ethiopians had enough revenue to raise soldiers and equip them with breech-loading and magazine rifles. In addition, they maintained a small artillery corps, whose deadly accuracy was evident at Adwa.

A fascination with firearms permeated Ethiopia's dominant Amhara culture to the point that rifle cartridges became a form of currency well into the 1930s. By stretching resources, Ethiopia could field military forces capable of fighting European imperialists until the 1920s, when the cost of technology soared beyond the ability of poor states to keep pace. China and Japan were exceptions to this trend—both found the means to build modern armies and used these to create their own empires. Under the Qing Dynasty, Chinese armies had expanded into Mongolia, Central Asia, and Tibet. Conquering these regions added numerous subjects, but as with all empires, exploitation fueled resentment. This was exacerbated by nationalism, a powerful force sweeping across the globe during the nineteenth century. Pride for one's language, culture, or country could morph into varying degrees of nationalism. These feelings could enhance solidarity and support an aggressive posture against all who resisted the obviously superior group. Contemporary critics in Britain and America labeled this "jingoism." A popular British song of the 1870s expressed this with the lines, "We don't want to fight but by Jingo if we do; We've got the ships, we've got the men, we've got the money too."

Although nationalism could support imperialism, more often it provided reasons to struggle against empires. The Qing discovered this when many of their Han (Chinese) subjects rose up during the **Taiping Heavenly Kingdom Movement** (1850–1864). This was the most violent war of the nineteenth century, causing the deaths of at least 10 million people. Simultaneously, Qing leaders had to deal with the second of two Opium Wars while surrendering over 230,000 square miles of territory along the Amur River to Russia. The foreign dynasty maintained control of China due to marshaling loyal Han supporters, divisions within the Taiping rebels, and military reforms that made Qing soldiers more effective. It even expanded in the early 1900s, ending an ambiguous relationship with Tibet by occupying the capital, Lhasa, and temporarily driving Tibet's theocratic leader, the Thirteenth Dali Lama, into exile. This was a short-lived triumph, as Tibetans joined with Han during the Double Ten Revolution of 1911, which ended Qing rule.

With its better educated and homogeneous population, Japan avoided some of Qing China's turmoil. Isolated from most of the world by choice since the early 1600s, Japan faced a major challenge when Commodore Matthew Perry arrived with an American naval squadron in 1853. This was a case of "gunboat diplomacy," as the Japanese were told they could open their ports to American trade or face bombardment. With no viable option for effective resistance, Japan's leaders granted Perry's "request." The humiliation was never forgotten and played an important role in changing Japan. The result was civil strife and the Meiji Restoration of the 1860s. A new Japan emerged, which embraced the catch phrase "rich country, strong military." Fukuzawa Yukichi, an influential journalist, is typical of this era; he called on Japan to "leave Asia" and embrace Western models of excellence. These included a German-style army and British-style navy. By 1894, Japan could fight a war with the much larger China, win battles on land and sea, and force China to surrender territory and cash. The latter was so significant, it more than covered the entire cost of the war. Ten years later, Japan thrashed Russia, joining that rare club of non-Western nations capable of defeating a European power. Commodore Perry had taught Japan so well that the road to Pearl Harbor was laid when Japanese imperialists identified America as a possible threat in 1911.

International Efforts to Limit War

While war raged across the globe, the nineteenth century also produced efforts to limit the destructiveness of battle. Horrified by the carnage he witnessed at Solferino (1859), Swiss businessman Jean-Henri Dunant directed a successful campaign to establish rules for treating wounded survivors of battle. From this emerged the First Geneva Convention (1864) and the International Red Cross. Peace Societies in Britain, America, and France were another example of this trend, as were provisions that made "conscientious objection" a legal defense for avoiding military service. The power of such efforts was reflected by the **First Hague Convention** of 1899: it called on nations to abstain from filling artillery rounds with poison gas or dropping bombs from balloons or other flying craft. So-called "dumdum" bullets, which would expand on hitting a body due to their soft metal, were also outlawed, although this rule did not apply if your army was fighting against enemies who were not signatories to the Hague Convention. This was very convenient for colonial powers, who could continue to use such ammunition against local groups opposed to domination and completely unaware of the Hague Convention.

The Impact of Industrialization on Militarism and War

Industrialization has played a major role in the conduct and perhaps the frequency or infrequency of wars the globe has experienced for centuries but most critically over the last three, as a result of the advanced and stronger weaponry and war materiel, and the arms race it engendered. In this context, for example, regarding the 1866 **Austro-Prussian War**, says David Ziegler, one of the most respected experts on the role of industrial technology in war, the decisive factor in the victory of the Prussians was not the superiority of the army in terms of armaments or explosives, but the *railroad*. Ziegler adds: "This was so important to the Prussian army that the general staff had a special Railway Subsection. It made possible rapid mobilization of troops from reserve status to front-line units … The railroad also enabled the Prussians, who lacked overall superiority in numbers, to achieve superiority in the one spot where it counted, the battlefield."[11] The second most important factor, Ziegler continues, was the *telegraph*, which accelerated and mobilized the "order to go out rapidly."

The deployment of the new war machinery whose use the French botched was a major factor in the Franco-Prussian War of 1870–1871. During the World Wars, new military technology was a major decisive innovation, exemplified by the use of chlorine gas poison, the introduction of submarines that could torpedo ships and boats, airplanes able to drop, for example, the two deadliest atomic bombs with precision on **Hiroshima** and **Nagasaki** on August 6 and 9, 1945, respectively, which ended the war between the United States and Japan. In fact, the Cold War (1950s–1990), actually "the long peace," as some have called it, was due in part to the nuclear arsenals both the

---

11   David Ziegler, *War, Peace, and International Politics* (New York: Longman, 1993), 24–25.

Soviet Union and the United States had accumulated. In sum, the new weapons facilitated by the second (or third) Industrial Revolution became at least temporarily a deterrent against war.

The issue of **militarism**, strengthened by the race to build and amass a big deadly arsenal from the military industrial complex (as some would say to defeat the enemy), was a major contributor to the several wars that were waged during the nineteenth and twentieth centuries in continental Europe, as this section will show. The first war worthy of mention was the Austro-Prussian War or the Seven Weeks' War in 1866. This was a tug of war engineered by Chancellor Otto von Bismarck of Prussia, using new or improved industrial weaponry, to decide who was going to control the future of the German states and principalities, made independent by the 1815 Congress of Vienna. The dispute centered on the control of Schleswig and Holstein provinces that had been taken from Denmark in 1864, which Prussia and Austria administered jointly. Italy had joined in alliance with Prussia, a move that stemmed from Austria's continued occupation of Venetia (Venice), which the Italian nationalists wanted unified with Italy. Consequently, after the war, Venice was ceded to Italy.

Second was the Franco-Prussian war, the result of France's declaration of war on Prussia on July 19, 1870, following the announcement that Prince Leopold of the Hohenzollern-Sigmaringen Dynasty was selected to occupy the Spanish throne. Given that Leopold was a member of the Hohenzollern family, France, through its ambassador to Berlin, refused to ever allow Leopold to sit on the Spanish throne, as King William of Prussia was asked by the French to guarantee. Bismarck purposely misinterpreted the message contained in the Ems Telegraph, or Ems Dispatch. This led to the brief but decisive victory of Prussia over France.

Even though the French used superior weaponry enhanced by the new industrial technology, including the breech-loading *Chassepot* rifle and the *mitrailleuse* (a new machine gun), the war ended in a humiliating defeat for France at Sedan on August 31, 1870, plus the surrender of General Patrice MacMahon and his troops to the Germans on September 2, 1870. Subsequently, to further humiliate the French, the Germans entered Paris triumphantly where they declared William I of Prussia emperor of Germany at the Palace of Versailles on January 18, 1871. Alsace and half of Lorraine were annexed by Germany; Napoleon III was forced to abdicate; and France was compelled to pay an indemnity of 5 billion francs, with all terms contained in the Treaty of Frankfurt signed between Germany and France on May 10, 1871. Prussia had been joined in the war by virtually every German state and principality, even (the northern states were an easy sell, these three needed the Ems Telegraph distortion) the states of Bavaria, Württemberg, and Baden in the south, convinced, as it were, by Bismarck that they had all been insulted as Germans by the French.

The war also sealed the good fortune of the Italian kingdom, which longed for unification. Without French protection that had been "guaranteed" by Napoleon III, now stripped of his power by the Germans, Italy annexed the Papal States, declaring Rome the capital of the kingdom of Italy under Victor Emmanuel II. As a result, Pius IX declared himself prisoner of the Vatican in 1870, an issue officially called the *Roman Question*, which was resolved by Benito Mussolini through the Lateran Treaties or the Lateran Pact of February 11, 1929. The treaties, declaring Italy as a Catholic nation, recognized the Vatican, a territory of some 44 hectares (109 acres) as an independent state, with the pope as its sovereign and the world leader of the Catholic Church.

World War I and World War II: Causes and Outcomes

In explaining the causes of World War I, most historians note the impact and imprint of industrialism on the tendency for nations to resolve conflict by resorting to war, even when diplomacy would have been able to solve it. A combination of industrial advances, technological changes in weaponry, fervent nationalism, a sense of military superiority, and imperialism or expansionist tendencies resulted in a precarious situation for international relations in Europe during the greater part of the twentieth century. Industrialization emboldened certain countries, especially, Germany, Austria-Hungary, France, Russia, Serbia in the Balkans, and even Great Britain, as the latter looked at the growth and the technological advances of its "mighty" navy in particular. By the time of the assassination of the heir apparent to the Austrian throne Archduke Franz Ferdinand in1914, as early as 1904, Europe had already divided itself into two distinct main rival camps: the Anglo-French Entente (France, Britain, and Russia) and the Triple Alliance of 1882 among Germany, Austria-Hungary, and Italy. To complicate the matter further, in 1893–1894, France and Russia agreed to a defense military pact.

Thus, for an intelligent observer or an astute diplomat, something catastrophic was bound to occur in the midst of such powerful and antagonistic international chaos. The fateful trigger was the archduke's assassination (which included his wife Sophie) by a Serbian nationalist, 19-year-old Gavrilo Princip, who fired the deadly shots in Sarajevo, the Serbian capital, when the apparent future emperor visited the city on June 28, 1914. However, war did not necessarily have to occur then, had it not been for the encouragement of Austria-Hungary by Germany to strike first. Germany advised Austria-Hungary to immediately deliver a stern 48-hour ultimatum, terms no country in Europe would have accepted. One critical request was that Austrian officials be allowed to come to Serbia and participate actively in the investigation. Serbia was willing to honor all terms of the ultimatum except its eleventh dictate, the investigation demand. Germany knew that the terms of the ultimatum would trigger a war, and she was prepared to assist Austria as part of the Greater Pan-German movement. On July 28, 1914, precisely one month after the archduke's assassination, Austria-Hungary declared war on Serbia.

This First World War was fought on two fronts: western and eastern Europe. In the west, Germany entered northwestward through Luxembourg and Belgium, intent, ultimately, on reaching France (as spelled out in the *Schlieffen Plan*) between August 4 and August 25, 1914. In France, however, the Germans were only able to occupy temporarily some of the most important industrial border cities and factories, as the inconclusive battles of the Western Frontiers raged on: the Battle of Lorraine (14–25 August 1914); the Battle of the Ardennes (21–28 August 1914); the Battle of Charleroi (21–23 August 1914); and the Battle of Mons (23 August 1914).

On the eastern front, Russia went after Germany and the Austrian Empire, while Austria-Hungary attacked Serbia in the south. By 1915–1918, trench warfare was the dominant strategy on both sides, using chemical weapons, heavy and constant machine-gun power, and heavy artillery propelled by the industrial and technological advances of the era in the military industrial complex, though no side was clearly winning the war. The United States declared war on Germany in 1917 almost two years after a German **U-boat** torpedoed the liner **RMS** *Lusitania*, killing 1,198 passengers onboard, including 128 Americans. President Woodrow Wilson, who asked

Congress for authorization to declare war on Germany on April 2, 1917, followed up with an official declaration four days later, April 6, 1917.

On the ground in Europe, the Bolsheviks overthrew their government in the revolution of November 7, 1917, making Russia a useless ally for either side. Subsequently, German and only a division of Austrians on the western front, seeing the tide of the war pivoting against them, began to pull back from their positions on the Western Front, and on November 11, 1918, the Germans were forced to ratify an armistice, which their own allies had done much earlier. The subsequent Treaty of Versailles (1919) was severely punitive for the losing side, especially Germany, as the following terms demonstrate: Article 231, or the "War Guilty Clause," declared that Germany was responsible for the war; Germany had to return Alsace-Lorraine, which it had annexed from France in the Franco-Prussian War of 1870; the highly industrialized Saarland would be administered by the League of Nations for 15 years; Eupen and Malmedy were to be ceded to Belgium, while Northern Schleswig was given to Denmark; Poland was to receive part of Silesia from Germany; the Rhineland was demilitarized; Danzig, a large German city, came under the authority of the League of Nations as a free city; all German colonies in Africa (western Cameroon, Togo, Tanganyika, Rwanda-Burundi, and South West Africa) were distributed among France, Britain, Belgium, and South Africa; and the German army was to be limited to 100,000 men, with conscription forbidden. While its fleet of navy vessels could not exceed 10,000 tons, Germany could not have a submarine arsenal or an air force.

There were other, less important punitive measures in the treaty. As a result, Germany lost 13 percent of its territory and one-tenth, or between 6.5 and 7 million, of its population. Most historians believe that the treaty was indeed so severe that it caused the declared guilty nation, Germany, to eventually reject it, as Adolf Hitler did during the 1930s. Germany's utter rejection of the terms of the treaty led to World War II. It seems clear that, by 1919, diplomacy had been severely weakened by the alliances formed among the European powers following the Napoleonic wars, reflecting the European penchant for resorting to war to resolve conflict as the primary instrument of international peace. The Allies—France, Britain, and the United States—created the League of Nations to emphasize the role of diplomacy rather than war for the future. The league, however, was too weak in structure and in its resolve to make a difference in the conduct of the international business of war and peace. The refusal of the US Congress to sign the treaty clauses, even though the major proponent of the new League of Nations was the very president of the United States, Woodrow Wilson, prompted both Benito Mussolini of Italy and Adolf Hitler of Germany to simply ignore it. As a consequence, while Italy invaded Ethiopia, also a League of Nations member, on October 3, 1935, Germany annexed Austria in 1938 and invaded Poland in 1939.

The Role of Diplomacy: The League of Nations and the United Nations

World War II, which involved 30 countries and killed between 50 and 85 million people, both military and civilian, began on September 1, 1939, after Adolf Hitler invaded Poland. It has remained the deadliest event in the history of humankind. Almost immediately, France and Britain declared war on Germany. Germany's allies, called the Axis Powers, consisted of Japan, Bulgaria, Hungary, Romania, Croatia, and Slovakia. Subsequently, in a surprise move following his change of mind about a direct attack on France, Hitler rolled his troops over Denmark and Norway first, crushing any resistance in Belgium and the Netherlands, and converged on and completely overran France, his mortal enemy, in June 1940. His troops then followed with an air bombardment of Britain across the Channel, in a failed tug of war known as the Battle of Britain.

Italy widened the war when Mussolini, Hitler's protégé, unnecessarily invaded Greece on October 28, 1940, and Egypt on September 13, 1940. However, Hitler had to rescue Mussolini and his paper tiger Italy in 1941. In a further unexpected move, frustrated by the Battle of Britain, Hitler ordered the invasion of Russia in July 1941, which ended in disaster for his troops at the battles of Stalingrad and Kursk, culminating in a Russian assault on BerlinApril 16-May 2, 1945. In December 1941, the United States entered the war with a massive armada, aircraft, and millions of soldiers along with the Allied forces, causing severe casualties in Normandy, France. On D-Day, June 6, 1944, 156,000 Americans joined by British and Canadian forces successfully landed on the five beachheads of Normandy in an assault called Operation Overlord, a move that caused the collapse of the German operations in Western Europe by the end of August of 1944. On August 25, 1945, Paris was liberated, and Charles de Gaulle, the leader of the French Resistance, paraded through the city amidst sporadic attacks in the countryside from isolated German soldiers.

FIGURE 3.5   American Troops Wade to Omaha Beach on D-Day.

Meanwhile, under orders from Joseph Stalin, the Soviet Union troops had been bombarding Berlin since April 16, 1945, while Hitler was hidden in his fortified bunker. It is widely accepted now that Adolf Hitler shot himself in the head after forcing his wife, Eva Braun, to ingest deadly poison in his underground bunker on April 30, 1945. On May 2, 1945, Berlin was liberated from the Nazis—not by the Americans but by the Soviets, who never left the city until almost 50 years later on August 31, 1994, following the breakup of the Soviet Union. In the Pacific war theater, deadly hostilities in the air, at sea, and on land between the United States and the Japanese continued until President Truman ordered two atomic bombs to be dropped, one on Hiroshima on August 6, 1945, and the other on Nagasaki, on August 9, 1945, killing 80,000 and 40,000 people, respectively.

The following documents are called primary sources because they are contemporaneous to the period, the people, the leaders, and the events; in this case, the bombing of Pearl Harbor by the Japanese on Sunday, December 7, 1941. Primary sources bring life and context to historical writing.

Primary Source 2

Following are the living excerpts of the conversations among the US State Department, the White House, and other relevant participating government entities trying to decide how to respond to Japanese aggression in 1945 and to explain to the American people why the action taken to end the war using an unprecedented weapon called the nuclear bomb was necessary. The reason for asking students to read these documents is to show them how difficult life and death decisions are made in the United States and who is ultimately responsible for them. Reading the actual record makes any reader feel as if he or she is witnessing the making of this ultimate step to end the World War that had started in 1939. Memoirs, government documents, and contemporary voices bring history to life and give us an insight into how people who made the decisions for us were thinking at the time. This exercise will provide a feeling that most people would not experience if they just read texts written by authors living in our era.

*The bombing of Hiroshima and Nagasaki in 1945 constitutes one of the worst and most frightening one-time events in the history of mankind. As you read these primary source excerpts of the event, focus on the suffering of the people who were the target of the two bombs; the agony and helplessness of those making the decision; and the reaction of the rest of the world even among those fighting against Adolf Hitler (already dead by then) and Emperor **Hirohito**. Consider as well the cruelty and deadly kamikaze attacks on Americans and their allies on the high seas and on land. If you do this, you will then understand the terrible state in which our own world finds itself and perhaps resolve to shout out loud to the world, as Pope Paul VI did at the United Nations, "No More War! No More War!" Indeed, if the 1945 horrific event was so devastating, just think what the nuclear war arsenals the United States and Russia have stockpiled might do to the entire world if either nation decides to destroy the other.*

Excerpts from the events that led to the first atomic bomb on Hiroshima and Nagasaki: 1945

National Security Archive Electronic Briefing Book No. 162
Edited by William Burr - 202/994-7000
Posted - August 5, 2005
First Updated - April 27, 2007
Latest Update, August 4, 2015
VI. The First Nuclear Strikes

Document 53: Memorandum from General L. R. Groves to the Chief of Staff, August 6, 1945, Top Secret
Source: RG 77, MED Records, Top Secret Documents, File no. 5b (copy from microfilm)

> The day after the bombing of Hiroshima, Groves provided Chief of Staff Marshall with a report which included messages from Captain William S. Parsons and others about the impact of the detonation which immediately killed at least 70,000, with many dying later from radiation sickness and other causes. [41]How influential the atomic bombings of Hiroshima and later Nagasaki compared to the impact of the Soviet declaration of war were on the Japanese decision to surrender has been the subject of controversy among historians. Sadao Asada emphasizes the shock of the atomic bombs, while Herbert Bix has suggested that Hiroshima and the Soviet declaration of war made Hirohito and his court believe that failure to end the war could lead to the destruction of the imperial house. Frank and Hasegawa divide over the impact of the Soviet declaration of war, with Frank declaring that the Soviet intervention was "significant but not decisive" and Hasegawa arguing that the two atomic bombs "were not sufficient to change the direction of Japanese diplomacy. The Soviet invasion was."[42]

Document 54: Memorandum of Conversation, "Atomic Bomb," August 7, 1945
Source: Library of Congress Manuscript Division, Papers of W. Averell Harriman, box181, Chron FileAug 5–9, 1945.

> The Soviets already knew about the US atomic project from espionage sources in the US and Britain so Molotov's comment to Ambassador Harriman about the secrecy surrounding the US atomic project can be taken with a grain of salt, although the Soviets may have been unaware of specific plans for nuclear use.

Documents 55a and 55b: Early High-level Reactions to the Hiroshima Bombing
Cabinet Meeting and Togo's Meeting with the Emperor, August 7–8, 1945
Source: Gaimusho (Ministry of Foreign Affairs) ed. Shusen Shiroku (The Historical Records of the End of the War), annotated by Jun Eto, volume 4, 57–60 [Excerpts] [Translation by Toshihiro Higuchi]

Diary Entry for Wednesday, August 8, 1945
Source: Takashi Itoh, ed., *Sokichi Takagi: Nikki to Joho* [Sokichi Takagi: Diary and Documents] (Tokyo, Japan: Misuzu-Shobo, 2000), 923–924 [Translation by Hikaru Tajima].

Excerpts from the Foreign Ministry's compilation about the end of the war show how news of the bombing reached Tokyo as well as how Foreign Minister'- Togo initially reacted to reports about Hiroshima. When he learned of the atomic bombing from the Domei News Agency, Togo believed that it was time to give up and advised the cabinet that the atomic attack provided the occasion for Japan to surrender on the basis of the Potsdam Declaration. Togo could not persuade the cabinet, however, and the Army wanted to delay any decisions until it had learned what had happened to Hiroshima. When the Foreign Minister met with the Emperor, Hirohito agreed with him; he declared that the top priority was an early end to the war, although it would be acceptable to seek better surrender terms—probably US acceptance of a figure-head emperor—if it did not interfere with that goal. In light of those instructions, Togo and Prime Minister Suzuki agreed that the Supreme War Council should meet the next day.[42a]

An entry from Admiral Tagaki's diary for August 8 conveys more information on the mood in elite Japanese circles after Hiroshima, but before the Soviet declaration of war and the bombing of Nagasaki. Seeing the bombing of Hiroshima as a sign of a worsening situation at home, Tagaki worried about further deterioration. Nevertheless, his diary suggests that military hard-liners were very much in charge and that Prime Minister Suzuki was talking tough against surrender, by evoking last ditch moments in Japanese history and warning of the danger that subordinate commanders might not obey surrender orders. The last remark aggravated Navy Minister Yonai who saw it as irresponsible. That the Soviets had made no responses to Sato's request for a meeting was understood as a bad sign; Yonai realized that the government had to prepare for the possibility that Moscow might not help. One of the visitors mentioned at the beginning of the entry was Iwao Yamazaki who became Minister of the Interior in the next cabinet.

Document 56: Navy Secretary James Forrestal to President Truman, August 8, 1945
Source: Naval Historical Center, Operational Archives, James Forrestal Diaries

General Douglas MacArthur had been slated as commander for military operations against Japan's mainland, but this letter to Truman from Forrestal shows that the latter believed that the matter was not so settled. Richard Frank sees this as evidence of the uncertainty felt by senior officials about the situation in early August; Forrestal would not have been so "audacious" to take an action that could ignite a "political firestorm" if he "seriously thought the end of the war was near."[43]

Document 57: Memorandum of Conversation, "Far Eastern War and General Situation," August 8, 1945, Top Secret.
Source: Library of Congress Manuscript Division, Papers of W. Averell Harriman, box 181, Chron File Aug 5–9, 1945

> Shortly after the Soviets declared war on Japan, in line with commitments made at the Yalta and Potsdam conferences, Ambassador Harriman met with Stalin, with George Kennan keeping the US record of the meeting. After Stalin reviewed in considerable detail Soviet military gains in the Far East, they discussed the possible impact of the atomic bombing on Japan's position (Nagasaki had not yet been attacked) and the dangers and difficulty of an atomic weapons program. According to Hasegawa, this was an important, even "startling," conversation: it showed that Stalin "took the atomic bomb seriously"; moreover, he disclosed that the Soviets were working on their own atomic program.[44]

Document 58: Memorandum of Conference with the President, August 8, 1945 at 10:45 AM.
Source: Henry Stimson Diary, Manuscripts and Archives, Yale University Library, Henry Lewis Stimson Papers (microfilm at Library of Congress)

> At their first meeting after the dropping of the bomb on Hiroshima, Stimson briefed Truman on the scale of the destruction, with Truman recognizing the "terrible responsibility" that was on his shoulder. Consistent with his earlier attempts, Stimson encouraged Truman to find ways to expedite Japan's surrender by using "kindness and tact" and not treating them in the same way as the Germans. They also discussed postwar legislation on the atom and the pending Henry D. Smyth report on the scientific work underlying the **Manhattan Project** and postwar domestic control of the atom.

Documents 59 a–c: The Attack on Nagasaki:

> **Cable APCOM 5445 from General Farrell to O'Leary [Groves assistant], August 9, 1945, Top Secret**
>
> **COMGENAAF 8 cable CMDW 576 to COMGENUSASTAF, for General Farrell, August 9, 1945, Top Secret**
>
> **COMGENAAF 20 Guam cable AIMCCR 5532 to COMGENUSASTAF Guam, August 10, 1945, Top Secret.**

Source: RG 77, Tinian Files, April-December 1945, box 20, Envelope G Tinian Files, Top Secret

> The prime target for the second atomic attack was Kokura, which had a large army arsenal and ordnance works, but various problems ruled that city out; instead, the crew of the B-29 that carried "Fat Man" flew to an alternate target at Nagasaki. These cables are the earliest reports of the mission; the bombing of Nagasaki killed

immediately at least 39,000 people with more dying later. According to Frank, the actual total of deaths due to the atomic bombs will never be known, but the "huge number" ranges somewhere between 100,000 and 200,000 people. Barton J. Bernstein and Martin Sherwin have argued that if top Washington policymakers had kept tight control of the delivery of the bomb instead of delegating it to Groves the attack on Nagasaki could have been avoided. The combination of the first bomb and the Soviet declaration of war would have been enough to induce Tokyo's surrender. By contrast, Maddox argues that Nagasaki was necessary so that Japanese "hardliners" could not "minimize the first explosion" or otherwise explain it away.[45]

Endnotes

[41] Frank, 273–74; Bernstein, "The Alarming Japanese Buildup on Southern Kyushu, Growing U.S. Fears and Counterfactual Analysis: Would the Planned November 1945 Invasion of Southern Kyushu Have Occurred?" *Pacific Historical Review* 68 (1999): 561–609.

[42] Sadao Asada, "The Shock of the Atomic Bomb and Japan's Decision to Surrender: A Reconsideration," *Pacific Historical Review* 67 (1998): 101–48; Bix, 523; Frank, 348; Hasegawa, 298. Recently, Bix appears to have moved toward a position like Hasegawa's; see Bix, "Japan's Surrender Decision and the Monarchy: Staying the Course in an Unwinnable War," *Japan Focus* at <japanfocus.org/article.asp?id=321>. For emphasis on the "shock" of the atomic bomb, see also Lawrence Freedman and Saki Dockrill, "Hiroshima: A Strategy of Shock," in Saki Dockrill, ed., *From Pearl Harbor to Hiroshima: The Second World War in Asia and the Pacific, 1941–1945* (New York: St. Martin's Press, 1994), 191–214.

[42a] For more on these developments, see Asada, "The Shock of the Atomic Bomb and Japan's Decision to Surrender: A Reconsideration," 486–88.

[43] Frank, 300.

[44] Hasegawa, 191–92. For the inception of the Soviet nuclear program and the role of espionage in facilitating it, see David Holloway, *Stalin and the Bomb* (New Haven, Yale University Press, 1994).

[45] Sherwin, 233–37; Bernstein (1995), 150; Maddox, 148.

Discussion Questions

1. Have a class debate where some students solely blame Germany and Adolf Hitler for World War II and some place it on **appeasement** and the cowardly nations of the time. Do you justify or condemn the dropping of the atomic bomb on Hiroshima and Nagasaki by US president Harry Truman in 1945?

2. Can you compare that war and its outcomes with the most recent civil war in the Democratic Republic of the Congo during the 1990s and 2000s as a global war, as some historians and political scientists have done? Explain why or why not?

Emperor Hirohito of Japan ignominiously had to surrender on August 15, 1945. As a result, Germany was occupied by the Western Allies, who divided the defeated enemy into four zones controlled by France in the southwest; Britain in the northwest; the United States in the south—all together called the Federal Republic of Germany—and the Soviet Union in the east, called East Germany or the Democratic Republic of Germany, thus effectively ending what Hitler termed the German Third Reich, or the Third Empire.

Furthermore, Germany was compelled to dismantle the naval and air forces, introduce democratic reforms, and pay $23 billion in reparations for the war, mainly in machinery and manufacturing plants. When the Allied Powers established the United Nations (UN) in September 1945, the two Germanys were intentionally excluded from membership in the General Assembly and the Security Council—the latter made up of the superpowers of the time, the United States, the Soviet Union, Britain, France, and the little but influential island of Formosa, known as Taiwan or the Republic of China (rather than the mainland People's Republic of China, as its internal conflict lingered). Only on September 18, 1973, did the two Germanys—the Democratic Republic of Germany (East Germany) and the Federal Republic of Germany (West Germany)—join the United Nations. They were subsequently reunited on October 3, 1990, as the Cold War came to an end.

The creation of the United Nations, consisting of a General Assembly, made up of all 193-member states and countries in the world where the majority vote carries the day, and the Security Council—a club of the five original powers, except that the People's Republic of China replaced Taiwan in 1971—served as a signal that wars would no longer be accepted by the international community. The council was to serve as the arbiter of all major conflicts on the globe and follow up on the vote of the General Assembly, if the case was deemed potentially a disturbance to international peace. The Security Council's decision became binding (at least on paper) when all five members cast a unanimous vote or if the majority voted "yes," even if one or two members abstained from voting. The establishment of the United Nations was an effort to permanently end wars among nations, resolving all conflicts through diplomacy, stemming from its mission and power that superseded that of the defunct League of Nations. It also signified putting an end to the previous secret treaties and alliances, having all nations working together toward the maintenance of global peace and security.

Unfortunately, despite its periodic peace-keeping force being sent often to countries at war or experiencing violent political conflicts that might potentially lead to a major war, the United Nations has been unable to prevent or stop internal massacres, genocides, and civil and international wars since its creation in 1945. Examples include the wars in Angola, Mozambique, the Democratic Republic of Congo, Ethiopia and Eritrea, Syria, Iraq, India and Pakistan over Kashmir, the violent confrontation between Ukraine and Russia, Afghanistan, Chad, the Central African Republic (CAR), Libya, Sierra Leone, El Salvador, Colombia, the two Koreas that drew American intervention in 1950, the two Vietnams that also caused a United States intervention on behalf of South Korea, and others. Only rarely has the United Nations been successful in the final stages of a conflict and on its humanitarian mission through the work of private or diplomatic intervention of its member states. This happened most notably in Zimbabwe (former Southern

Rhodesia), South West Africa (now Namibia), and Sudan, which led to the independence of South Sudan in 2011.

One must emphasize that the world had never before witnessed the magnitude of the devastation caused by the First and Second World Wars and their global impact. It would appear therefore that the causes of the relatively global peace experienced after World War II have indirectly been the proliferation of the nuclear arsenals in the United States, the Soviet Union (now Russia), and the several smaller powers (i.e., North Korea, India, Pakistan, Israel, and perhaps South Africa) as deterrents that have the ability to inflict a catastrophic and mortal blow to our planet. As Ziegler once wrote:

> Without question, the work of diplomats on many occasions has helped prevent small wars and emerging conflicts from becoming full-blown wars. On the other hand, there have been cases to demonstrate that diplomacy alone is not enough to prevent war. Perhaps the assumption of a basic harmony of interests is mistaken; perhaps political leaders are not yet rational enough to recognize such basic harmony. Whatever the reason, historical experience should not make US optimistic about the ability of diplomats alone to prevent all wars.[12] (2001: 343)

The greatest disappointment most likely caused by World War II was the failure of high-level diplomacy, which poses a question about the usefulness of diplomacy when leaders confront a man as delusional as Adolf Hitler, the Führer, was. The months preceding the impending international drama were full of anticipation, anxiety, and fear. Thus, in order to resolve the conflict over Germany's imminent annexation of Czechoslovakia, Neville Chamberlain, the prime minister of Great Britain, left London on September 15, 1938; on September 29, 1938, he visited Hitler alone in his private Berchtesgaden mountain retreat. The next day, September 30, 1938, Adolf Hitler, Benito Mussolini, Neville Chamberlain, and French premier Édouard Daladier met and signed the Munich Pact, which allowed the Führer to annex the Sudetenland, home to some 30 million people who spoke German, along with a concession to Germany of 66 percent of the Czech coal industry, 70 percent of its iron and steel, and 70 percent of its electric power.

Upon his triumphant return to England, Chamberlain announced that through his daring solo diplomatic trip to meet Hitler, he had secured "the Peace of our Time" for Europe. The diplomatic concession, however, did not satisfy Hitler, and by the time the Führer made his move into Poland on September 1, 1939, Czechoslovakia no longer existed as such. The mood in Europe had totally changed for the worse. Chamberlain was not only blamed for Hitler's evil boldness but he was called the "Great Appeaser." With his reputation thrown out the window, Chamberlain was soon removed from his position as prime minister and replaced by Winston Churchill. The case simply proved that diplomacy works only when1) a negotiator knows how strong the other is and the consequences of war for either side; 2) both know the other's future interests; 3) both are of sound mind; 4) both are willing to compromise; and 5) the negotiator is unafraid of speaking clearly and with confidence about what would happen if the other side refused to abide by a written agreement. Unfortunately, all along, Hitler was intent on pursuing his goals by force;

---

12   Ziegler. *War, Peace, and International Politics.*

sadly, his homologues were simply scared of another war and were therefore easily susceptible to being fooled and outmaneuvered.

The modern European wars, which began with the Thirty Years' War (1618–1648) that concluded with the Treaty of Westphalia, up to the end of the two World Wars, shaped the world of today—namely, the constellation of the nations that now constitute west and eastern Europe and the developing countries of Africa, Latin America, and Asia and those on the continent of Australia. It is important to stress here that, regarding the participation of Africans during the two World Wars up to the time they achieved independence between 1957 and the early 1970s, there was an interesting interlude of virtually no war but skirmishes, if any, occurring among the colonial powers, as they used diplomacy and not war to solve their colonial conflicts following the dictates of the Berlin Conference (1884–1885). Thus, the colonial powers fought in Africa just as an extension of the two World Wars, and their intention then was not primarily to take each other's territory by force but to weaken the enemy. Africans, of course, had no choice but to fight on the side of their colonial master against his enemy, as was the case between France and Italy in Chad, Britain and Germany in Cameroon, France and Germany in Togoland, Britain and Germany in Tanganyika, and Portugal and Germany in Angola and Mozambique.

Indeed, the first closest-to-war incident among the European powers in Africa was the Fashoda (present-day Kodok) confrontation on the banks of the Nile River between Captain Jean Baptiste Marchand and General Sir Herbert Kitchener (September 18-November 3, 1898) for control of Sudan. Kitchener ordered Marchand to retreat, which he finally did on November 3, 1898, "because the French government was not in a position to fight a war at the moment and Marchand's forces had no chance of winning a skirmish no matter how insignificant."[13] The tense situation was, however, diffused when, on March 21, 1899, France renounced claims over any territory along the Nile in exchange for a few unproductive desert portions near present-day Chad.

The second incident worthy of mention, which resulted in a humiliating to following the British ultimatum (to Lisbon) on January 11, 1899, was the confrontation between Portugal and Great Britain over Mashonaland and the Shire River, which the British considered to be theirs, following Portuguese explorer Serpa Pinto's annexation of the Macololo people in Nyasaland. A British ship made anchor in Lisbon on the Tagus River, waiting for an immediate reply of full compliance to the ultimatum. Portugal's quick capitulation led to a diplomatic settlement of the borders of Nyasaland, Southern Rhodesia, and Mozambique on June 11, 1891.

However, the humiliating capitulation"...brought down the government of Prime Minister Jose Luciano de Castro in Lisbon...and is still viewed as one of the worst humiliations the Portuguese have ever suffered."[14] The present warlike Portuguese national anthem (A Portuguesa) "Herois do Mar" (Sea Heroes), composed by Alfredo Keil (of German descent), poet, drawer, and photographer, and Henrique Lopes de Mendonça, who wrote the lyrics, came out of this debasing incident, as Portugal's national pride was hurt to the core. In fact, the anthem's original chorus

---

13 Mario J. Azevedo, *Africana Studies: A Survey of Africa and Its Diaspora* (Durham, NC: Carolina Academic Press, 2005), 115.

14 Ibid.

words read: "To arms, to arms against the Bretons, "which years later were softened to "Against cannons, March, March!"

While the League of Nations had upheld the right to self-determination, the United Nations not only defended people's right to independence but also upheld the universal rights of men. These two noble organizations were the indirect outcomes of the two World Wars. Can one then conclude that something good came out of the wars and thus put aside the accepted claim that "two wrongs do not make a right"? Indeed, as historians are quick to point out, from the wars of the Napoleonic era came the democratic and nationalist revolutions of the 1820s and 1840s on the one hand. From the two World Wars, on the other hand, emerged the permanent democratic unification of Germany along with the acceptance of the geographic and national contours of France, Russia, Germany, Austria, Poland, and of most eastern European states.

In Latin America, where the various former colonies achieved their independence from Spain during the period 1810–1820, new nations waged war against each other aimed at increasing the size of the territory rather than as domination or conquest of the other. If these often bloody forays can be given a name, they ought to be called simply "border conflicts" that at times led to violence. In fact, the *Oxford Research Encyclopaedia of Latin America* notes: "…every South American nation engaged in at least one war against one or more of its neighbors during the nineteenth century in an attempt to maximize or stabilize its borders…European countries, and especially Great Britain, inserted themselves into these disputes to protect commercial advantages. As a consequence, almost every decade saw an international border conflict that ultimately redrew the boundaries."[15] Examples of conflict include the Ecuador and Peru skirmishes of 1828 and 1829, which lingered until 1941; the border conflicts among Peru, Bolivia, and Chile of 1835 and 1879–1884; the violent boundary encounters of the 1870s between Chile and Argentina, which were resolved only in 1904; the 1825–1828 Uruguay border problems with Brazil; and the War of the Triple Alliance of Paraguay, Argentina, and Brazil in 1864–1870.

Scholars Philip Adler and Randall Pouwels thus summarize the extent and impact of industrialization and globalization in Latin America:

> The agrarian economy became dependent on the exports to Western European and North American states. The rural majority lived in agrarian villages or on haciendas in conditions that differed little from serfdom. Little manufacturing could develop because of both the widespread poverty of the internal market and the openness of that market to imports from abroad. By the end of the nineteenth century, Latin America was tied perhaps more closely to foreign economic interests than it had ever been in the colonial era. The newly formed nations could not become truly politically independent because of their economic dependence on countries such as the US and Britain led to interference in their internal political affairs.[16]

---

15   *Oxford University Encyclopedia of Latin America* (see htpp://latinamericanhistory.oxfordre.com/view/10.1093/acrefore/9780199366439.001.0001/acrefore-9780199366439-e-36: 2/13).

16   PhilipAdler and Randall Pouwels. *History of Civilizations*, 7th ed. (Boston, MA: Cengage Learning, 2008), 33.

War, Medicine, and Public Health[17]

Throughout history, the treatment of war casualties and victims taught societies many medical lessons—of course, this is not to say that war is needed for the advancement of medical and public health science and practice. However, just as we learned the horrors of war from the Crimean War (1852–1854) and the work of Florence Nightingale in that violent conflict, which revolutionized the way hospitals are run, so did the world learn from the major war scenes, including the American Civil War.

Indeed, in spite of the awful circumstances surrounding people's physical suffering at war during the nineteenth century and thereafter, physicians and surgeons, as well as nurses and all other medical personnel learned invaluable lessons from the experience, both in combating disease and in treating potentially deadly injuries that needed surgery. Both the efficacy of quinine, used sparingly against malaria, and aggressive vaccinations against infectious diseases spread the adoption of the most efficacious personnel assignment procedures, as well as the new treatment methods that were to be later improved in a peaceful setting; namely, in civilian hospitals and health care centers at home. As the *Encyclopaedia of the Civil War* in "Medical Care, Battle Wounds, and Disease" notes:

> Throughout the war, both the South and the North struggled to improve the level of medical care given to their men. In many ways, their efforts assisted in the birth of modern medicine in the US. More complete records on medical and surgical activities were kept during the war than ever before, doctors became more adept at surgery and at the use of anesthesia, and perhaps most importantly, a greater understanding of the relationship between cleanliness, diet, and disease was gained not only by the medical establishment but by the public at large.[18]

Unbeknownst to most, a number of infection-related preventive practices, such as hygiene and cleanliness, proper diet, appropriate use of anesthesia, and better protective gear, were major outcomes of the two Worlds Wars. Suffice it to point to a few important war developments that impacted humankind positively. According to scientists and public health experts, World War I forced the Allies to improve their administrative operations in health, to further appreciate the importance of hygiene and sanitation, and to modify or enhance their surgical procedures. Thus, they learned that health services on the battlefield and at home had to be increased by at least twentyfold, compelling the United States to deploy some 29,602 physicians "as reserve officers"; streamline and better organize doctors for the effective and rapid treatment of soldiers; list some physicians "in charge of wounds" for a more effective organizational scheme; create fracture clinics in general hospitals by 1917; and perform "reconstructive surgery of bones and joints, while enhancing their practice with an accelerated and improved usage of X-rays."

---

17   Adapted from Mario J. Azevedo, *The State of Health and Health Care in Mississippi*, pp. 9-13. Copyright © 2015 by University Press of Mississippi. Reprinted with permission.

18   *Encyclopaedia of the Civil War Medicine*, "Medical Care, Battle Wounds, and Diseases" (Civil War Society, 1996–2018), 1.

In England, at the urging of Prime Minister Lloyd George (1918–1922), public health and health services received a major boost when health centers came to prominence, while the emphasis shifted to the need to "bring preventing and curative medicine together."[19] Antiseptic practices to treat wounds were upgraded, and only specific physicians with the necessary training and experience "in the substitution of hypertonic salt solutions for antiseptic, auto-inoculations, vaccines, etc." could provide these services, all accompanied by techniques for the "cleansing and removal of debris and loose devitalized tissues from the wound."[20]

This resulted in an agreement among the armies and their governments at home about "the need for complete excision of dead, badly damaged or grossly infected tissue"[21] from the patient. Hygiene continued to be refined with better ways of purifying water, waste disposal, and field sanitation and the administration of vaccine against tetanus, typhoid, and paratyphoid ailments. Overall, as a result, the number of deaths in World War I from typhoid decreased by 90 percent, while claiming 30 to 51 times more victims among the non-vaccinated on the battlefield than among the vaccinated. We may note here the historical fact that typhoid fever killed more soldiers in the Crimean War (1852–1854) than the war itself.

Among the British troops, who numbered some 1,200,000, typhoid cases fell to 7,423 and caused only 266 casualties. Blood transfusion, an indispensable medical feature of our times, was used for the first time in World War I; trench fever, transmitted by human body lice, was discovered and treated; trench foot, whose symptoms were cold, swollen red feet, rendering them numb and blistered, was resolved through dry boots, anti-frostbite grease, and foot powder; and gout was studied and treated more effectively. All improvements in health brought about by the harsh and deadly conditions of the First World War contributed to concrete and positive health results, including much lower infant mortality rates in Europe and America.

World War II unwittingly helped perfect the techniques and improve the discoveries brought about by the treatment of wounds, illnesses, and deaths of soldiers who fought in the war. The use of sulfonamide antibacterial indication (also called M&B at the time) in adequate dosages produced for the first time in great quantities by pharmaceuticals for treatment against sore throat, pneumonia, and gonorrhea, of which many soldiers suffered, saved many lives. Penicillin had already been discovered by British physician Alexander Fleming in 1928, but companies were urged to produce it on a larger scale, which by 1945 had become 20 times more potent and effective and could be administered faster than ever before.

Burn centers, skin grafts, and blood transfusions became a "sophisticated well-oiled machine at the end of the war"[22] in the treatment of the wounded. The changes also included blood storage and distribution and the massive inoculations against tetanus that had started during World War I. All this proceeded at an accelerated pace. It was also during the Second World War that chemical warfare protection brought about the development of face and head gas masks against

---

19   Abraham S. Bennett, "Medical Advances Consequent to the Great War, 1914–1918." *Journal of the Royal Society of Medicine*, 83, 11(1990), 741.

20   Ibid., 739.

21   Ibid.

22   "Medicine and World War Two" (www.historyleaningsite.co.uk.), Retrieved 2020.

gas poison. The earnest research against mosquito bites was also a legacy of the last of the two Great Wars, answer many other medical advances.

Conclusion

The Industrial Revolution has been associated with exploitative capitalism, class differentiations, dependency, militarism, extreme nationalism, and imperialism, which are considered by many experts as the propelling forces behind wars and people's violent revolts against tyrannical regimes. These conditions were underscored by the last two World Wars, particularly in Europe, and by the conflicts in such continents as Central America, South America, and Africa, all of which unfortunately weakened the relevance of diplomacy and gave prominence to the rise and unchecked use of deadly weaponry created just for the purpose of killing and overcoming the enemy in the name of the nation. The conditions created by the changes contributed to an international environment that explains the precipitous waning of the League of Nations following World War I and the often ineffective work of the United Nations on a global scale in our times.

Chapter Summary

There is no doubt that the globalized Industrial Revolution had a most profound impact—perhaps greater than any other event in the history of the evolution of our world and the lifestyles we enjoy on this planet. While the introduction of colonialism prevented an industrialization takeoff in most regions of the world, including Africa, Latin America, and the Far East, the forced introduction of communism partially slowed its pace and scope in several other parts of the world, including China, North Vietnam, North Korea, Russia, and Cuba, forcing them to eventually try to catch up with the economic developments of the industrialized world—until then confined mostly to what are now the British Isles, western Europe, and North America, the latter dominated by the United States and Canada. Other areas, such as Australia, New Zealand, Japan, Taiwan, and Singapore, benefited from their contact with the West, assisted at times by their racial affinity as well as their strategic location. If there is any merit in the preceding developmental assumptions and theories discussed here, one thing is absolutely clear: Africa, Latin America, Amerindia, and most of Asia would have been completely different from what they are now as nations and perhaps be listed as the least economically developed regions of the world.

However, one cannot dispute the assertion of many experts that aggressive industrialism also whetted an appetite for wars among nations as well as their tendency to forcibly dominate less-advanced societies. One of its many consequences was the accelerated phenomenon known as "globalization," which can be seen as a two-sided sharp sword. While the developed world has been pushing this concept, touting it as benefiting the whole world—especially in the economic arena such as unfettered trade—the developing world has continued to see it as a control mechanism designed to keep in check the "wretched of the world," to use Walter Rodney's characterization of imperialism and globalization in his book *How Europe Underdeveloped Africa*.

Discussion Questions

1. Define the following concepts: mercantilism, capitalism, socialism, and communism. Which nations today might be classified as fitting one of the concepts that are provided in this chapter? Give the reasons.
2. What is the meaning of nationalism, industrialism, capitalism, and militarism in the context of Europe during the twentieth century?
3. Could you name and elaborate on the intellectual and material cultural elements that spurred industrialization in Europe and globally? Which element do you think was more critical in the process?
4. What were the major factors that contributed to the rise of western European industrial development, particularly during the second Industrial Revolution (1870–1914)?
5. What do you think are the reasons why some countries and continents achieved more industrialization than others? Do you believe that some parts of the world are intellectually more endowed than others? What is the basis of your negative or positive answer?

References

Using the Sources

Beyond the primary sources provided in this chapter, students will benefit from analyzing maps and images provided and additional readings and materials cited below. Students and instructors may find film and literary adaptations particularly helpful in the classroom or as additional assignments. References and suggested supplementary sources are provided.

Primary Sources

"The New Act on Juvenile Labour." 1867. *Ragged School Union Magazine, Jan.1849–Dec. 1875* 10, 233–35. https://alliance-primo.hosted.exlibrisgroup.com/permalink/f/lvbsh/TN_proquest3877003

US Department of State. "National Security Archive Electronic Briefing Book No. 162." In *The National Security Archive: The Atomic Bomb and the End of World War II: A Collection of Primary Sources: VI. The First Nuclear Strikes*, edited by William Burr.https://nsarchive2.gwu.edu//NSAEBB/NSAEBB162/index.htm

Film and Television

Der Magische Gürtel (The Enchanted Circle). 1917. German film about successful *U-Boot* patrol (see https://www.iwm.org.uk/collections/item/object/1060008290).

Understanding 9/11 – A Television News Archive.https://archive.org/details/911

Secondary Sources

Adler, Philip, and Randall Pouwels. 2008. *World Civilizations*. Volume II, 7th ed. Stamford, CT: Cengage Learning.

Anderson, Eugene. 1964. *Nineteenth Century Europe—Crisis and Contribution*. 2nd ed. P. # 29. Washington, DC: Service Center for Teachers of History, American Historical Association.

Anderson, M.S. 2014. *Europe in the Eighteenth Century 1713–1789*. 4th ed. New York: Routledge.

Auletta, K. October 1997."American Keiretsu." *The New Yorker.*

———."The Industrial Revolution."https://www.khanacademy.org/partner-contnet/big-history-project/ acceleration/bhp-acceleration/a/the/-indUStrial-revolution. Retrieved March 29, 2018.

Azevedo, Mario J. 2005. *Africana Studies: A Survey of Africa and Its Diaspora.* Durham, NC: Carolina Academic Press.

Bennett, Abraham S. 1990."Medical Advances Consequent to the Great War, 1914–1918." *Journal of the Royal Society of Medicine,* Vol. 83, 11, 738–41.

Bowen, H. V. 2002. "Sinews of Trade and Empire: The Supply of Commodity Exports to the East." The *Economic History Review,* Vol. 55, 3(August 2002): 466–486.

Browne, Cynthia Stoke. 2018.*The Industrial Revolution.* Mountain View, CA: Khan Academy.

Burns, Edward M., and Philip L. Ralph. 1974. *World Civilizations: From Ancient to Contemporary.* 4th ed. New York: Norton & Company.

Crist, David. 2013. *The Twilight War: The Secret History of America's Thirty-Year Conflict with Iran.* Baltimore, MD: Penguin.

Dyer, J.H. July-August 1996. "How Chrysler Created an American Keiretsu." *Harvard Business Review.*

"East India Company during the Late Eighteenth Century." 2002. *Economic History Review,* Vol. LV, 3, 466–86.

Encyclopaedia Britannica. 2018. "Industrial Revolution." London: UK.

Encyclopaedia of the Civil War Medicine Mississippi Health). 1996–2018. "Medical Care, Battle Wounds, and Diseases", 1. Civil War Society, Amazon.com.

Fall, Bernard B. 1961. *Street without Joy: Indochina at War, 1946–54.* Harrisburg, PA: Stackpole.

Giangreco, Dennis M. *2009. Hell to Pay: Operation Downfall and the Invasion of Japan, 1945–1947.* Annapolis, MD: Naval Institute Press.

Harley, C. Knick. 1998. "Cotton Textile Prices and the Industrial Revolution." *Economic History Review,* Vol. LI, 1, 49–63.

Henderson, Peter V.N. "Border Wars in South America during the 19th Century." *Oxford Research of Encyclopaedia of Latin America.* (2/13,

Hopley, Claire. July 29, 2006. "British Textiles Clothe the World." https://britishheritage.com/ british-textiles-cloth-the-world/

Hudson, Pat. 2006. "The Limits of Wool and the Potential of Cotton in the Eighteenth and Nineteenth Centuries." www.Lse.ca.uic/Economic-History/Assets/Documents/.../HelsnimkiHudson.pdf.Retrieved March 27, 2018.

"Industrial Revolution." *Geography.*http://geography.name/industrial-revolution/

"Keiretsu." 2009. *Economist.* https://www.economist.com/news/2009/10/16/keiretsu.

Labonté, R. 2011. "Interrogating Globalization, Health, and Development." https://doi. org/10.1080/09581590500186117, Online Article Retrieved in 2015.

Miscamble, Wilson D. 2011. *The Most Controversial Decision: Truman, the Atomic Bombs, and the Defeat of Japan.* New York: Cambridge University Press.

Parshall, Jonathan, and Tully, Anthony. 2005. *Shattered Sword: The Untold Story of the Battle of Midway.* Dulles, VA: Potomac Books.

Remarque, Erich Maria. English version, 1929. *All Quiet on the Western Front.* Boston: Little Brown and Co.

Shin, Jang-Sup. 2002. "The East Asian Industrialization in the Gerschenkronian Mirror: Catching-Up Strategies and Institutional Transition." Singapore: National University of Singapore, Department of Economics, Working Paper No. 0208, 1–41.

"A Short History of Merino Wool." https://www.littleflockofhorrors.com/blog/a-short-history-of-merino-wool/Stoker, Donald. 2019. *Why America Loses Wars: Limited War and US Strategy from the Korean War to the Present*. New York: Cambridge University Press.

Tooze, Adam. 2006. *The Wages of Destruction: The Making and Breaking of the Nazi Economy*.Allen Lane.

Westad, Odd Arne. 2017. *The Cold War: A World History*. New York: Basic Books.

Wilde, Robert. 2018. "Coal in Industrial Revolution."THOUGHTCO.https://www.thoughtco.com/about-us#ContactUs

Williamson, Murray, and Robert Scales. 2005. *The Iraq War*. Cambridge, MA: Belknap Press.

Woodward, D.,N. Draeger, R. Beaglehole, and D. Lispon. 2001. "Globalization and Health: A Framework for Analysis and Action." *Bulletin of the World Organization* 79, 875–81.

Ziegler, David. 1993. *War, Peace, and International Politics*. 6th ed. New York: Longman.

Zimmerer, Jürgen. 2005. "Annihilation in Africa: The 'Race War' in German Southwest Africa (1904–1908) and Its Significance for a Global History of Genocide." *Bulletin of the German Historical Institute, Issue 37*, 51–57.

Credits

Fig. 3.1: Source: https://commons.wikimedia.org/wiki/File:Ford_1921.jpg.

Fig. 3.2: Source: https://commons.wikimedia.org/wiki/File:Missionaries_and_steam_train%2C_Congo%2C_ca._1900-1915_%28IMP-CSCNWW33-OS10-83%29.jpg.

Fig. 3.3: Source: https://commons.wikimedia.org/wiki/File:Robert_Whitehead_with_battered_test_torpedo_Fiume_c1875.jpg.

Fig. 3.4: Source: https://commons.wikimedia.org/wiki/File:Timbre_penny_post_Canada_1898.jpg.

Fig. 3.5: Source: https://commons.wikimedia.org/wiki/File:Into_the_Jaws_of_Death_23-0455M_edit.jpg.

Chapter 4

The Twentieth Century

Introduction to Chapter Themes

This chapter focuses on the twentieth century, a century noted for unprecedented development in areas such as science, technology, and human rights, yet marred by continuing global inequities created by imperialism, racism, sexism, and ethnic conflict. This chapter examines the twentieth century through the themes of this textbook: geography and environment; material culture; science and technology; gender and sexuality; and war, peace, and diplomacy. Geography and Environment are discussed in relation to globalization and global environmental concerns, including climate change. The section on Material Culture examines human-made objects that helped revolutionize human culture and civilization during the twentieth century, such as new forms of transportation and communication. Science and Technology, often spurred by wartime innovations, initiated unprecedented advances in communications, transportation, and daily life. The section on Gender and Sexuality examines global women's rights, with a focus on women's right to vote, and the uneven progress of women's rights around the world. Sections on War, Peace, and Diplomacy examine global wars, such as World War I, World War II, and the Cold War, as well as the many smaller conflicts that marked the years before and after these global wars. This section also makes clear that advances in technology were linked to the devastation of twentieth-century warfare despite efforts to secure global peace.

Student Learning Objectives

After reading this chapter students should be able to describe and discuss:

- Twentieth century advances in human rights and science and technology
- How global warfare, inequities, and destruction marred the twentieth century
- The pros and cons of modern globalization
- Trends and conflicts in global warfare in the twentieth century

Timeline of Selected Dates

1908   Ford Motor Company introduces Model T
1914   Terrorist action starts chain of events leading to World War I

1917	Start of Russian Revolution
1918	World War I concludes with defeat of the Central Powers
1922	Bolsheviks create first Communist state, the USSR
1927	First "talkie" film
1929	Wall Street Crash—start of the Great Depression
1933	Adolf Hitler made German chancellor
1935	Italy invades Ethiopia
1937	Second Sino-Japanese War begins
1939	Germany invades Poland; start of World War II in Europe
1945	World War II ends; United Nations established; Cold War begins
1969	Internet created
1989	Collapse of Soviet Bloc; Tiananmen Square Massacre in Red China
1992	European Union created
1994	End of South African apartheid
2001	Al-Qaeda launches 9/11 attacks against the United States

Geography and Environment

Globalization

In 1992, sociologist Roland Robertson described "globalization" as "the compression of the world and the intensification of consciousness of the world as a whole."[1] Robertson argues a cultural approach to the concept of globalization allows it to be applied to concepts of geography as a social science in a twentieth-century historical context.

Technology drove globalization. Faster means of transportation and communication made the world feel smaller and more integrated to many people. Globalization, however, did not play out around the world in an even manner for all. Regardless, there is a sense, for better or worse, that twentieth-century globalization heralded a new kind of global consciousness.

Historians recognize that globalization processes are not new. Defined broadly, globalization occurred from the beginning of human existence with the spread of *Homo sapiens* from Africa to other continents and during what scholars describe as a series of developments of world systems and cross-cultural connections. These may include the Silk Roads from the first century BCE, the Indian Ocean system from the third century BCE, and global trade following 1571.

Modern globalization made a start during the Industrial Revolution but waned during the World Wars of the early to mid-twentieth century. Its popularity as a concept (although definitions are widely contested) grew in the late twentieth century, and today globalization has become a buzzword in many regions.

Globalization's impact became particularly noticeable after the fall of the Berlin Wall in 1989. This marked the end of competition between US- and Soviet-led systems, while the World Wide

---

1   Roland Robertson, *Globalization: Social Theory and Global Culture.* Theory, Culture & Society. (London: Sage, 1992), 8.

Web became publicly available on the internet two years later. By 1998, CNN reported 147 million global internet users in North America and western Europe, as well as China, Japan, and Taiwan.[2] Because the internet allowed instantaneous access to commerce, professional and social connections, and information—at least to those who gained internet access—it became a central focus of the globalization process and created, as Robertson argues, a new culture of global geographical compression and consciousness.

Globalization's Global Inequities

The *Encyclopaedia Britannica* explains globalization through focus on the spread of rapid transportation, communication, and scientific and technological advances, which are said to result in a natural integration of the regions of the world. Globalization, however, is sometimes a contentious concept among scholars, business leaders, and politicians. For some, globalization simply means interdependence, a spread of economic benefits on a global scale, which do not respect boundaries, forcing people to adopt and adapt to their prescribed uses. In other words, many proponents of globalization see only benefits in a world that does not discriminate on the basis of national boundaries, color, religious creed, region, political affiliation, or sexual orientation.

To others, however, globalization means an uneven distribution of the world's resources for the benefit of the West and its allies and the imposition of cultural elements of one part of the world on the other, to the extent that, no matter the degree of the spread and touted benefits sharing, there is only one world that determines the flow of goods that may trickle down to others. This one-dimensional direction creates in the process the haves and the have-nots. The end result of such asymmetric movement is that the loser will continue to be the developing world, which, no matter how hard it might try to catch up with the dominant and already privileged counterpart, will continue to fall behind. Such conditions will maintain a perpetual imbalance that only a cataclysmic terrestrial event might reverse, making unrealistic the claim of a global village.

Canadian medical researcher Ronald Labonté defines the phenomenon thus: "At its simplest," globalization is "… the constellation of processes by which nations, businesses and people are becoming more connected and interdependent across the globe through increased economic integration and communication exchange, cultural diffusion" (especially from the West) and travel.[3] Scholar David Woodward et al continue on this theme, noting:

> Economic globalization has been the fundamental force behind the overall process of globalization over the last two decades. It has been characterized both by a dramatic growth in the volume of cross-border flows and by major changes in their nature. International trade has grown at an accelerated pace—nearly 8.6 percent per year over the

---

2   Cheri Paquet, "Report Counts 147 Million Global Net Users," CNN.com, February 12, 1999. http://edition. cnn.com/TECH/computing/9902/12/globalnet.idg/index.html

3   R. Labonté, "Globalization, Health, and Development: The Right Prescription," 2011. (http://idrc.ca/en/en-67832-201-I-DO_TOPIC.html), 1–11.

period 1990–1999—with the proportion accentuated by services increasing steadily, reaching nearly 19 percent in 1999.[4]

They add, "this transformation has largely by-passed low-income countries, most of which remain critically dependent on aid flows."[5]

Global Environmental Concerns and the Anthropocene

Humans have always impacted on their environment. Since antiquity, human use and manipulation of natural resources have led to deforestation, pollution, and human-changed ecosystems. In the modern age, European imperialism created new world systems, which disrupted older patterns. As European colonization, industrialization, and economic systems spread across the globe, indigenous peoples, their land, and their resources fell to European control during the Columbian Exchange and by processes of ecological imperialism. Plantation agriculture in colonial lands in the Americas, Africa, and Asia led to environmental degradation. The German economic historian and founder of communism, Karl Marx, argued plantation systems were not "the natural destinies" of these regions. The long-term repercussions of global power and economic systems based on European imperialism set the stage for global inequalities tied to globalization trends and environmental changes.[6] Industrialization sped these processes up to the point that some scholars now propose humans have initiated a new geological age, the Anthropocene, defined by *Merriam-Webster* as "the period of time during which human activities have had an environmental impact on the Earth regarded as constituting a distinct geological age." Although scholars debate the starting date of this age, many locate it in the Industrial Revolution or the Atomic Age.

Ryuichi Fukuhara, a Japanese academic, argues, "No one would refute the Industrial Revolution opened up a Pandora's Box that caused unintended and unpredictable enormous environmental changes."[7] He locates the Anthropocene in the mid-twentieth century and notes European industrialization once meant "'deindustrialization'" of other parts of the world, but as China and India substantially increased their global industrial and economic power in the twentieth century, this came at the cost of additional environmental degradation.[8]

While some scholars maintain that historical inequities continue to shape globalization's global effects on the environment, others argue that globalization will prove beneficial as the world's people find common cause with one another; for example, in recognizing and fighting global climate change.

---

4   D. Woodward, N. Draeger, R. Beaglehole, and D. Lispon, "Globalization and Health: A Framework for Analysis and Action." *Bulletin of the World Organization*, 79, 2001: 875–81.

5   Woodward et al., "Globalization and Health."

6   Karl Marx and David McLellan, *Selected Writings* (Oxford; New York: Oxford University Press, 2000), 295.

7   Ryuichi Fukuhara, "Human and Nature Revisited: The Industrial Revolution, Modern Economics and the Anthropocene." In S. Yamash'ta, T. Yagi, and S. Hill, Eds., *The Kyoto Manifesto for Global Economics* (Singapore: Springer, 2018), 46.

8   Fukuhara, 52.

FIGURE 4.1　September 2019 Climate Strike in Sydney, Australia.

Climate Change and Environmental Activism

Following the work of scientists and activists as early as the eighteenth century, the concept of anthropogenic global climate change came to the forefront of global concerns in the twentieth century as global scientists, activists, and leaders studied and popularized the issue. A series of transnational agreements on issues like air pollution led to international agreements such as the UN Framework Convention on Climate Change of 1992, signed at the Rio Earth Summit. The 1992 agreement began a process of international policy decisions, leading to the 1997 **Kyoto Protocol**.

The recognition of human-caused climate change is often credited to the Swedish Nobel Prize–winning physicist Svante Arrhenius whose 1896 findings, building on the work of earlier scientists, set precedents for twentieth-century work on **climatology**. Rachel Carson, the American scientist and author (Figure 4.2), is often credited with alerting the general public to the crisis, specifically by outlining the dangers of chemical pesticides to the environment in her globally best-selling book, *Silent Spring* (1962). Her work is credited with sparking

FIGURE 4.2　Marine Biologist Rachel Carson, Author of *Silent Spring*, Working with Bob Hines in the Atlantic Ocean.

significant environmental movements in the United States, eventually leading to the creation of the US Environmental Protection Agency (EPA). Carson's work was part of a postwar global environmental movement that took hold in the 1960s and by 1972 saw the first United Nations (UN) Conference on the Human Environment (Stockholm Conference) held in Sweden, attended by delegates from 114 governments. The Stockholm Declaration of the United Nations Conference on the Human Environment proclaimed:

> Man is both creature and moulder of his environment, which gives him physical sustenance and affords him the opportunity for intellectual, moral, social and spiritual growth. In the long and tortuous evolution of the human race on this planet a stage has been reached when, through the rapid acceleration of science and technology, man has acquired the power to transform his environment in countless ways and on an unprecedented scale. Both aspects of man's environment, the natural and the man-made, are essential to his well-being and to the enjoyment of basic human rights the right to life itself.[9]

By 1997 a landmark international treaty, the **Kyoto Protocol to the United Nations Framework Convention on Climate Change**, was ratified by 192 nation-states to help mitigate the effects of greenhouse gases on global climate change. While the agreement was an important step forward in global environmental policy, it was ultimately ineffective without the participation of China and the United States, who never agreed to its terms.

Grassroots movements for environmental protection and halting climate change should not be discounted. For example, indigenous groups around the world contributed not only to local movements from the Americas to New Zealand, but to international indigenous efforts for water protection and rights. In fact, local environmental movements were often the impetus for global efforts in the post–World War II era. Greenpeace, an internationally recognized environmental organization, for example, began as the "Don't Make a Wave Committee," when in 1971, "12 angry men," as they called themselves, fearing earthquakes, tsunamis, and radiation leaks, sailed a halibut boat from Vancouver, British Columbia, to protest US underground nuclear testing in the Aleutian islands.[10]

Primary Source 1

L. H. Bailey (1858–1954) was a botanist, writer, and teacher whose work influenced farmers, gardeners, scientists, and conservationists. In The Holy Earth *(1915), Bailey argued for the moral imperative of human regard for nature and the earth. The book would influence ecologists and environmentalists. In this excerpt, he discusses humankind's destructive tendencies.*

---

9   "Declaration of the United Nations Conference on the Human Environment," 1972. https://www.ipcc.ch/apps/njlite/srex/njlite_download.php?id=6471

10   Jay Walz, "12 Sail for Amchitka to Fight Atom Test," *The New York Times*, October 3, 1971, 14. https://www.nytimes.com/1971/10/03/archives/12-sail-for-amchitka-to-fight-atom-test.html

"The Habit of Destruction"

L. H. Bailey

The first observation that must be apparent to all men is that our dominion has been mostly destructive.

We have been greatly engaged in digging up the stored resources, and in destroying vast products of the earth for some small kernel that we can apply to our necessities or add to our enjoyments. We excavate the best of the coal and cast away the remainder; blast the minerals and metals from underneath the crust, and leave the earth raw and sore; we box the pines for turpentine and abandon the growths of limitless years to fire and devastation; sweep the forests with the besom of destruction; pull the fish from the rivers and ponds without making any adequate provision for renewal; exterminate whole races of animals; choke the streams with refuse and dross; rob the land of its available stores, denuding the surface, exposing great areas to erosion.

Nor do we exercise the care and thrift of good housekeepers. We do not clean up our work or leave the earth in order. The remnants and accumulation of mining-camps are left to ruin and decay; the deserted phosphate excavations are ragged, barren, and unfilled; vast areas of forested lands are left in brush and waste, unthoughtful of the future, unmindful of the years that must be consumed to reduce the refuse to mould and to cover the surface respectably, uncharitable to those who must clear away the wastes and put the place in order; and so thoughtless are we with these natural resources that even the establishments that manufacture them—the mills, the factories of many kinds—are likely to be offensive objects in the landscape, unclean, unkempt, displaying the unconcern of the owners to the obligation that the use of the materials imposes and to the sensibilities of the community for the way in which they handle them. The burden of proof seems always to have been rested on those who partake little in the benefits, although we know that these non-partakers have been real owners of the resources; and yet so undeveloped has been the public conscience in these matters that the blame—if blame there be—cannot be laid on one group more than on the other. Strange it is, however, that we should not have insisted at least that those who appropriate the accumulations of the earth should complete their work, cleaning up the remainders, leaving the areas wholesome, inoffensive, and safe. How many and many are the years required to grow a forest and to fill the pockets of the rocks, and how satisfying are the landscapes, and yet how desperately soon may men reduce it all to ruin and to emptiness, and how slatternly may they violate the scenery!

All this habit of destructiveness is uneconomic in the best sense, unsocial, unmoral.

L. H. Bailey, "The Habit of Destruction," *The Holy Earth,* pp. 18-20, Charles Scribner's Sons, 1916.

Society now begins to demand a constructive process. With care and with regard for other men, we must produce the food and the other supplies in regularity and sufficiency; and we must clean up after our work, that the earth may not be depleted, scarred, or repulsive.

Discussion Questions

1. According to Bailey, how do humans destroy their surroundings? Give specific examples of human actions.
2. Reading between the lines, how does Bailey suggest humans could mediate or repair the destruction they cause?
3. What are the moral imperatives Bailey argues should compel humans to be "good house-keepers" of the earth?

Conclusion

Globalization and the environment became key global concerns in the twentieth century. While both concepts have a long global history, the Columbian Exchange, imperialism, and industrialization sped up the processes of globalization and environmental degradation, leading to global concerns about economic, political, and social inequities. These inequities were often tied to environmental degradation in former colonies and less industrialized nations, while continuing industrial globalization added to environmental concerns. Scholars, governments, and local communities have addressed the pros and cons of globalization as a concept and a phenomenon, while also addressing the growing concerns of global environmental issues such as climate change on local and international levels.

Material Culture

For long, the study of material culture was left to artists, anthropologists, and archaeologists and included the influences from discoveries—as has been the case when ancient cities and ruins are discovered—the importance of the shape of furniture and its uses, messages left by our ancestors in ceramics and museum exhibits, the intriguing nature of roads that have become famous, and the learning we get, for example, from the examination of objects we take for granted such as airplanes. Even though flying machines have played a major role in our modern and contemporary civilization as we interact with them, yet as a subject matter, the impact of airplanes, for example, has often been neglected in the books we read.

The reason for the neglect, as Janice Tauer Wass writes in her *Teaching History with Material Culture*, is that generally:

> Methods for studying material culture and exploration are experimental ... No scholarly doctrines are yet established, although several scholars have different research models ... Researchers agree [now] that its study needs to be built on a rigorous and

systematic examination of evidence that proceeds from discovery, identification, and classification of material culture to the thoughtful analysis and interpretation of the artifact in cultural content.[11] (Wass, 1998: 3)

In this section, we will explore critical objects created or invented by humans, which have revolutionized the trajectory of our planet's culture and civilization from the twentieth century to the first decades of the twenty-first century. We will focus specifically on the changes brought about by the airplane, television, the computer, the motorized vehicle, the modern ship, the film industry, war weaponry, penicillin, musical instruments, drugs, the disco culture, the video games and other important material objects that have transformed our lives and given new meaning to human existence.[12] The issue of their role in society cannot be considered to be a simple appendage in the discipline of history, as they are all a part of the human experience on the planet.

From the beginning of humankind, there has been a competitive effort to reach perfection, efficiency, and effectiveness in the means of defense and offense, or the making of weapons of war—first made of crude sticks, stones, and primitive bows and arrows. With time, these have evolved into **weapons of mass destruction** (WMDs), as is the case today with our chemical and biological arsenals. These exponentially compound military lethality. For example, consider a 1918 raid by 12 British aircraft against the headquarters of their enemy, Kaiser Wilhelm II. Nearly every bomb missed, and the others did very little damage. During the next World War, a single B-29 bomber dropped an atomic bomb on Hiroshima, Japan, which killed at least 70,000 people and destroyed much of the city.

Hiroshima ushered in the Atomic Age, which encouraged all powers to gather weapons of mass destruction. The nuclear club, those nations possessing atomic weapons, quickly expanded from America to the Soviet Union, Great Britain, France, Red China, India, Pakistan, South Africa, and Israel. Surrounded by hostile neighbors, the latter viewed nuclear weapons as insurance against catastrophe in a conventional war. These neighbors, who lost four such conflicts between 1947–1973, sought their own WMDs as a balance. The 2003 American-led invasion of Iraq was "fallout" from this arms race, when faulty intelligence led President George W. Bush to topple Saddam Hussein and halt Iraqi production of WMDs. Iran's poor relations with America and Israel, along with efforts to develop nuclear weapons, are creating similar tensions in 2019–2020.

As chemical and biological agents are also classified as WMDs, these have been employed by Iraq, Syria, and the Soviet Union after World War II. Despite the horror of WMDs, if one weighs the balance between beneficial and harmful material

FIGURE 4.3   Rotary Dial Telephone, ca. 1940s.

---

11   Janice Tauer Wass, "Teaching History with Material Culture." 1998. https://www.lib.niu.edu/1998/iht529802.html

12   Wass, "Teaching History with Material Culture."

culture during the twentieth century, it can be argued the good outweighs the evil. The sewing machine, airplane, motorcar, and other inventions have been beneficial to humankind. These advances brought the people of the world closer together than ever before, increasing and facilitating a new level of communication and dialogue among the nations of the globe. Since 1945, technology has contributed to a peaceful resolution of some human problems, and possibly the fear of WMDs kept great powers from initiating another "total war."

Obviously, the momentous inventions of the computer and the internet have been the precursors of the now popular Facebook, Twitter, What's App, Instagram, and Snapchat, even though, by facilitating our communication, these gadgets have also contributed to some unpleasant experiences at times, particularly when people misuse them. While communication through Facebook, for instance, has widened our knowledge, it has also enhanced the spread of unfounded rumors and the wrong information, robbing, for example, many children of the opportunity to communicate meaningfully or preserve a sound family environment to which we had been accustomed prior to the mid-twentieth century.

We have equally seen the potential negative impact of robots in the workplace. The invention has tended to take over employees' jobs needed to sustain and protect family livelihood, honor, and respect—benefits that a job brings to communities and nations. Unfortunately, these practices enrich employers and big business to the detriment of the lower classes and the poor. Yet even though this seems to be an inherent setback, robots can also spur ingenuity and inventiveness. Playing with robots, men and women can find new ways of preserving the concept of work and satisfaction through further training, targeted schooling, and the search for more suitable employment dictated by one's level of education and experience. How reassuring is the fact, for example, that our current personal computer or laptop is able to check one's correct spelling and advise us instantaneously to choose the most grammatically accepted sentences and paragraphs.

It is also clear from experience that the internet has been misused by many unscrupulous individuals who plan to hurt others, but overall, its benefits outweigh its negative impact. Indeed, as a result of the internet, databases are now easily accessible to almost anyone, and important information in our fields of study is at our fingertips in a few seconds, allowing us to instantly know almost anything happening on our planet. In the field of health, diagnostic tools of the twentieth century can give the physician or the patient an immediate answer, while prognosticating the future has become more accurate, a process that was either impossible to undertake before or took too long to do. Many more lives have been saved as a result of the discovery in the realm of health, just as happens with an ultrasound test and analysis.

Early detection of cancer, made easier by modern instruments in hospitals, continues to save thousands of lives throughout the world daily. Likewise, lifesaving has been the discovery of penicillin, which has become a most welcome addition to the arsenal against sexually transmitted diseases. In the same vein, the study of genetics promises humankind a bright future in our ability to forecast or map the **pathogenesis** of health problems that could be avoided. Space travel and exploration are new features of the twentieth century, as is also the almost supersonic speed of modern trains available in such countries as France, Germany, the United States, Japan, and China. Fortunately, our developing world is beginning to catch up in these astonishing new frontiers as is happening in such countries as Kenya and Brazil. Amazon, a phenomenon that started a few decades ago, has revolutionized the way we do business, which is now faster, cheaper, and more reliable while making driving to physical stores and groceries less attractive given the consumers' waste of thousands of hours while waiting to be served.

Film continues to entertain people and is more attractive through high-definition screens, colorful pictures, and fabulous sound systems. The video game industry has provided an excellent and easy mode of entertainment; it can, on the other, easily make children game addicts who lose control of what is most important in their upbringing, such as going to school and the need for concentration on the most critical activities in life, like being part of a family. Likewise, the perfection and improvement of musical instruments and their harmonic synchronization have given inner and indescribable joy to many people, just as music in the form of disco spots and dances provides fun and exercise and relieves stress.

Much more can be said about the nature of the material culture of our century: The global positioning system (GPS), for instance, makes travel directions easier; "mobile money" is becoming more popular every minute these days in international transactions; think of eBay buying and the availability of e-books, access to electronic journals and newspapers, which we can read at any time we wish for free. These are dramatic changes, just like electronic travel visa applications are a blessing to frequent globetrotters; surveillance cameras at home make us feel more secure; the easy availability of fax machines, still an efficient way of sending information quickly, has made communication more efficient and fast; and home printing of information and documents every time we need to do so is a major leap into the future.

Yet there is no doubt that whatever material culture our century has come up with can also be misused if left in the wrong hands and minds. GPS, for example, can be deployed to hurt innocent people when it is used indiscriminately as a spy tool by the police, the government, or a criminal gang. Indeed, even the science of cloning and altering people's pictures can endanger the reputation of law-abiding citizens and their personal integrity. By the same token, our advanced cyber technology can be used to steal information or shut down a critical system we rely on to harm specifically targeted people or businesses; and travel in space can bring or contribute to future space warfare and therefore to loss of life and ultimately the total annihilation of the human race from the globe. Under these conditions, one just hopes that human decency and values will prevail as we move into a future where more stunning developments will certainly occur.

Finally, to be fair and objective, we might also point here to some of the worst aspects of the material culture of our century, such as those practices attributed to the 1960s—namely, the culture of drug abuse, excessive consumption of alcohol, and careless sexual activities in and outside the communes and Woodstock events, where trash, open defecation, and urination were of no concern among some members of the younger generation of the time. Indeed, experts also posit that the sexual practices of the 1960s may have had an impact on the emerging sexually transmitted diseases like HIV/AIDS in the 1980s and the increase in the rates of syphilis and gonorrhea, which still plague our world today, including the West.

The twentieth century has seen a phenomenal leap in material culture that has made our lives much more comfortable, enjoyable, and infinitely safer overall than the preceding centuries. Unfortunately, not every human being has benefited from the enriching positive changes that have occurred over the past one hundred years. In fact, the overwhelming majority of the people in the world today still live in misery, and when they choose to own at all costs one of the advanced gadgets they think they need, such as a cell phone, they may not be able to afford a day's meal or a physician's visit. This is the sad and unfair reality of life, as those who have get more and those who do not continue to have less. What solution do you suggest to remedy the situation?

Science and Technology

Technology in the Twentieth Century

History took a sharp turn on July 25, 1939, when Polish, French and British spies met in the Kabaty Woods outside of Warsaw. The Poles, expecting invasion by Nazi Germany, handed over a working copy of the German Enigma machine (Figure 4.4), which allowed for the transmission of coded radio messages. In addition, they provided their own *bomba kryptologiczna* ("Cryptographic Bomb"), a computer that allowed users to decipher messages sent via Enigma.

Work remained to perfect what became the Ultra Program. Prime Minister Winston Churchill claimed the finished product "won the war." General Dwight D. Eisenhower agreed, calling Ultra's contribution "decisive." Historians maintain a lively debate over the exact value of Poland's *bomba* and subsequent efforts by Allied cryptologists at top-secret Bletchley Park, but few dispute the tremendous value of being able to know Axis plans from the start.

FIGURE 4.4   General Heinz Guderian and the Enigma Machine.

The *bomba* was a significant contribution to the Allied war effort, yet its computing power is minuscule compared to a Texas Instruments calculator from the 1970s. This marks a critical aspect of the twentieth century—what American academic Clayton M. Christensen calls "**disruptive innovation**." Christensen argues that change was rapid, and corporations needed a very nimble approach to survive resulting change. For example, pay phones were once ubiquitous in America. A caller inserted coins, just like a vending machine, and could then place a call for a specific number of minutes. In 1995, the United States had 2.6 million pay phones; by 2018, less than 100,000 remained. Cell phones made pay phones unprofitable.

Twentieth-century technology advanced at breakneck speeds. Orville Wright made the first powered aircraft flight in 1903; 41 years later, he flew a Lockheed Constellation. Wright commented the Constellation's wingspan was longer than the distance of his historic flight. Twenty-five years later, US astronaut Neil Armstrong became the first human to walk on the moon.

Innovators like Wright were celebrity figures of the twentieth century. Another example was Henry Ford, who embraced the assembly line, where employees in his factory specialized on one task while his Model T automobile was moved from one work station to the next. Ford also argued that his workforce needed good pay, as he would get the best, while encouraging them to become consumers, boosting demand for products and growing the economy. This combination of large factories with assembly lines, plus well-paid workers, was highly successful. Ford's cars were ubiquitous, and his techniques were studied across the globe. Diametrically opposed systems like Soviet Russia and Nazi Germany lauded his accomplishments and sought to copy his success.

As more people purchased automobiles, demand rose for gasoline stations, auto mechanics, and improved roads. These in turn supported tourism and trucking, plus mechanization of the armed forces. State and federal governments became involved in highway construction, and as more people drove automobiles on vacation, railways saw a decline in passenger service—another example of disruptive innovation.

Building highways required national support. Electrification also required the deep pockets of the state. Electric power stations first started in Britain, quickly followed by Germany and America. Creating an electrical grid to power a region was expensive and complicated. It also dramatically improved labor productivity, comfort, and safety. Electricity illuminated dark streets, powered refrigerators, and supported movie theaters, whose films promoted new technology for the masses.

Electrification made other technologies popular. Guglielmo Marconi produced the first successful radio in 1900 and a year later was sending messages across the Atlantic. Within 20 years, radio stations broadcast music, news, and advertisements. About the same time in Japan, Britain, America, and Russia, inventors created technology that soon morphed into television.

The need for electricity even had international consequences. During the 1920s–1930s, America and the Soviet Union embraced hydroelectric power. This required massive dams holding vast quantities of water, followed by the controlled release of such over spinning turbines. The Dnieper Hydroelectric Station and Hoover Dam dramatically expanded Soviet and American power grids upon their completion in the 1930s.

Gamal Abdel Nasser, charismatic leader of the Free Officers whose coup ended a century of monarchy in 1952, also wanted hydroelectric power. Driven by Nasser's economic and nationalist vision for Egypt, the nation embraced the Aswan High Dam. A gigantic undertaking, it sought to end dangerous Nile River floods. It would store water for irrigation and generate electricity for industrial growth.

The costly project required foreign capital at a time when Nasser also sought weapons to improve the Egyptian armed forces for a second round against their Israeli neighbors. Unwilling to accept American restrictions on the use of these weapons, Nasser turned to the Soviet Union. He came away with plenty of weapons and financial support for building his dam.

Encouraged by Soviet support, Nasser took over the Suez Canal, a mainly British- and French-owned private company, arguing this was a vestige of imperialism and incompatible with Egyptian sovereignty. Nasser hoped canal revenues would help Egypt pay off Soviet loans, but instead, the confiscation led to an alliance of Israel, the United Kingdom, and France, who launched military strikes against Egyptian positions in the Sinai and along the canal in 1956. This second of the four Arab-Israeli Wars ended after Soviet and American leaders applied considerable pressure against the victorious allies.

Construction of the Aswan High Dam lasted from 1960–1970. Filling the reservoir required moving 100,000 people along with the statue of Ramses the Great at Abu Simbel. Although critics argue the dam created environmental challenges, the overall impact on Egypt was positive.

When construction on the Great Ethiopian Renaissance Dam started in 2011, another ancient African polity sought hydroelectric power from the Nile. Would this impact on Egypt's share of river water? Egyptian leaders clearly demonstrated this worry and suggested economic, diplomatic, and even military responses were possible if Ethiopia's dam reduced Egypt's share of Nile water. Yet another example of disruptive innovation.

A different example of government support for technology was America's Manhattan Project (1942–1946). Lobbying by Hungarian-born physicist Leó Szilárd convinced the world-famous Albert Einstein to write American president Franklin Roosevelt in 1939. He described the possibility of Germany creating a super explosive based on uranium. The United Kingdom's Maud Committee made a similar argument in 1940.

The Manhattan Project grew from Roosevelt's support of Einstein's letter. It employed thousands of scientists and support personnel, spread across numerous sites in the United States and Canada. They delivered four atomic bombs at a cost of $500 million each, second in cost only to the B-29 Superfortress bomber program, which was used to drop the bombs on Hiroshima and Nagasaki in 1945.

Fears that Germany would produce an atomic weapon proved unfounded. The Nazi regime's virulent anti-Semitism, combined with a disdain for theoretical science, drove some of its best physicists into exile and service with the Allies. Germany's atomic bomb was not even on the drawing board at war's end in 1945, although its V-2 guided ballistic missile served as a model for postwar nuclear bomb delivery systems.

Called Intercontinental Ballistic Missiles (**ICBMs**), these were constructed in quantity by both the United States and the Soviet Union. As these Cold War rivals sought to increase ICBM capabilities, we witness the strange paradox of twentieth-century military technology, which could spin off into peaceful innovations like your microwave, duct tape, or digital cameras. ICBM spinoffs led to *Sputnik I*, the first successful satellite and a tremendous propaganda coup for the Soviet Union.

Fueled by the Cold War and fears of a "missile gap," Americans sought to defeat Soviet technology in a "space race." They lost round two in 1961, when *Cosmonaut* Yuri Gagarin became the first person to travel in outer space. Round three went to the United States, whose Apollo program allowed Neil Armstrong to walk on the moon in 1969.

Conclusion

Scientific technology continues to shape the twenty-first century. The Human Genome Project, completed in 2003, allows research into genes and offers the possibility of combating deadly illness. *Mars Exploratory Rover* successfully landed in 2004, beginning a remarkable career that lasted until 2018. The same year, *SpaceShipOne* became the first successful private spacecraft. Four years later, work crews completed the largest machine in the world near Geneva, Switzerland. Called the Large Hadron Collider, it is a particle collider allowing physicists to use 17 miles of tunnels to study quarks, dark matter, and the nature of time and space.

Twenty-first-century technological change was not restricted to outer space. Kenya's Safaricom provided another example of disruptive innovation. Traditional telephones relying on land lines require serious infrastructure investment and maintenance. These are a daunting challenge to poor nations. Embracing the cell phone revolution was not cheap but allowed Safaricom to piggyback on First World satellites and create a reliable communications system in East Africa. In 2007, Safaricom launched M-Pesa, a mobile banking system tied to its cell phone network. M-Pesa expanded to Egypt, Afghanistan, and Romania in the second decade of the twenty-first century. Proponents cite M-Pesa for empowering poor people who can't participate in traditional banking systems. Detractors argue it charges usurious fees for each financial transaction.

Although the internet dates to the 1960s and its origins are yet another spinoff from military technology, it became internationally significant in the 1990s. After that decade, Google and Photoshop became verbs, Myspace came and went in four years, surpassed by social media platforms like Facebook or Twitter. The economic potential of the internet was dramatic, as witnessed by the growth of Amazon.com; its political power was equally significant. Those too poor to afford internet access or are located in rural zones with small populations complained of a "digital divide," or "internet poverty." Better-off citizens had to deal with cyberbullying and "sexting."

The Arab Spring, a series of protests and revolutions that spread from Tunisia to Syria, provides a sense of how electronic words can be weapons. Social media platforms weaponized mass anger over the social, economic, and political failings of authoritarian leaders like Muammar Gaddafi of Libya. The Arab Spring resulted in regime changes for Tunisia, Libya, and Egypt, plus a Syrian civil war still ongoing in 2020.

The writers of this text hope twenty-first-century technology will take you on a pleasant journey, like *Voyager I*, an American space probe, launched in 1977 to study the outer solar system. In November 2019, still functioning with vigor, it was 13.7 billion miles from Earth and headed for the Oort Cloud. Barring mishaps, *Voyager 1* will reach that destination in about 300 years. If technology continues to advance exponentially, perhaps your descendants will already be there, throwing a party to celebrate its arrival.

Discussion Question

1. Do you concur with Christensen's disruptive innovation theory? If yes, could you suggest some current technologies that could go the way of the typewriter or pay phone? If no, what's wrong with his theory?

Gender and Sexuality

Global Women's Rights

In 1791, the revolutionary feminist Olympe de Gouges argued, "Woman is born free and remains equal to man in rights."[13] As an Enlightenment thinker, De Gouges worked to reshape women's

---

13 "19. Olympe de Gouges (1748–1793), Declaration of the Rights of Woman and the Female Citizen, 1791." In *Tolerance: The Beacon of the Enlightenment* [online] Cambridge: Open Book Publishers, 2016. http://books.openedition.org/obp/2972

rights in the political and social spheres. As noted in Chapter 1, De Gouges's "Declaration of the Rights of Woman" (1791) and Mary Wollstonecraft's "A Vindication of the Rights of Woman" (1792) were some of the earliest treatises declaring the natural rights of women and helped lay the groundwork for the call for global women's rights in the modern age.

The twentieth century saw the growth of women's rights around the world, although like many trends in the twentieth century, their growth was uneven and often based on localized cultural, social, and political concerns. The United States, for example, saw the slow spread of women's suffrage (the right to vote) from state to state before the federal government gave women the national vote in 1920; even then, African American women (and men) still faced local discrimination and attempts to curtail their voting rights.

Other rights for women in the spheres of labor and sex and attempts to end domestic and sexual violence, also saw gains, but as the United Nations Convention on the Elimination of All Forms of Discrimination against Women (CEDAW) made clear in 1979, "despite various … [international human rights declarations, covenants and specialized agencies] extensive discrimination against women continues to exist."[14] The 1979 convention, sometimes called an "international bill of rights for women," worked to expand, restate, and internationalize a wide swath of women's rights, noting that the phrase "'discrimination against women' shall mean any distinction, exclusion or restriction made on the basis of sex which has the effect or purpose of impairing or nullifying the recognition, enjoyment or exercise by women, irrespective of their marital status, on a basis of equality of men and women, of human rights and fundamental freedoms in the political, economic, social, cultural, civil or any other field."[15] By 1999, 163 countries had ratified CEDAW, with notable exceptions, such as the United States. Many countries, including those who ratified, had (and lodged) reservations about sections of the agreement that conflicted with local laws or customs.[16] As with many international agreements, the ability to monitor and regulate adherence to CEDAW, as well as track international progress, hindered its overall international effectiveness. Regardless, CEDAW remained a lodestar for comprehensive international women's rights.

Women's Suffrage

In the twentieth century, women's suffrage— a key right—(the right of women to vote in elections) had become a reality led by New Zealand, where women were guaranteed on a national level the right to vote in 1893. Thirteen years later, the first female members of a parliament were elected in Finland. Following the end of World War I, a number of European nations in addition to Australia and Canada allowed women the vote, and in 1920, the United States passed the Nineteenth Amendment to the Constitution, which stated, "The right of citizens of the United

---

14 "Convention on the Elimination of All Forms of Discrimination against Women New York, 18 December 1979." United Nations Human Rights: Office of the Commissioner. https://www.ohchr.org/en/professionalinterest/pages/cedaw.aspx

15 "Convention on the Elimination of All Forms of Discrimination against Women."

16 "Convention on the Elimination of All Forms of Discrimination against Women (CEDAW): A Fact Sheet (RS20097)." EveryCRSReport.com. https://www.everycrsreport.com/reports/RS20097.html

States to vote shall not be denied or abridged by the United States or by any State on account of sex."[17] By 1945, when the United Nations' charter "determined … the equal rights of men and women," some 50 nations had approved women's suffrage, although some limited women's right to vote by age, education, or race.[18]

Timeline of Women's Right to Vote by Country 1893–1945[19]

Year	Country	Year	Country
1893	New Zealand	1922	Ireland
1902	Australia	1924	Mongolia
1906	Finland	1928	United Kingdom
1907	Norway	1929	Ecuador
1915	Denmark Iceland	1930	South Africa Turkey
1917	Canada Estonia Russia/Soviet Union	1931	Spain Ceylon/Sri Lanka
1918	Austria Czechoslovakia Germany Hungary Luxembourg Poland United Kingdom	1932	Brazil Thailand Uruguay
1919	Netherlands Rhodesia Sweden	1933	Portugal
1920	Belgium Iceland United States	1934	Cuba

---

17 "Transcript of 19th Amendment to the U.S. Constitution: Women's Right to Vote (1920)." https://www.ourdocuments.gov/doc.php?flash=false&doc=63&page=transcript. Some states continued means to deny African Americans the vote.

18 United Nations, "UN Charter (full text)." https://www.un.org/en/sections/un-charter/un-charter-full-text/

19 "Women and the Vote: Page 5—World Suffrage Timeline." New Zealand History. https://nzhistory.govt.nz/politics/womens-suffrage/world-suffrage-timeline. Their list of dates from C. Daley and M. Nolan (eds.), *Suffrage and Beyond: International Feminist Perspectives* (Auckland: Auckland University Press, 1994).

Year	Country	Year	Country
1935	India	1942	Dominican Republic
1937	Philippines	1944	France
			Jamaica
1939	El Salvador	1945	Bulgaria
			Guatemala
			Italy
1941	Indonesia		Japan
			Panama
			Trinidad and Tobago

The second half of the twentieth century saw the spread of women's suffrage as international, national, and individual pressure to expand women's rights continued in regions where cultural and religious systems had slowed the growth of women's rights. In the twenty-first century, holdouts like Kuwait (2005), United Arab Emirates (2006), Afghanistan (2014), and Saudi Arabia (2015) gave women the vote. Despite these gains, women around the world still faced social and political pressure and violence as they tried to affirm their rights.

Limitations to International Women's Rights

In 1998, the Human Rights Watch Women's Rights Project argued that despite impressive progress made by women's human rights movements, "Throughout the world, women are still relegated to second-class status that makes them more vulnerable to abuse and less able to protect themselves from discrimination."[20] Their study reported abuses, including rape as a weapon of war, sexual assault against refugee and displaced women, sexual trafficking, forced prostitution and marriage, reproductive and sexual rights violations, domestic violence, and other cases of abuses against women at work.

Refugee, displaced, and indigenous women were often the most vulnerable groups as they faced intersectional discrimination. Migrants, for example, may be fleeing violence while also facing abuses abroad related to their sex and perceived identities. Indigenous women face discrimination as women and as indigenous people. In addition, the abuse toward these groups often goes undocumented. Indigenous women have organized to fight this discrimination.

On Valentine's Day in 1992, following the murder of a local indigenous women, residents of downtown Eastside Vancouver, British Columbia, began the Women's Memorial March to recognize and honor women who are now recognized as Murdered and Missing Indigenous Women (MMIW) by a growing international community. It was only in the early twenty-first century, however, that MMIW was recognized as national and international crises by governments such as those in the United States and Canada. In the 2010s, official statistics revealed that indigenous

---

20   Human Rights Watch Women's Rights Project. *The Human Rights Watch Global Report on Women's Human Rights* (New Delhi; Oxford: Oxford University Press, 1998), xiv.

FIGURE 4.5   Women Celebrating International Women's Day in Cameroon.

women in Canada were six times more likely to be murdered, and that in the United States, they were 2.5 times more likely to be victims of sexual assault.[21]

Conclusion

Women's rights have been at the forefront of gender and sexual movements in the twentieth century. Although impressive gains have been made in women's suffrage and in recognizing women's rights as human rights by the end of the twentieth century, additional work was required. Women's rights remained uneven across social, economic, racial, and religious lines, with specific concerns about refugee, migrant, and/or indigenous women who faced myriad forms of abuse tied to their often-intersectional identities.

War, Peace, and Diplomacy

Global Warfare in the Twentieth Century

Despite genuine efforts like the Hague Convention to limit the impact of war, the twentieth century featured the most destructive global conflicts in history. Two World Wars, massive spinoff

---

21   Global Indigenous Council, "GIC Issues—#MMIW Missing and Murdered Indigenous Women." https://www.globalindigenouscouncil.com/mmiw

revolutions in Russia and China, plus wars of national liberation are but a few of the many conflicts fought between 1900–2000. The effects of imperialism, nationalism, and the Industrial Revolution increased the possibility for violence and aided perpetrators with propaganda and technology to make this century so deadly. The cost was 187 million killed.

Jan Bloch, a Polish banker and delegate to the Hague Convention, published *Is War Now Impossible?* in 1898. He argued the Industrial Revolution made mass armies so large and gave soldiers such devastating weapons, like the Maxim machine gun or quick-fire artillery, that combat on a grand scale could only result in stalemate for all sides. This stalemate would consume vast quantities of blood and treasure, produce economic collapse, and revolutionary violence among disgruntled citizens of all parties.

Considering results from the Second Boer War (1899–1902), the Russo-Japanese War (1904–1905), and World War I (1914–1918), it is obvious Bloch was a visionary. His limitations were assumptions that world leaders were logical and that technology would not find solutions for breaking a stalemate. The world we live in today would be a very different place if the kaisers, tsars, and prime ministers of 1914 had taken Bloch seriously.

Instead, jingoism convinced all participants in the political and diplomatic decision-making of summer 1914, that their army would quickly defeat the enemy, and the boys would be home by Christmas. Most of these soldiers were conscripts, previously called to duty when they turned 18, trained for combat, then returned to the civilian world until called back to the colors by a general mobilization.

Conscription allowed nations to maintain large armies at more reasonable cost, since once trained, soldiers returned to their civilian jobs. Keeping millions of men in arms was very expensive, not only from salaries and rations, but also for taking the men from the labor pool, which played havoc with the national economy.

The armies of 1914 maintained specialists usually found in the general staff. These highly trained officers planed future conflicts, organized railways for the rapid mobilization of conscripts, and helped their generals implement plans during wartime. Facing the possibility of fighting both Russia and France simultaneously, the German general staff had some of the most complex plans. These called for taking advantage of the nation's superior railway system for a rapid mobilization, then defeating France quickly before Russia's torpid mobilization placed millions of soldiers on Germany's eastern frontier.

Russian and French general staffs hoped war on several fronts would stymie the Germans, and to provide extra preparation time had directed the construction of fortifications along the German frontier. Attacking these defenses would slow the offensive, allowing the two allies a chance to employ superior numbers against their common foe.

This dilemma vexed German staff officers from the 1890s onward. They argued fully mobilized enemy forces would be very difficult to defeat and that it was vital to first crush France, then turn on Russia. Attacking through French defensive works was problematic, but a solution was possible if Germany was willing to violate an international agreement dating back to 1839.

Belgium became independent that year, under the proviso that it would remain neutral in world affairs. In exchange, the great powers promised to support Belgian independence. French fortifications ended at the Belgian frontier, and German planners saw this as the solution to their dilemma. Even though Germany had inherited Prussian guarantees to back the 1839 agreement, this was dismissed as "a mere scrap of paper."

Germany invaded Belgium on August 4, 1914, meeting more resistance than expected. While mobilization of German manpower had been very efficient, fighting French, Belgian, and British troops took longer than expected. This ended any chance for a rapid victory in the west, as German military strength was partially diverted to fight Russia on the Eastern Front.

Thus, generals on both sides created a good replica of what Bloch described in 1898. Sadly for the soldiers, war was not impossible but frightfully costly, and lasting four years, very difficult to conclude. On the Western Front, where Belgians, French, and British mainly fought Germans, titanic struggles pitted millions of troops, created massive casualties, and did so with very few consequences.

It is difficult to study battles like **Verdun** and determine who "won" or "lost." The Battle of Verdun lasted 303 days during 1916, causing 70,000 casualties a month. When concluded, neither Germany nor France had gained significant territory, nor had the casualties sapped either nation's willingness to fight another Verdun.

The same year, along the Somme River in northern France, an even bloodier contest pitted French and British forces against German defenders. When concluded, nearly 1 million soldiers were dead or wounded, while the Allies advanced 7 miles. To place this battle in an American perspective, think of the Vietnam War Memorial in Washington, DC. It honors US service personnel who died in the Vietnam War from 1955–1975 and bears 58,320 names. On the first day of the **Battle of the Somme** (July 1, 1916), the British army recorded 19,240 fatalities.

Verdun and the Somme featured large numbers of soldiers forced to attack heavily fortified positions. Elaborate trenches, fronted with lines of barbed wire and defended by machine guns and artillery, made attacks costly. The millions of men in the armies of major powers meant there was a continuous front, from the Swiss frontier to the English Channel. There were no flanks where a dashing commander could sneak around and upset enemy defenses.

Instead, soldiers had to go "over the top"—out of their trenches and into **no-man's-land**. The latter, the space between the two trench lines, was a moonscape of shell craters, fallen trees, and dead bodies. Add a little rain or snow, and the advance became even more difficult as soldiers attempted to charge through sheets of fire while lugging all their heavy gear.

Could technology provide a solution, some special weapon that could break the deadlock? Germany, a powerhouse of chemistry, answered with poison gas. Dispersed in massive clouds when the wind blew toward enemy lines, it caused horrific casualties and panic but was quickly mimicked by all sides.

The *U-Boot* (submarine) was another game-changing weapon that did so, but not as intended by German admirals. First used to hunt enemy warships, these were diverted for attacks on slow-moving merchant ships. Firing torpedoes from underwater, *U-Boot* captains were very successful. One sank 194 ships from 1915–1918. Despite heavy losses, *U-Boot* attacks on civilian vessels like the *RMS Lusitania* in 1915 were in the end counterproductive, as they were a major factor which brought America onto the side of Germany's enemies in 1917.

British and French militaries employed poison gas and submarines but also mechanized vehicles. These played a role in 1914, when 600 taxicabs left Paris carrying soldiers to a key battle that stopped the German advance. In France and Britain, engineers asked if motorized vehicles could be armored and equipped with weapons. *Tank* originally meant a large cylindrical water holder. In 1915, it was code for top-secret British efforts to create a tracked armored vehicle carrying machine guns or small cannons. Working models were unleashed on German defenders a year later at the Battle of the Somme. Continually improved, had Germany not collapsed for political reasons in 1918, enemy tanks were poised to create tremendous challenges in 1919.

The Eastern Front, where Russia fought Germany and Austria-Hungary, also demonstrates Bloch's prescience. While a continuous line of trenches was not possible due to the vast space of the Russian Empire, heavy casualties wore down loyalties to both the tsar and the kaiser. By 1917, as Lenin, head of the Bolsheviks describes it, the Russian army "voted with its feet." Thousands deserted, and many more joined anti-regime political parties like the Bolsheviks.

Along with food and fuel shortages, economic misery exacerbated problems across the empire, leading to the February and October Revolutions of 1917. The first dethroned a tsar; the second eliminated Russian democracy. A civil war followed in the next five years. Combined with epidemics, famine, and political executions, Russia's grim share of casualties from World War I and this spinoff were the largest of any participant.

While Austrian and German generals might have smiled on hearing how the Russian revolutions drove their enemy from the conflict, their own nations collapsed a year later. The simple but effective Bolshevik (Communist) political message of "Peace, Land, and Bread" played well in many nations. As Bloch predicted, modern industrialized war promised horrific casualties, economic collapse, and revolutionary unrest. Autocratic empires could not survive the costs of World War I.

"Peace, Land, and Bread" were on the minds of many in 1919 as diplomats negotiated an end to the Great War at Versailles, the Sun King's Palace near Paris, France. It created both a League of Nations, enjoined with a mission to prevent future conflicts, and the seeds for another round of fighting. When you read about the ongoing struggle between Israelis and Palestinians, remember that a partial cause for this strife came from decisions made at Versailles. Nor was this the only flaw. French Marshal Ferdinand Foch argued the Versailles Peace Conference produced enough humiliation to guarantee a second war with Germany and not enough restrictions to make a German comeback impossible.

Even the most optimistic diplomats saw tremendous challenges for the League of Nations. The Great War might be over, but Mexico, Russia, and China had ongoing civil wars; the latter is still ongoing in 2019, and why there is a People's Republic of China and a Republic of China (Taiwan). Shorter but equally violent conflicts over territory, like the Russo-Polish War or the Chaco War, spread across the 1920s–1930s.

Imperial powers found it more difficult to maintain colonial hegemony. Britain granted de facto independence to Catholic Ireland. Spain and Italy defeated African insurrections, but only by intervening with significant military assets. Even China would no longer kowtow to unequal treaties forced on the Qing Dynasty during the nineteenth century.

Chinese resistance generated concern in neighboring Japan. Having embraced the Industrial Revolution, nationalism, gunboat diplomacy, and imperialism, Japanese efforts to dominate China were threatened. Army leaders, who held considerable political power under the Japanese constitution, argued China's growing power would end a very favorable relationship with the northeast portion of China outsiders called Manchuria.

Rich in mineral and food products vital to the Japanese economy, Manchuria was the scene for the League of Nations' first major failure and the start of World War II in Asia. Japanese troops occupied the region in 1931 but faced stiff opposition from guerrillas, who were never completely quashed. The Republic of China, distracted by internal discord between "warlords," plus Communist and nationalist political factions, agreed to a truce in 1933. Four years later, skirmishing between Chinese and Japanese soldiers—dubbed the Marco Polo Bridge Incident—led to all-out war. This continued unabated until Japan's surrender in 1945.

Next, Italy successfully challenged the League of Nations in 1935, launching an invasion of Ethiopia despite tepid opposition from France and Britain. Although poison gas was considered especially barbarous, Italian aviators dropped gas bombs with abandon. Mechanized infantry, automatic weapons, and vastly superior artillery made it nearly impossible for Ethiopians to repeat their 1896 victory at Adwa.

Another conflict foreshadowing the Second World War was a civil war in Spain. Fought from 1936–1939, it drew international official support for both sides. The government obtained military aid from the Soviet Union, while rebel forces gained arms and soldiers from Germany and Italy. Reflecting anti-Fascist, pro-Communist, and romantic ideals, government forces were also augmented by the **International Brigades**—40,000 men and women from across the globe who volunteered for combat service.

Claude Bowers, the American ambassador to Spain, called this conflict a "dress rehearsal" for World War II. It provided lessons for using tanks, mechanized units, aircraft, and artillery. It ended in rebel victory and only five months before the Second World War broke out in Europe.

Although Chinese, Ethiopian, and Spanish victims would cite an earlier date, Europeans entered a second World War on September 1, 1939, when German forces invaded Poland. Deep criticism of Great War tactics encouraged 1920s–1930s German military leaders to embrace new technologies that provided considerable firepower and mobility advantages. Motorized vehicles from trucks to tanks, along with aircraft, provided German generals with fast-moving and hard-hitting elite forces. These were never the majority, and for the entire war, most German soldiers did a lot of marching on foot, with their heavy gear in carts or wagons pulled by horses.

Still, the elites were enough to allow rapid victories over numerous enemies between 1939 and 1941. In the space of 46 days, German soldiers conquered France and drove British soldiers off the continent. Compared to the long stalemate over the same terrain during World War I, this was revolutionary. Journalists called this *Blitzkrieg*—"lightning warfare"—and it was the hallmark of German operations across Europe.

Simultaneously, Japanese forces, fighting with mainly infantry units, were involved in a protracted struggle against Chinese opponents who lost battle after battle but would not surrender. Instead, China was willing to trade space for time, hoping to gain allies who could alter the balance of power. Frustrated by their failure to gain a quick victory, Japanese generals ordered their troops to murder civilians in the **Nanjing Massacre**. Taking place in December 1937, these actions resulted in the death of at least 40,000 people, and upwards of 300,000.

Nanjing was but one of many World War II military campaigns directed specifically against civilians. German South West Africa at the start of the century and the Armenian portions of the Ottoman Empire during World War I were earlier zones of directed mass murder, but these horrific events pale in comparison to violence during the Second World War.

Mass murder continued in China and spread through Asia and the Pacific when Japan widened the war in 1941. Between 3 and 10 million civilians died as a result. Others were brutalized in chemical weapons experiments conducted by Unit 731 or forced into sexual slavery as "comfort women." Even 75 years after the war's end, Japan has difficult relations with neighboring countries whose people suffered from these actions.

Europe also witnessed mass brutality. Under Soviet dictator **Joseph Stalin**, 9 million people were shot, starved, or beaten to death. Whether through state-induced famine, like the Ukrainian *Holodomor*, the Gulag prison system, or death camps like Katyn, the Soviet Union suffered terribly under Stalin, the so-called "man of steel."

The war against civilians, however, reached its apex in Germany. From the first day of fighting, as German forces swept into Poland, they were followed by *Einsatzgruppen*, uniformed death squads tasked with liquidating groups deemed unfit to live in Adolf Hitler's empire. These focused on Jews but also targeted Slavic intellectuals, Gypsies, and the mentally handicapped. When mass shootings were deemed uneconomical, victims were rounded up for termination in death camps like Auschwitz or Treblinka. Between 1939 and 1945, Germans murdered at least 11 million people during what historians describe as the **Holocaust**.

Primary Source 2

Nazi Regulation of German Youth

Totalitarian regimes, no matter what their political persuasion, earn the title by attempting to dominate all aspects of life. Making sure citizens were focused on the state's version of reality was a paramount goal. Even hobbies and entertainment were controlled for this purpose; thus, stamp collecting could get you sent to prison in Stalin's Russia, as you might be following international norms and seeking stamps from outside the Soviet Union, which could come with information contrary to official doctrines.

Nazi Germany added a racial twist to tyranny, seeking to exclude young Germans form the corrupting influence of "degenerate" music and art, described as the work of "blacks and Jews."[1] American jazz and swing music fell in this category and was defended by Swingjugend (swing kids). The latter sported English- or American-style clothing and liked dancing to swing music.

---

1 Michael H. Kater, "Forbidden Fruit? Jazz in the Third Reich." In *The American Historical Review*, Vol. 94 (1989): 11–43.

Nazis produced legislation like this ordinance, with its hefty fine and possible jail times, to discourage Swingjugend.[2]

> Police directive relating to the prevention of juveniles from using public dance halls. From the 29th of November 1939
>
> As per Reich Minister of Police Regulations from 14 November 1938 (Reich Statute Book I, p. 1582), the following is decreed:
>
> #1
>
> (From the draft of #6 of the Police Regulations for the Protection of Youth of 9. 3. 1939 – Reich Statute Book I, p. 499–)
>
> (1) Juveniles under 18 may only participate in public dancing, inside or out, when in the company of a certified educator or an adult guardian, and then only until 11 p.m.
>
> (2) This prohibition from paragraph 1 does not apply to members of the Armed Forces or the Reich Labor Service.
>
> #2
>
> Operators of outdoor and indoor public dancing must display a clearly perceptible notice of the prohibition in paragraph # 1.
>
> #3
>
> By order of the Local Police, selected establishments from paragraph number 1 can be closed, especially on national holidays.
>
> #4
>
> The following will be punished with a fine of up to 150 Reich Marks, and in especially serious cases, arrest for up to six weeks.
>
> 1) Juveniles who willfully violate the prohibition in paragraph # 1.

Discussion Question

1. Nazi hostility to jazz and swing music came from their non-European origins, plus a belief that Jewish or Black composers were creators of such. At the same time, German police enforced laws aimed at keeping teens out of dance halls, American police looked the other way as servicemen on leave beat up jazz-loving Mexican American teens for wearing zoot suits in 1943 California. Polish policemen harassed *Bikiniarze* a decade later for their own flamboyant costumes and fascination with American beatniks. A similar history comes out of the 1960s Soviet Union over *Stilyagi*. Can you identify twenty-first century music or recreational activities that create hostile blowback?

---

2   For additional information, see Jonathan Grant, "The Socialist Construction of Philately in the Early Soviet Era." In *Comparative Studies in Society and History* 37, no. 3 (1995): 476–93; and Michael H. Kater, "Forbidden Fruit? Jazz in the Third Reich." In *The American Historical Review*, 94, no.1 (1989): 11–43.

Such violence was found on all fronts of World War II. While it was mainly land battles that ended the war for Germany and its European allies, Japan was only brought down after extensive naval campaigns across the Pacific.

World War II naval battles demonstrate the rapid pace of twentieth-century technology. Battleships were large, heavily armored gun platforms; Japan built the greatest ever constructed—the *Yamato* (Figure 4.6), with its gigantic 18-inch cannons. Designed to outshoot every American battleship afloat, the *Yamato* was sunk in 1945 by a bomb- and torpedo-carrying aircraft.

Based on **aircraft carriers**, naval aviation proved far more formidable than the best battleships. The British made this clear at Taranto (1940) when 21 planes sank or heavily damaged three Italian battleships. A year later, Japanese carriers gained a great victory over the Americans at Pearl Harbor. Between June 4–7 1942, the decisive naval battle of World War II ended any chance of a Japanese victory when American naval aviators sank most of Japan's carriers off the island of Midway.

Defeats like Midway or the German disaster at the massive tank battle near Kursk (1943) clearly demonstrate another decisive factor of World War II. Germany, Japan, Italy, and their lesser allies had but a fraction of the economic power possessed by their enemies. In the time it took Japan to produce three aircraft carriers, the United States launched two dozen. Even with

FIGURE 4.6   Yamato.

good fortune and mistake-free leadership, it is difficult to imagine how the Germans or Japanese could have won after America and the Soviet Union entered the war in 1941.

Victory was not easy, and hard-fought battles continued into the summer of 1945. Japanese resistance was intense, as many military men believed the "Imperial Rescript to Soldiers and Sailors" that argued "duty was as heavy as a mountain, and death as light as a feather."[22] American strategy for defeating Japan called for "island hopping"—securing Pacific bases that could support an advance against the Japanese home island. Between 1943–1945, numerous Japanese-held islands were invaded. Americans were uniformly successful, albeit at heavy costs. To give one example, **Tarawa Atoll**, about 2 miles long and 800 yards wide, was one of the smallest battlefields of World War II. In 76 hours, 3,976 Americans were killed or wounded. Of 2,636 Japanese defenders, only 17 surrendered.

Island battles continued, each skillfully defended by Japanese soldiers and sailors fighting almost to the last man. When American forces were finally poised to invade Japan in the summer of 1945, grim statistics faced President Harry S. Truman. He was told to expect a tenacious defense that would cause massive casualties for both sides. To give one example, US authorities, expecting a long campaign lasting until 1947, ordered 500,000 Purple Hearts—medals issued to military personnel wounded in combat.

Truman and his military advisers were not sure the American public would support two more years of bloody conflict. Thus, casualties, plus fear of a voter backlash, fueled support for employing new technology—the atomic bomb. On August 6, 1945, the first bomb, "Little Boy," was dropped on Hiroshima. Three days later, "Fat Man" hit Nagasaki. Upward of 226,000 people were killed, mainly civilians, including 20 Allied prisoners of war.

On August 15, 1945, Hirohito became the first Japanese emperor to broadcast over the radio. Informing his subjects that "the war situation has developed not necessarily to Japan's advantage," he called on them to "endure the unendurable" and accept surrender as Japan's only option. Was Hirohito acting due to the destruction of Hiroshima and Nagasaki? The recent Soviet declaration of war and invasion of Manchuria? The conventional devastation of other Japanese cities by American bombing raids, and loss of almost the entire merchant navy to submarine attacks? Or a combination of all these things? To this day, a tremendous debate continues among historians over the decision to use atomic weapons in 1945. Were they necessary, or were the other factors enough to bring about a Japanese surrender during that fateful summer?

Post-World War II Decolonization

This section can only provide a general discussion of the decolonization process, given the complexity of the subject matter and the vast number of colonial possessions that achieved independence during the twentieth century. The term *decolonization* means the process of letting a colony be independent from the colonizer. Colonization was maintained by using force—the state police, the army, or both. Colonialism in the twentieth century was the result of what historians call the "new imperialism" of the nineteenth century. It was mainly a European phenomenon, epitomized

---

22 "Imperial Rescript to Soldiers and Sailors, 1882," "Documents on Japanese Imperialism," http://www.professorcampbell.org/sources/japan.html.

FIGURE 4.7   50 Rupie Banknote of the German East African Bank, 1905.

by the Berlin Conference of 1884–1885, which divided almost all of Africa between Britain, France, Germany, Portugal, Italy, Spain, and Belgium.

It would be a mistake, however, to see colonialism as a purely European institution. China took over Tibet and parts of Central Asia during the same time period, while the Ottoman Empire expanded into the Arabian Peninsula. The pair of African states that escaped European imperialism, Ethiopia and Liberia, took lands from neighboring peoples. All these powers shared an ultimate political aim—the destruction of local, traditional political and social structures and to force the conquered people to adopt the colonizer's ethnocentric and often racist civilization and practices.

The scramble for an overseas empire came in different models. Sometimes, local elites were co-opted to provide some government functions. The British were especially adroit at this; for example, their "veiled protectorate" over Egypt (1882–1914) helped obscure the fact that all important decisions rested with London. South Africa, Rhodesia, or Australia were more traditional colonial ventures, where local peoples had little to no political power, and British settlers held the reins of power.

Colonies provided economic, military, or political value to their imperial owners. European settlers could also benefit from this setup. A settler colony was destined to allow the colonizing population and its descendants to settle in the new land forever, usually a fertile area with the best and the healthiest climate, where cash crops could be grown easily or critical minerals were abundant. The division of the colonial spoils was contingent upon the will of the colonizer, who rarely respected the natural geographic, ethnic, and linguistic boundaries. Often, colonizers would split kin groups to create a new colonial border while displacing others from their original habitat. African and Middle Eastern boundary disputes of today often reflect on maps created by imperial diplomats in Paris, Rome, or London.

Take, for example, the Aouzou Strip—44,000 square miles of Saharan desert described by a *New York Times* writer as "the world's largest sandbox." Situated between Libya and Chad, it was part of a complex series of negotiations between Italy and France, the colonial masters of those African states before World War II. In a 1935 effort to reward Italy for joining the Allies during the Great War and prevent more friendly relations with Germany, France agreed to separate the Aouzou Strip from Chad, allowing it to be part of Italian Libya.

World War II allowed France to reoccupy the territory, but the 1935 agreement was never annulled. Now speed your time machine to the 1970s. Libya and Chad are independent nations, with the former ruled by Muammar Ghaddafi. He was focused on expanding Libyan power in northern Africa, and on learning there could be uranium deposits in the Aouzou Strip, used the 1935 agreement as legal grounds for its occupation by his army. The resulting Libya-Chad War was fought from 1978–1987, mainly due to Ghaddafi's imperialistic strategy but buttressed by European-imposed boundaries.

After the Great War, critics of colonialism were powerful enough to force some window-dressing on empires. When German and Ottoman colonies were distributed among the victorious Allies, they came not as colonies, but "protectorates." The latter were supposedly temporary arrangements, with locals being trained for independence by their new governors. After the Second World War, colonies were even less palatable, yet smart operators in London or Paris figured how to tie strings that kept local economies tied to the former imperial master in what historians describe as neocolonialism.

Colonialism continued because it was profitable. American president Woodrow Wilson had warned colleagues at the Versailles Peace Conference, "No peace can last, which does not accept the principle that governments derive all their just powers from the consent of the governed, and that no right anywhere exists to hand about peoples from sovereignty to sovereignty as if they were property." Even though critics claimed Wilson was only speaking of Europe, such ideas encouraged non-Europeans to struggle against colonialism.

The newly created United Nations expanded on this argument in 1945, stating "all people had the right to self-determination." Two years later as the West entered into a cold war with the Soviet Bloc, standing against self-determination could undermine efforts to win this conflict. Soviet propaganda played this card skillfully in the 1950s–1960s until it came back to haunt them during their own efforts to dominate Afghanistan in the 1980s. Adding to these international developments was the fact that Europeans had spent considerable resources and energies to win the two World Wars to the extent that their willpower to sustain the colonial territories at all costs diminished.

The maintenance of colonialism over the indigenous people relied on the use of force. It was maintained against the will of the majority. Force was freely employed to maintain order, but force costs money. If there were too much resistance, then colonies were no longer profitable. Britain's American colonies provide an eighteenth-century example of this. With all due respect to George

Washington's excellent generalship, independence was at least partially the result of the high costs of maintaining British control.

The path toward decolonization, self-government, and independence took several forms—from outright force or violence used by the colonized against the colonizers, as was the case in several of the Portuguese colonies in Africa, or **Indochina** against the French—to peaceful demonstrations and acts of disobedience, exemplified by Ghana, the first sub-Saharan British colony to become independent in 1957. At times, a simple demand for independence by the indigenous population, usually led by the educated new elite (as was the case in several French colonies in Africa during the early 1960s), was enough to trigger the achievement of independence.

Southern Africa provides two quite different histories of decolonization in South Africa and Rhodesia. The former had European colonial roots stretching back to 1652. Numerous wars of conquest followed, including two between rival European settlers—the British and the Boers. Large quantities of gold and diamonds, plus excellent farmlands and a powerful strategic position made this land a great prize. Seeking local allies, London created the Union of South Africa in 1910, allowing Boers and Britons voting rights while forcing back Africans into small "homelands," often the least desirable real estate, and excluding them from any political power.

By 1934, for Whites, South Africa was an independent nation and member of the British Commonwealth. Fourteen years later, the government embraced *apartheid* ("separateness"), which created a segregated system designed to completely empower Whites over Blacks. The latter formed an African National Congress (ANC), which used strikes, boycotts, sabotage, and limited acts of terrorism to undermine the *apartheid* system. Nelson Mandela, who led ANC's fighters, became even more famous after his arrest and 1964 sentence to life in prison. The struggle continued, with ANC strategists hoping to enlist help from outside powers. Early ties to the Communist Party of South Africa made the Soviet Union a possibility but also made it easier for the *apartheid* regime to present themselves as stalwart Cold Warriors whose strategic mineral wealth should be preserved from Communist takeover.

By the 1980s, this argument was no longer potent, and sanctions from a host of nations began to crush the South African economy. The collapse of the Soviet Bloc in 1989 removed any Cold War arguments, and in the next two years, apartheid laws were dismantled. Released in 1990, after 27 years behind bars, Mandela was elected president of South Africa in 1993.

To the north, also blessed with agricultural and mineral wealth, Rhodesia presented a different path toward decolonization. Unlike South Africa, which had a sizable White minority, Rhodesian Whites were much smaller in number. Agitated over independence plans for neighboring British colonies, Rhodesia's Whites, possibly 5 percent of the total population, declared their independence in 1965. Fourteen years of conflict followed, until the costs of fighting crushed the economy and forced surrender. Unlike South Africa, the transition to majority rule was very difficult. Renamed Zimbabwe, the former Rhodesia replaced one authoritarian government with another. Under President Robert Mugabe, Zimbabwe saw its economy collapse in the worst case of hyperinflation in world history. By 2008, the national currency was replaced by American dollars, and Zimbabwe, once the breadbasket of southern Africa, needed food aid for its citizens. Mugabe's death in 2019 gives hope that new leadership will steer Zimbabwe on a better path.

Eritrea, in the Horn of Africa, provides yet another example of how European powers drew boundaries that created tensions in postcolonial Africa. The local people were mainly Muslims, while their next-door neighbor, Ethiopia, was dominated by Christians. There was a long history of border conflicts between these groups. Italy grabbed Eritrea in 1889, using it as a base to attack Ethiopia in 1895 and 1935. The latter campaign was successful until Italy entered the Second World War and was driven out of East Africa by British forces in 1941.

Great Britain's ten-year administration witnessed push and play between herself, seeking to benefit Anglo-Egyptian Sudan, Ethiopia, and local Eritrean leaders. A United Nations compromise allowed Eritrea to join Ethiopia as an autonomous province. Ethiopia was not only a victim of imperialism but also a perpetrator, with Ethiopian armies subjugating different ethnicities since the 1890s. Eritrea was no exception and lost autonomy in 1961 as Haile Selassie I strove to centralize his empire. This produced a 1961–1991 war of independence that continued despite dramatic changes in Ethiopia, as the ancient Solomonic dynasty was overthrown by the pro-Communist *Derg* ("Committee"). In the end, the cost of maintaining control over Eritrea was too high, and Eritrea was independent.

Southeast Asia had a similar history of colonization. Much of this region had fallen to British, French, and Dutch armies during the nineteenth century. Southeast Asia represented a uniquely strategic area on the other side of the globe, full of valuable products like rice, oil, rubber, tin, and spices. World War II replaced the Europeans with Japanese overlords. While it is debatable as to Japan's long-term goals, Tokyo gained advantages with local people by presenting World War II as a struggle to free Asians from European domination. Japanese support of nationalist leaders in Burma, the Philippines, India, and Indonesia allowed enough political development that these forces could contest a return of their old masters after 1945.

French Indochina provides an example of the power vacuum that was Southeast Asia in 1945. The colonial regime was devastated by the many twists and turns of France during World War II. British and Chinese soldiers had to disarm Japanese troops, as there were not enough French soldiers for these duties. This near complete elimination of French power allowed an icon of anti-imperialists to enter the world stage.

Ho Chi Minh, a dedicated Communist since the 1920s, was also a Vietnamese nationalist who greatly resented French domination. He helped create the *Viet Minh* in 1941 to fight against both French and Japanese forces. He used *Viet Minh* cadres to eliminate Vietnamese political rivals while gathering abandoned Japanese military stockpiles in the chaotic days of August 1945. Ho's famous September 2 Declaration of Independence drew from eighteenth-century American and French revolutionary rhetoric while reminding the Vietnamese that France had sold them out to the Japanese and did not deserve their support.

France was unwilling to give up her empire without a fight and invested significant military assets to crush Ho's revolution. For all practical purposes, the *Viet Minh's* defeat of the elite paratroopers and Foreign Legion on May 7, 1954, at Dien Bien Phu marked the end of the French empire in Asia, which included Laos, Cambodia, and Vietnam. The latter divided into North Vietnam and South Vietnam as independent states, who became proxies for the Soviets and Americans during the 1950s–1970s.

The Vietnam War (1954–1975), while more connected to the Cold War, has some roots in the story of colonialism. American leaders saw Ho as part of a monolithic Communist conspiracy to dominate the globe. Despite advice from experts who worked with Ho during World War II, every American president, from Eisenhower to Nixon, could not accept that their Vietnamese enemies were genuine nationalists and not tools of Red China or the Soviet Union. The final collapse of South Vietnam in 1975 demonstrated the strong nationalist credentials of the revolutionaries inspired by Ho, who had passed away a decade earlier.

Like France, British and Dutch power, tremendously weakened by World War II, withdrew from the subcontinent and Southeast Asian colonies in the 1940s–1950s. The demise of the British Empire may have been the most dramatic. The "Jewel in the Crown," India, was handed over to nationalists like Mahatma Gandhi, who had embraced nonviolent resistance to British imperialism. Britain's 1947 withdrawal led to the creation of Pakistan, with mainly Muslim citizens, and India, with Hindus in the majority but significant Muslim minorities. It was easier to get the British out than to settle boundaries between the new nations, especially regarding the status of Kashmir. To this day, neither country is poised to end their conflict, or even discuss the status of Kashmir.

While European colonialism had nearly disappeared by the 1980s, there are still decolonization issues in the twenty-first century. Despite rhetoric and outright support for anti-colonial freedom fighters in Africa and the Middle East during the 1960s, Red China has its own subject people. Tibet, an independent Himalayan polity from 1911, was invaded in 1950; to the north, Xinjiang was conquered by imperial Chinese armies in the 1870s. Both provinces remain ethnically, religiously, and linguistically separate from the dominant Han culture. Red Chinese treatment of Tibetans and the Uyghur people of Xinjiang sadly proves that imperialism is not just a European malady, but rather a human malady.

Primary Source 3

On June 26, 1945, delegates of 50 nations signed the Charter of the United Nations, concluding the United Nations Conference on International Organization. Article 73 referred to UN members' responsibilities to administer territories regarded as having not yet attained "a full measure of self-government."

Article 73 of Chapter XI, June 26, 1945 of The United Nations Declaration Regarding Non-Self-Governing Territories

Members of the United Nations which have or assume responsibilities for the administration of territories whose peoples have not yet attained a full measure of self-government recognize the principle that the interests of the inhabitants of these territories are paramount, and accept as a sacred trust the obligation to promote to the utmost, within the system of international peace and security established by the present Charter, the well-being of the inhabitants of these territories, and, to this end:

a. to ensure, with due respect for the culture of the peoples concerned, their political, economic, social, and educational advancement, their just treatment, and their protection against abuses;

b. to develop self-government, to take due account of the political aspirations of the peoples, and to assist them in the progressive development of their free political institutions, according to the particular circumstances of each territory and its peoples and their varying stages of advancement;

c. to further international peace and security;

d. to promote constructive measures of development, to encourage research, and to co-operate with one another and, when and where appropriate, with specialized international bodies with a view to the practical achievement of the social, economic, and scientific purposes set forth in this Article; and

e. to transmit regularly to the Secretary-General for information purposes, subject to such limitation as security and constitutional considerations may require, statistical and other information of a technical nature relating to economic, social, and educational conditions in the territories for which they are respectively responsible other than those territories to which Chapters XII and XIII apply.

Discussion Question

1. What are the pros and cons of the United Nations Article 73 regarding non-self-governing territories?

The Cold War

Historian Gar Alperovitz argues the 1945 decision to use nuclear weapons had little to do with Japan and was much more focused on providing diplomatic leverage for America to use against the Soviet Union, perceived by policy makers as the postwar threat to national security. While this view is debated, historians agree that America and the Soviet Union entered a cold war in 1947.

This conflict featured diplomatic, economic, and cultural strategies, but never large-scale military actions between the two superpowers. Proxy wars across the globe, like American efforts to defeat local Communists in Vietnam or Soviet efforts to create a friendly regime in Afghanistan, proved bloody and demonstrate the difficulties of defeating enemies with friends too dangerous to attack directly.

An American-Soviet War, especially after the latter developed nuclear weapons in 1949, could have become more deadly than World War II. Both nations maintained large conventional military forces, plus a growing stockpile of atomic bombs and sophisticated delivery systems.

The latter started with large transcontinental aircraft, but soon included missiles launched from submarines and by the 1960s, Intercontinental Ballistic Missiles (ICBMs). By that point the United States and the Soviet Union had so many nuclear weapons, along with a multitude of delivery options, that both reached a stage of "mutually assured destruction" (MAD) in the case of a nuclear war.

Antiballistic missiles were designed to shoot down ICBMs, and by the 1980s, America launched the Strategic Defense Initiative, designed to create laser weapons that could destroy incoming missiles. Despite the growth of antimissile technology, Britain, France, Red China, India, Pakistan, Israel, South Africa, and North Korea created nuclear weapons in the last 50 years.

MAD possibly kept each side from launching their ICBMs, but if this balance of terror prevented nuclear war, what about conventional conflict? Both sides of the Cold War also built up traditional military forces. Tanks, aircraft, submarines, and a host of other weapon systems established what American president Dwight Eisenhower warned was "a military industrial complex," with a vested interest in keeping new weapons on the design boards and large militaries to purchase them.

Like pre-1914 Europe, the Cold War spawned alliance systems which tied the interests of many states into two camps. The West introduced the North Atlantic Treaty Organization (NATO) in 1949, while the East created its Warsaw Pact six years later. By the 1960s, NATO and the Warsaw Pact had enough soldiers in Europe to create battles larger than any seen in World War II.

It would be a mistake, however, to see the Cold War as all about atomic bombs or armored divisions. It was also a contest of propaganda, technology, espionage, and proxy wars. Each side attempted to present its culture in the most positive light. Soviets claimed space exploits proved their system was better, while Americans argued their consumer culture was evidence a planned economy could not work. "Invasions" of one culture into another created Red scares in America or police actions to keep "decadent" rock and roll music from seeping into the Soviet Bloc.

Globalization played a part in ending the Cold War. Despite flaws in Western democracies, some very evident to Americans watching the news in the summer of 2020, these were robust structures with potent economies. The Soviet model, which openly espoused one-party rule and made authoritarian leadership likely, was less flexible. Keeping up with Western military technology—vital for Warsaw Pact grand strategy—required television, radios, computers, access to international scientific literature, and a host of other data streams.

Access alerted locals of the significant economic disparities between their "workers' paradise" and that of the "Capitalist exploiters." Blue jeans, cowboy movies, Beatles records, and even chewing gum became subversive tools that pried Soviet Bloc citizens from the Party line. Why can't we have these also? was a hard question to answer with a quote from Marx or Lenin. Faced with consumer demands, the Soviet Bloc was incapable of providing both guns and butter.

As we suggest in our section on decolonization, oppression is costly and can reach a point of very limited returns. Soviet leaders clearly understood that they could not return to the days of

Stalin. Was reform possible? Mikhail Gorbachev, eighth leader of the Soviet Union, argued *glasnost* ("openness") and *perestroika* ("restructuring") were the solutions. Martin McCauley, an Irish historian and expert on Soviet Russia, argues they were the exact opposite and "set reforms in motion without understanding where they could lead."

Gorbachev's good intentions dismantled the Soviet Union, while at the

FIGURE4.8 Perestroika Stamp

same time, national forces within the Warsaw Pact, resentful of Soviet domination, began to unravel the status quo. These trends accelerated in 1989's "Autumn of Nations," when from Poland to Bulgaria, local Communist regimes were replaced by nationalist governments supporting political pluralism. The collapse was violent in Romania and Yugoslavia but relatively peaceful elsewhere. Gorbachev had to accept the failure of communism when Baltic, Ukrainian, and Central Asian citizens demanded independence from the Soviet Union.

Regional Warfare

While nuclear weapons were deterrents to all-out conflict between the superpowers, they did not end regional wars. The post-1945 world witnessed many conflicts, mainly in the non-Western world, and often connected to the history of imperialism. These ranged from guerrilla campaigns designed to overthrow colonial regimes in Algeria or Kenya to conventional wars in China or Palestine.

China witnessed the culmination of a decades-long struggle between *Guomindang* (Nationalist) and Communist armies. Although the former managed to maintain control of Taiwan, they were driven off the mainland by 1950. In the same year, Communist troops invaded Tibet, driving the 14th Dalai Lama into exile. To the south, French Indochina saw the pro-Communist Viet-Minh slowly gain enough strength to fight a set-piece battle at Dien Bien Phu (1954), where they destroyed a large contingent of elite French soldiers. Within a year, the French departed, only to be replaced by Americans attempting to buttress local anti-Communist politicians.

India and Pakistan went through four conflicts between 1947 and 1999. India's larger economy and population were somewhat balanced by American support for Pakistan, but the last two conflicts indicate Pakistan would fare poorly in a future struggle. Today's complex relationships between Pakistan, the Afghan *Taliban*, and America's war on terror are a result of this reality.

Arabs and Israelis produced four wars also. Between 1947 and 1973, these were quick and showed Israel far better prepared for combat. Blowback from repeated Arab defeats fueled political instability and was at least partially responsible for regime changes in Iraq, Syria, and Egypt.

The **Palestine Liberation Organization** (PLO) was another result of failure. Picking up on the playbook of older revolutionary groups like Serbia's Black Hand, PLO fighters used terror as a weapon, attacking civilian targets to break Israeli resolve. Europe's Red Brigades, the Tupamaros in Uruguay, or Shining Path in Peru are but a few examples of similar groups who plagued world peace in the 1970s–1990s.

Conventional wars featured prominently in the 1980s. Argentine forces staged a coup de main in 1982, occupying the Falkland Islands in hopes that the United Kingdom would surrender this far-away colony. Instead, the world witnessed the most intense air-sea battles since the Second World War. Vertical take-off Harrier "jump jets" allowed Britain's Royal Navy vital air cover and the ability to end Argentine attacks with deadly Exocet anti-ship missiles.

The Falkland War was over in ten weeks, while the **Iran-Iraq War** lasted nearly eight years and threatened to expand, when both sides attacked tankers carrying Middle Eastern oil to Japan and Europe. Ending with no clear victor, this war cost over a million casualties, expended more than a trillion dollars, and destabilized both nations. The two American invasions of Iraq (1990, 2003) were directly connected to events and outcomes of the Iran-Iraq War.

Terrorists scored their greatest success on September 11, 2001, when **Al-Qaeda** operatives hijacked airliners for suicide missions against buildings in New York and Washington, DC. Nearly 9,000 people were killed or injured. Events of 9/11 have shaped the first two decades of the twenty-first century, leading to occupations of Iraq and Afghanistan, plus a seemingly endless global war on terror.

Initial blows fell on Afghanistan, where the Taliban regime provided a haven for Al-Qaeda. Former allies in the fight against Soviet invaders (1979–1989), Al-Qaeda and the Taliban shared a common worldview while embracing a deeply conservative Sunni-Muslim version of Islam. With ethnic minorities, Shia Muslims, and local warlords resisting the Taliban, it was not difficult for American operatives to gain support for an operation aimed at the overthrow of Taliban leadership and the destruction of Al-Qaeda.

Between November and December 2001, US air power, plus special forces units, some mounted on Afghan ponies, joined with local allies to take over Afghanistan. This happened with minimal casualties, but what next? The Al-Qaeda leadership had escaped, but could a nation-building strategy create a strong pro-Western Afghanistan that would not harbor future terrorists?

Two years later, partially from claims Iraq had given aid to Al-Qaeda, America went to war in the Fertile Crescent for a second time. Easily defeating the Iraqi military, could this be a chance to sweep out the old regime and create a democratic substitute? While it is easy to look back at 2001–2003 and find strong contrarian evidence that remaking Afghanistan and Iraq would be very difficult, America was still celebrating the heady victory over communism after the 1989 collapse of the Soviet Union. "Victory fever," to use a Japanese expression from 1941–1942, had swept through American leaders.

America found more enemies in a collection of Islamic terrorist organizations ranging from *Boko Haram* in Nigeria to ISIS in Syria. The latter benefited from the seeming collapse of the Assad regime and soon was sending columns of "**technicals**," small trucks mounting heavy weapons, that could defeat American-trained members of the new Iraqi army. Simultaneously, ISIS drove government forces from eastern Syria.

Russia returned to the world stage crushing jihadist forces in Chechnya during a decade-long struggle than ended in 2009. A year earlier, Russian forces defeated the Republic of Georgia in a border conflict, and from 2014–2019 was involved in a larger operation directed against Ukraine. The latter continues as this book goes to press, with Russian special forces units supporting local militias in eastern Ukraine.

Conclusion

War continues across the globe. It is very different from the 1453 Siege of Constantinople, with operators in air-conditioned offices directing Predator drones to launch Hellfire missiles against a terrorist bunker in Yemen. The writer hopes that war will one day be reserved just for historians, but suspects it will be some time before, as Isaiah 11:6 puts it, "… The wolf also shall dwell with the lamb, and the leopard shall lie down with the kid; and the calf and the young lion and the fatling together; and a little child shall lead them."

Chapter Summary

As this chapter makes clear, the twentieth century was a juxtaposition of human ingenuity and aggression as humankind achieved amazing technological feats, such as space travel, while at the same time inflicting catastrophic violence on themselves and their home planet. The good news is that on balance, the twentieth century saw progress, rather than the regression, of human behavior. In the early twenty-first century, humankind continued to grapple with the positive and negative consequences of the twentieth century, including globalization, climate change, international human rights, science and technology, and global warfare.

Discussion Questions

1. What where the pros and cons of globalization in the twentieth century?
2. Why have scholars identified the twentieth century as part the Anthropocene era?
3. How did individuals, nations, and international organizations work to increase human and civil rights in the twentieth century?
4. Give examples of further inventions or improvements of discoveries that have occurred during the twentieth century that might show how beneficial or harmful they have been to humankind. What actions would you take if you were a powerful president of a country?
5. What do you think the social consequences of the scientific evolution or revolution of our age have been? Elaborate on your ideas. Have you personally benefited socially and economically from it? If not, why not; if yes, explain.
6. Using the internet and your textbook, please find the areas that were colonized by France, Britain, and Portugal, which became independent during the twentieth century.
7. Can you differentiate the concepts of decolonization, self-government, and independence from your readings and class discussions?
8. How did military technology and warfare shape global history in the twentieth century?
9. Many Western nations no longer employ conscription, which compelled young people to provide two to four years of military service. All-volunteer forces were deemed more effective but tend to attract about 1 percent of the general public. With the vast majority of citizens not directly impacted by the demands and dangers of military service, politicians have been emboldened to fight very long conflicts, like America in Iraq or Afghanistan. Do you think it would be as simple to sell "forever wars" if you and your friends were subject to a draft?

References

Using the Sources

Beyond the primary sources provided in this chapter, students will benefit from analyzing maps and images provided in the textbook and additional readings and materials cited below. Students and instructors may find film and literary adaptations particularly helpful in the classroom or as additional assignments. References and suggested supplementary sources are provided.

Primary Sources

"19. Olympe de Gouges (1748–1793), Declaration of the Rights of Woman and the Female Citizen, 1791." In *Tolerance: The Beacon of the Enlightenment* [online] ed. Caroline Warman. 2016. Cambridge: Open Book Publishers. http://books.openedition.org/obp/2972

Bailey, L. H. *The Holy Earth*. 1915. New York: Charles Scribner's Sons. Project Gutenberg eBooks, 2010. http://www.gutenberg.org/files/33178/33178-h/33178-h.htm

"Declaration of the United Nations Conference on the Human Environment." 1972. https://www.ipcc.ch/apps/njlite/srex/njlite_download.php?id=6471

"Police Directive Relating to the Prevention of Juveniles from Using Public Dance Halls." November 29, 1939. Translated by John Dunn from original German.

"Transcript of 19th Amendment to the U.S. Constitution: Women's Right to Vote (1920)." https://www.ourdocuments.gov/doc.php?flash=false&doc=63&page=transcript

United Nations. 2020. "Declaration Regarding Non-Self-Governing Territories." Article 73, Chapter XI, June 26, 1945. *United Nations at 70, DPA Online Newsletter*, 2020. New York: United Nations.

United Nations. "UN Charter (full text)." https://www.un.org/en/sections/un-charter/un-charter-full-text/

Secondary Sources

Berger, Arthur Asa. 2017. *Reading Matter: Multidisciplinary Perspectives on Material Culture*. New York: Routledge.

Burns, Edward McNall, and Philip Lee Ralph. 1955. *World Civilizations*. Vol. 2, 5th ed. New York: Norton and Company.

Christensen, Clayton M. 1997. *The Innovator's Dilemma: When New Technologies Cause Great Firms to Fail*. Boston: Harvard Business School Press.

"Convention on the Elimination of All Forms of Discrimination against Women (CEDAW): A Fact Sheet (RS20097)." EveryCRSReport.com. https://www.everycrsreport.com/reports/RS20097.html

"Convention on the Elimination of All Forms of Discrimination against Women New York, 18 December 1979." United Nations Human Rights: Office of the Commissioner. https://www.ohchr.org/en/professionalinterest/pages/cedaw.aspx

Crist, David. 2013. *The Twilight War: The Secret History of America's Thirty-Year Conflict with Iran*. Penguin.

Daley, Caroline, and Melanie Nolan. 1994. *Suffrage and Beyond: International Feminist Perspectives*. Auckland, NZ: Auckland University Press.

Fall, Bernard B. 1961. *Street without Joy: Indochina at War, 1946–54*. Harrisburg, PA: Stackpole.

Fukuhara, Ryuichi. 2018. "Human and Nature Revisited: The Industrial Revolution, Modern Economics and the Anthropocene." In S. Yamash'ta, T. Yagi, and S. Hill, eds., *The Kyoto Manifesto for Global Economics*. Singapore: Springer.

Giangreco, Dennis M. 2009. *Hell to Pay: Operation Downfall and the Invasion of Japan, 1945–1947.* Annapolis, MD: Naval Institute Press.

Global Indigenous Council. "GIC Issues—#MMIW Missing and Murdered Indigenous Women." https://www.globalindigenouscouncil.com/mmiw

Gonzalez-Ruibal, Alfredo, Almudean Hernando, and Gustavo Politis. 2011. "Ontology of the Self and Material Culture: Arrow-Making among the Awa Hunter-Gatherers (Brazil). *Journal of Anthropological Archaeology,* Vol. 30, 1(2011): 1–16.

Hill, Mitchell. 1995. "What the Principle of Self-Determination Means Today." *ILSA Journal of International and Comparative Law,* Vol. 1(1995): 120–33.

"Imperial Rescript to Soldiers and Sailors, 1882." *Documents on Japanese Imperialism.* http://www.professorcampbell.org/sources/japan.html.

Kozaczuk, Władysław. *Enigma: How the German Machine Cipher Was Broken, and How It Was Read by the Allies in World War Two.* Edited and translated by Christopher Kasparek. 1984. Frederick, MD: University Publications of America.

Labonté, R. "Globalization, Health, and Development: The Right Prescription." 2011. http://idrc.ca/en/en-67832-201-I-DO_TOPIC.html: 1–11.

Marx, Karl, and David McLellan. 2000. *Selected Writings.* Oxford; New York: Oxford University Press.

Miscamble, Wilson D. 2011. *The Most Controversial Decision: Truman, the Atomic Bombs, and the Defeat of Japan.* New York: Cambridge University Press.

O'Toole, Paddy, and Prisca and Were. 2008. "Observing Places: Using Space and Material Culture in Qualitative Research." *Qualitative Research,* Vol. 8, 5(2008): 616–34.

Paquet, Cheri. February 12, 1999. "Report Counts 147 Million Global Net Users." CNN.com, http://edition.cnn.com/TECH/computing/9902/12/globalnet.idg/index.html

Parshall, Jonathan, and Anthony Tully. 2005. *Shattered Sword: The Untold Story of the Battle of Midway.* Dulles, VA: Potomac Books.

Robertson, Roland. 1992. *Globalization: Social Theory and Global Culture.* Theory, Culture & Society. London: Sage.

Slatin, Sonia. 1979. "Opera and Revolution: La Muette de Portici and the Belgian Revolution of 1830 Revisited." In *Journal of Musicological Research,* Vol. 3: 45–62.

Stoker, Donald. 2019. *Why America Loses Wars: Limited War and US Strategy from the Korean War to the Present.* New York: Cambridge University Press.

Tooze, Adam. 2006. *The Wages of Destruction: The Making and Breaking of the Nazi Economy.* Allen Lane.

Walker, Mark. 1993. *German National Socialism and the Quest for Nuclear Power, 1939–1949.* Cambridge.

Wass, Janice Tauer. 1998. "Teaching History with Material Culture." https://www.lib.niu.edu/1998/iht529802.html

Westad, Odd Arne. 2017. *The Cold War: A World History.* New York: Basic Books.

Williamson, Murray, and Robert Scales. 2005. *The Iraq War.* Cambridge, MA: Belknap Press.

"Women and the Vote: Page 5—World Suffrage Timeline." New Zealand History. https://nzhistory.govt.nz/politics/womens-suffrage/world-suffrage-timeline

Women's Rights Project and Human Rights Watch. 1998. *The Human Rights Watch Global Report on Women's Human Rights.* New Delhi; Oxford: Oxford University Press.

Woodward, David, Nick Drager, Robert Beaglehole, and Debra Lipson. 2001. "Globalization and Health: A Framework for Analysis and Action." *World Health Organization. Bulletin of the World Health Organization* 79, no. 9, 875–81.

Zimmerer, Jürgen. 2005. "Annihilation in Africa: The 'Race War' in German Southwest Africa (1904–1908) and Its Significance for a Global History of Genocide." *Bulletin of the German Historical Institute Issue* 37 (2005): 51–57.

Film and Television

Der Magische Gürtel (The Enchanted Circle). 1917. German film about successful *U-Boot* patrol (see https://www.iwm.org.uk/collections/item/object/1060008290).

The Journeys of Apollo [NASA Documentary on YouTube].

Understanding 9/11 – A Television News Archive. https://archive.org/details/911.

Credits

Chapter 5

Africa on the World Stage

Introduction to Chapter Themes

Globally, the history of Africa can figuratively be compared to a ping-pong ball, constantly in an up-and-down motion whose trajectory is difficult to predict. If one reads what has been written from the beginning of modern history to the present, the general narrative on Africa has been negative, and its achievements have been either ignored or distorted to fit an image that those outside the continent have decided to project and maintain, often for very obvious motives. This chapter attempts to straighten the unfair wrongs Africa has suffered, highlight its accomplishments, expose its serious challenges and past unforgivable decisions, and provide a personal perspective of its future, using the broadest acceptable and hopefully objective criteria that have been applied to other people of the world.

Many reasons justify why Africa should take a special place in the contemporary world and in history books. It is strategically located—right at the center of the world—between Europe and the Middle East, Asia, and the Americas. Africa straddles the Mediterranean Sea, the Atlantic and Indian oceans, and the Suez Canal, which serve as the major routes to the rest of the globe. This is why Africans traded with India, China, and the Arab world long before the Europeans slowly entered the continent during the fifteenth century. Africa is also the fastest-growing continent, home to 1.3 billion people, half of whom are less than 25 years of age, at a time when virtually all other continents are experiencing a reduction in population births. Its weight at the United Nations continues to grow, and Africa can no longer be ignored when major decisions are made in the deliberations of the Security Council and the General Assembly. It is the ancestral home of over 40 million people in the United States—the African Americans—who stand as the most critical group that helped build this country. Interest in Africa is growing throughout the world, which most observers no longer call the "sleeping giant," but the world's "rising giant," while it continues to take full advantage of the unprecedented technological advancements offered today, including the new mobile economy. Above all perhaps is the fact that, in mineral resources, it is the richest continent in the world. Indeed, of the 54 African countries, more than 20 have oil reserves, the resource that fuels our world today, and several are endowed with diamonds, gold, uranium, platinum, and iron. Finally, one cannot overlook either that Africa is a continent with the greatest diversity in geographic systems and ecosystems, cultural and linguistic manifestations, and abundance in its animal kingdom.

The themes of this chapter, as are those of all chapters in the volume, will be an examination of the impact of geography and environment on the continent of Africa and its people; a critical look at the material culture that has prevailed on the continent over the centuries, which has often caused resistance to nefarious outside and inside influences; delving into the relation and treatment of the more than 1,000 major ethnic groups, as well as the specific gender roles that have persisted over the millennia; gauging the state of Africa's technology and application of scientific innovations that have benefited other people of the world; and weighing the nature and impact of the themes of war, peace, and diplomacy, which have been a part of human history as people attempt to adapt, adopt, and improve new rational ways of preserving life and enhancing global progress.

Student Learning Objectives

After reading this chapter students should be able to describe and discuss:

- The geographic and human resources of the continent of Africa and how they can be used to benefit all people

- The challenges that Africa as a continent has had in the past and explain how these have shaped its history and the present

- The remaining political, social, military, economic, and technological issues Africa must overcome in order to successfully play its role among the nations of the world

- The likely future of Africa

- Trends in war, peace, and diplomacy in modern Africa

Timeline of Selected Dates

1884–1885	Berlin Conference divides Africa among European powers
1859–1879	Introduction of the telegraph in Africa
1860s–1880s	Tukolor and Mandinka rebel against French rule
1890s	Zulus rebel against British rule in South Africa
1901	Uganda-Kenya railroad completed
1901–1902	First steamboat on Lake Victoria
1905	Maji Maji Rebellion in Tanganyika against German rule
1960s	Africa enters the "age of globalization"
1960s–1975	Violent resistance against Portuguese in Angola, Guinea-Bissau, and Mozambique
1962–1964	Algerians resist French rule
1966–1990	Namibia resists White South African rule
1974–1980	Southern Rhodesia (Zimbabwe) resists White rule
1992	End of apartheid in South Africa
2006	Ellen Johnson becomes first female president in Africa (Liberia)
2018	Somaliland passes law making rape, forced marriage, and sex trafficking a crime

Ancient Africa through the Sixteenth Century

For centuries, the African continent remained both a forbidding and a forgotten place in the eyes of the Europeans and of most other people of the world. It was a forbidden place for several reasons. First is its harsh topography, a predominantly rising **plateau** as one leaves the coast inland, which, combined with the sometimes dense vegetation, forest, and even jungle in parts of the west and the central contours prevented easy travel virtually everywhere. Second is the major obstacle caused by some of the largest deserts in the world—the Sahara and the Kalahari in the north and south, respectively—made more intimidating by the vast waters of the Atlantic Ocean in the west, the Indian Ocean in the east, and the Mediterranean Sea in the north, which few seafarers dared to venture to travel to reach the interior and the mainland, until Portuguese navigator Vasco da Gama reached India in 1498.

The slave trade and subsequent European conquest, particularly during the mid-1880s, and the slow invasion of Islam in the north that had begun during the fifth and seventh centuries in North and East Africa, punctuated by the arrival of a few more European adventurers, opened the so-called "Dark" or "Old Continent" to the whole world. Indeed, since then, Africa had continued to be forgotten, ignored and therefore irrelevant. Things changed dramatically, however, when its vast human, mineral, animal, and agricultural resources were "discovered" and subsequently exploited by intrepid conquerors and destitute colonizers, making Africa a preferred destination for those seeking to be rich quickly and to live "a splendid life," with some areas being more inviting than others due to their climate, the hospitality of their people, and the richness of the soil, as the following chapter will show.

Africa's World Image and the Academy[1]

Historians, anthropologists, artists, socio-behaviorists, philosophers, and theologians, as well as sociologists have, for a century, shaped our understanding of African cultures, Africa's medical practices, and Africans' lifestyles across the continent. Said differently, social scientists and humanists have played an unparalleled role in people's accurate or distorted understanding of "alien" practices, especially African, given the prevailing unequal relationships between the Africans and their colonizers who overpowered them on their own continent 150 years ago. History, at times called the "queen" of the social sciences, or the humanities, according to some, has been more responsible for the restoration of the African past than any other discipline, as it has also on the understanding of the African American past in the United States. With its rigorous methodology of data collection using all available primary and secondary sources, government documents, diaries, memoirs, books, newspapers, oral traditions, witnesses or contemporary actors, relevant fossils, pictorial data, and artifacts, from archives, libraries, excavations, and corroborative materials from other disciplines, the Africanist historian, insisting on objectivity, has pioneered the systematic understanding of Africa and provided a foundation for the other social sciences and the

---

1   Adapted from Mario J. Azevedo, *Africana Studies: A Survey of the African Diaspora*, pp. 8-12. Copyright © 1993 by Carolina Academic Press. Reprinted with permission.

humanities to utilize and sharpen their own methodologies, thus reaching a more comprehensive understanding of the continent and its people over time.

The historiography of the colonial period treated Africa primarily as an extension of Europe, using European concepts and a Eurocentric point of view. The new Africanist historians brought Africans to center stage, treating them as the primary focus of their work. However, pioneering Africanist historians have been criticized by a younger generation of Africans and "radical" scholars, who insist that the discipline is too conservative and irrelevant to Africa's current problems partly because it still employs a Eurocentric rather than an Afri- or Afro-centric approach to the study of the continent. On methodology, the neo-historians, who wish to revise traditional history, argue that the claim of objectivity leads the Africanist historian to nothing; or, as historians A. Temu and B. Swai of the School of Dar-es-Salaam, Tanzania, put it in their *Historians and Africanist History: A Critique* (1981), it reduces history to a cul-de-sac, never venturing "beyond a timid empiricism"—that is, a description of facts without analysis or vision of the world. They maintain that ideology and methodology cannot be separated because the mere choice of a specific focus betrays the historian's predisposition, values, and partisanship, thus shattering the claim of objectivity. Temu and Swai, noted above, sarcastically conclude that the historian's objectivity has been the "objectivity of a eunuch"(or that of a castrated man who brags about his sexual escapades). The claim of the universal applicability of their theories and conclusions (i.e., that generalizations about European history necessarily apply to African history as well) has likewise come under attack. Western academics have, in fact, unwittingly tended to generalize about all societies and cultures using ethnocentric standards, which have often distorted the reality of the world under study, as is the case with the characterization of African medical practices as nothing but witchcraft, just to cite one example.

This is clear, for example, when political scientists, sociologists, and economists applied the supposed universality of the European modernization theory and development trajectory to Africa during the 1960s. On medical history in Africa, the first historians who looked at culture to understand public health over time emerged during the 1960s and picked up steam thereafter. The reason for the slow study of health and disease by historians is that public health, a combination of the principles and canons of the natural sciences, and to a large extent, the socio-behavioral sciences, grew as a respected field of study only during the 1960s and 1970s.The Ibadan and Dar-es-Salaam schools of Africanist historians, of which the late Walter Rodney was the major exponent, have further complained that the present historiography is dominated by Western historians who continue to misinterpret Africa, just as the first anthropologists did. Temu and Swai go farther in their criticism and make the interesting point that, even though Leopold von Ranke, the "father of modern historiography," advocated objectivity and a dispassionate approach to the study of the past, he himself glorified his Prussian state.

Anthropology, or the study of cultures, first in the form of ethnography (a focus on technologically less advanced societies or what the field used to call "primitive societies") began studying Africa before history did. However, the anthropological methodology has encountered the ire of even the most fair-minded Africanists both on the continent and in the West. The first ethnographers, who worked during the 1920s through the 1940s, did their research in collaboration with the colonial administrators whose aim was to understand the African cultures they encountered and facilitate colonization. In most cases, anthropologists presented a picture of timeless, static, small, savage, tribal societies, characterizing them as "exotic curiosities." While they popularized the so-called scientific method of fieldwork and participant-observation (a method whereby researchers observe and participate in the culture they are studying) and sometimes criticized the colonial status quo, up to the 1950s, anthropologists were seen as allies of colonialism, who propagated the idea that nothing was worth in African traditional medical knowledge and practices, which they attributed all to witchcraft and sorcery. Anthropology is therefore one discipline that is said to have inflicted irreparable damage to Africa's image at home and abroad.

E. E. Evans-Pritchard, for example, earned instant academic and world notoriety for his works on the Nuer and Azande of Sudan. The humiliating and pornographic nature of the pictures, neatly interspersed throughout his book on *Nuer Religion* (1956), in which grown men and children, ostensibly—but most likely forced to—exhibit their genitalia to the colonial camera. Another critical query that lingers in one's mind refers to the feelings of the families whose parents, grandparents, brothers, and sisters appear and will continue to appear in the pictures almost in perpetuity. The unauthorized posting of the pictures seems like a clear violation of the human rights of the people of South Sudan as well as those of the country's future generations. These degrading writings and ethnocentric tendencies were reinforced by the work of the misguided missionaries who were sent to Africa in large numbers during the nineteenth century. The reader can appreciate how far the Africa of today has come to liberate itself from the unfair images with which it has had to contend for over a century.

Geography and Environment

The African Continent

A concerted and organized social effort to address the needs of a settled population began with the invention of agriculture during the Neolithic Age, most likely around 5000 BC in North Africa, notably in Egypt, and in Asia—here, precisely in Mesopotamia, in parts of East and Southern Africa—and the rest of the world. As individuals aggregated and public needs emergencies arose, specialized structures and trained individuals were empowered to make decisions for the community. As a result, Neolithic men and women established the rudiments of such institutions as schools to ensure the transmission of culture and acquired knowledge to the next generations. To maintain law and order and fight crime, often in the form of theft and violence related to food and often to women, a government was formed, whether by an informal or a formal social contract. As societies, governments, or states multiplied, the need for the defense of the population was entrusted to an army that protected the frontiers and provided people's security inside the sometimes-visible community or state walls.

As the common interpretation of the cosmos and the meaning of life provided social cohesiveness, organized religion began to emerge through the work of local priests and the establishment of buildings of worship. So it was for economic survival: Granaries under specialized individuals were built to prepare for drought, famine, and hunger; tax collectors, along with early "economists," ensured that the state would have resources, some in kind and others in currency. As the

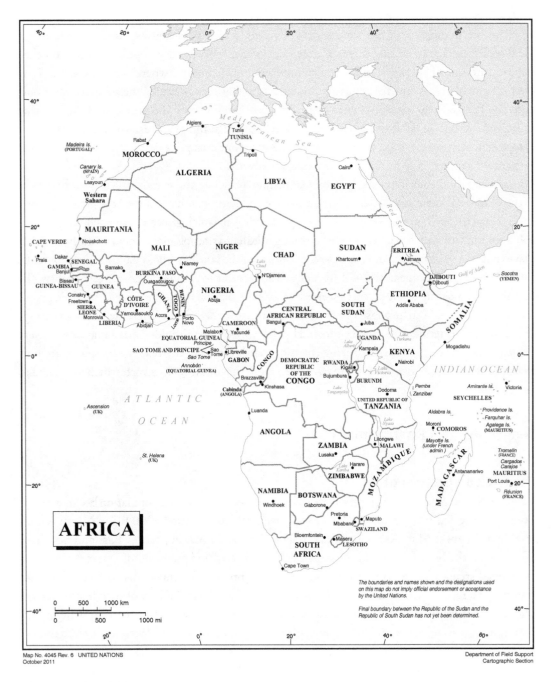

FIGURE 5.1 Map of Africa.

spread of epidemics endangered the health of the community, the once-scattered healers or the early physicians, herbalists, diviners, and magicians were called upon to prevent disease, cure the sick, and preserve the health of the population through health facilities, isolating some people and warning others about the dangers of contagion. The slave trade that began during the fifteenth century and lasted until the nineteenth century had its negative impact on the image of Africa on the world stage. The merchant caravans, the proselytizers who crisscrossed the Sahara Desert, and the continuous and unhindered number of traders that sailed on dhows from the Indian Ocean to the coast at times carrying crews of 12 to 30 people, and then the subsequent daring movement of intrepid strangers to the African interior of East and Central Africa, began slowly changing the continent's social, economic, and health fabric.

With time, namely beginning in the late nineteenth century, the forced introduction of colonialism bought with it such unintended allies as diseases in the form of syphilis and smallpox, as well as new strains of measles and influenza, as happened during World War I. Though some may have been endemic to Africa for centuries, the newcomers changed the balance between humans and their ecosystem, infecting and decimating in the process thousands of Africans. This was an event similar to what befell American Indians following the Spanish conquest of Central and South America with the 1492 landing of Christopher Columbus and the conquistadors in the New World, who introduced smallpox, measles, and syphilis. The accompanying development schemes could not but bring with them the harmful changes that historically have often resulted from a state of disequilibrium between humans and their environment. On the continent of Africa, these changes often contributed to hunger, misery, disease, suffering, death, and depopulation.

The Land and Its People[2]

Africa is the world's second largest continent, inhabited by some 1.3 billion people, and constitutes the fastest-growing population in the world, surpassing even Asia, including the demographic growth of China. Geographically, Africa is located between the Mediterranean Sea in the north, the Suez Canal and the Indian Ocean in the east, and the Atlantic Ocean in the west. The distance between north and south is about 5,200 miles and that between east and west is around 4,600 miles, with the total surface area of 11,730 million square miles.

Africa is best described as rich in geographic and demographic diversity. Yet, life has not been easy on the continent. Even at the dawn of the third millennium, about 75 percent of the African population are still engaged in and live off subsistence agriculture, producing primarily to feed the family rather than to sell their yield in the marketplace. Given that only about 6 percent is actually arable (plowable) land throughout the year, most of the farming is still agriculture intensive rather than extensive, characterized by shifting and slash-and-burn practices, in which the tools are still simple—the hoe and the ax—where such resources as fertilizers are often nonexistent. In the arable areas—parts of the savanna and highlands of East Africa—a pastoral lifestyle, at times combined with nomadic transhumance, is a way of life for many people. By contrast, a tiny percentage of the population in Central Africa (as is the case among the Bambuti and the Twa) and in the Namib and the Kalahari deserts lives essentially from hunting.

As a result of the harsh reality of life in the farms of the countryside and the lure of an urban lifestyle brought about by Western colonization, African cities began to grow steadily since the arrival of the Europeans. As a result, presently, the constant waves of rural immigrants to the urban enclaves make life even more miserable, reflected in overcrowding, slums, and poverty,

---

2   Adapted from Mario Azevedo and Gwendolyn Prater, *Africa and Its People: An Interdisciplinary Survey of the Continent*, pp. 59-83. Copyright © 1982 by Mario Azevedo and Gwendolyn Prater. Reprinted with permission.

and in increasingly violent crime in such large cities as Lagos (21 million people, Africa's largest), Cairo (20 million), Johannesburg (4.4 million), Lusaka (1.270 million), Abidjan (4.707 million), Luanda (6.5 million), and Kinshasa (13.3 million) in 2017. In Zambia, for example, urbanization has occurred so rapidly that by 2017, over 41.8 percent (from 15 percent in 1960) of the country's population lived in the urban areas.

The African continent has been described by geographers as a high plateau, with 90 percent of its land mass located 500 feet above sea level (compared to Europe's 50 percent), with 80 percent of it located within the tropics of Cancer and Capricorn and divided almost in half by the equator. Some experts have characterized the soil of Africa as a virtual "chunk of iron ore," although of lower grade, but rendering agricultural activity more difficult and less productive. Major geographical features include the Great Rift Valley, which extends from the Red Sea through the Ethiopian Mountains to East Africa's lakes, and out to the Indian Ocean in Mozambique. Parts of its plateau are made of isolated mountains or mountain chains: Kilimanjaro (19,340 feet), Rwenzori (16,000 feet), Kenya (17,000 feet), Cameroon (13,000 feet), the Drakensberg mountains of South Africa (11,000 feet), the Atlas mountain chains of Northwest Africa (13,000 feet), and the Manica Plateau of Mozambique and Zimbabwe (7,874 feet).

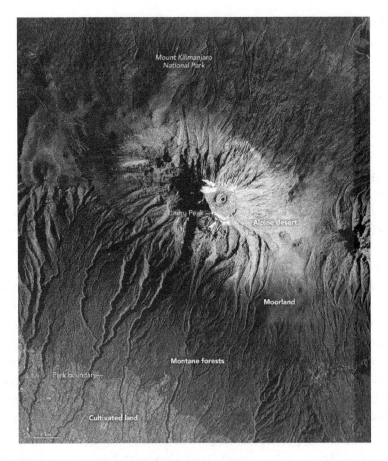

FIGURE 5.2   Mt. Kilimanjaro from Space.

Even though water is becoming less abundant elsewhere, rivers and lakes still constitute the greatest natural resources on the continent. Africa's long rivers (Nile, 4,000 miles; Congo, 2,718 miles; Niger, 2,600 miles; Zambezi, 1,600 miles) and large freshwater lakes (Victoria, 130 feet in depth; Tanganyika, 1,2704 square miles in surface, 450 miles long; Lake Malawi, 360 miles long and 11,429 square miles in surface; Turkana (formerly Rudolf), 50 square miles in surface and 180.2 square miles in size and 1,230 feet above sea level; and Chad, 520 square miles in surface and 400 miles long) that have created several internal basins, such as the Djouf of the middle Upper Niger River; the Chad Basin around **Lake Chad**; the Sudan Basin of the Upper Nile; the Congo Basin, mainly in Congo-Kinshasa or the Democratic Republic of the Congo; and the Kalahari Basin of Southern Africa. Although Africa's rivers range in length from over 4,000 miles, as is the case with the Nile, to over 1,600 miles for the Zambezi, as noted above, they are not entirely navigable. However, where they are, they constitute an important means of communication, transportation, and trading activities. Likewise, both rivers and lakes provide fishing opportunities to the surrounding populations and represent great hydroelectric potential for the entire continent. Unfortunately, except for the Aswan Dam in Egypt, the Cahora Bassa Dam in Mozambique, and the Upper Volta Dam in Southeastern Ghana, Africa has been unable to effectively harness the tremendous resources its waters offer. Indeed:

> The water power resources of Africa are tremendous and are estimated at about 40 percent of the world's total (275 of 688 million horsepower). It is somewhat ironic that this continent, plagued with aridity over such great areas, should at the same time have such a magnificent hydroelectric potential. The high rainfall in the rainforest and savanna areas, and their high average elevation, combine to explain this wealth. About 18 percent of the world total and 45 percent of the total African potential are in the Congo Basin. The 217-mile stretch of the Lower Congo River from Leopoldville to Matadi has an estimated potential of 85 million horsepower.[3]

The problem is, of course, related to the topography, which forces rivers to meander through flat regions. Dams are very costly to build and maintain and are rarely efficient options. The unpredictability of heavy rain and its absence or short duration in many parts of the continent make life difficult. A. T. Grove thus expressed this complexity:

> In January inflows of unstable moist air from the South Atlantic bring rain to the Congo/Zaire basin while the Indian Ocean is the source of rain for the countries stretching from Natal to Tanzania. As the sun moves north, so the inter-tropical converging zone (ITCZ) follows. By March the rainy season is over in Botswana and Zimbabwe and is beginning in a zone stretching across the continent from Kenya to Sierra Leone. By July/August the ITCZ has reached furthest north and Atlantic air occupies much of the continent between a few degrees north of the equator and the tropic of Cancer; rain falls over most of west Africa and Ethiopia with occasional

---

3   William Hance, *African Economic Development* (New York: Praeger, 1967).

showers even on the Tibesti mountains in the Sahara. In September and October, the rain belt moves rapidly south again, bringing a second rainy season to the equatorial zone. Then the cycle starts again.[4]

Laymen can best understand the geographic complexity of Africa by examining its four or five almost distinct climatic and vegetation zones. First is the tropical rainforest (with the highest population density in Africa, up to 94 square miles straddling the equator from the Atlantic Ocean up to the fringes of the East African highlands, where, throughout the year, temperatures never fall below 68°F. This region is characterized by heavy and constant rainfall, receiving over 50 inches (127 mm) of rain per year. As a result, it has no dry season. Because the constant heavy clouds reflect the sunlight, average temperatures remain between 84°F and 90°F in this zone.

Here, the vegetation is made up of thick, heavy trees, at times becoming a jungle (currently covering 15 percent of Africa), brushes, ferns (as tall as 10 feet), palm trees, wood climbers, or lianas, that may reach a height of 60 feet, and a canopy of broad-leaved evergreens up to 150 feet tall. Soils of the tropical rainforest are not the best because they lack humus and are low in organic nutrients and essential minerals, but they can sustain enough agricultural activity to feed millions of people. Rainforest crops include cassava; yams; sweet potatoes; grains, such as rice and corn; fruits, including plantains and bananas; coffee; cotton; palm oil; sesame; squash; melon; peanuts; peas; beans; onions; tomatoes; tobacco; mushrooms; edible leaves; snails; and termites. Mahogany and ebony trees are abundant in this region and constitute important export items in the form of wood and lumber. Rubber trees also produce sap, and quinine is extracted from certain known trees in the forest, while livestock and poultry include goats, sheep, pigs, and chickens. Mineral resources consist of iron, uranium, copper, gold, petroleum, diamonds, gold, zinc, bauxite, and titanium, among others.

Next comes the savanna, which covers most of Africa's land mass and lies just above and below the (equatorial) tropical rainforest, on the so-called "poleward sides" of Africa. Here, the rainy season, called the high sun, is long, and is followed by a short dry season, called the low sun, the coolest period of the year but with temperatures never dropping below 65°F. The soils are capable of high agricultural yield, and crops include sorghum, wheat, cotton, bananas, and cashew nuts. Livestock production includes cattle and sheep, which are sources of milk, butter, and blood for the Maasai, and are high in protein content. Minerals range from phosphates and chromite to diamonds, tin, gold, coal, zinc, copper, manganese, iron, and petroleum (some of which is exported). Vegetation in the savanna is varied, but the essential features are shrubs, grasses, scattered thorn trees, and acacias in the dry areas. Life in the savanna is pleasant, and most of the large game (elephants, giraffes, lions, rhinoceroses, and hippopotamuses) are found here, some of which live in national parks, as is the case in Kenya, Tanzania, Uganda, and South Africa. Unfortunately, many areas of the savanna are infested with mosquitoes, flies, and other insects that cause such diseases as malaria (the greatest killer of African children), yellow fever, river blindness, and sleeping sickness.

The desert or low-lying zone contains the Sahara Desert (about 3 million square miles) in the north. The Namib and the Kalahari deserts are located in Southern Africa and form parts of the

---

4   A.T. Grove, *The Changing Geography of Africa* (London: Oxford University Press, 1989).

countries of Namibia, Botswana, Zimbabwe, and South Africa. The desert, especially the Sahara, is hot during the day, reaching over 120°F, but can be as cool as 50°F at night. In the Sahara, resources such as oil, gas, uranium, and phosphates have been found, while the Kalahari and the Namib deserts are rich in diamonds, copper, coal, nickel, asbestos, kyanite, manganese, gold, barite, limestone, and chrome. Vegetation is almost nonexistent here; if present, it is very sparse. The few meager crops raised in this zone include sorghum, millet, beans, cowpeas, peanuts, and sunflowers in the Namib and Kalahari deserts, with dates and livestock, such as sheep and goats, found in the Sahara Desert.

The fringes of the Sahara Desert are less barren and receive between 8 and 80 inches of rain yearly, but droughts are recurring phenomena negatively affecting such countries as Senegal, Mali, Niger, Mauritania, Chad, Burkina Faso, Kenya, Somalia, and Sudan. The **Sahel** constitutes a transitional zone between the desert and the savanna and is located between 0° and 150° latitude north and continues to expand from the east to the west coasts of Africa. Sahelian soils lack humus and are much less productive than elsewhere, except when irrigated. Crops include peanuts, millet, corn, sesame, tobacco, barley, wheat, and cotton. The Sahel hosts many nomadic groups, such as the Tuareg and the Tubu, who raise camels, cattle, sheep, and goats along the sparse oases. Phosphate, iron, and salt, as well as oil, have been found in several areas of the zone. However, the bad news is that, while some scientists have estimated that every year desertification around the Sahara grows at a pace of half a mile, some claim that the annual rate of desertification in the southern fringes of the Sahara has actually reached 30 miles.

The Mediterranean climate zone is found on both extremities of Africa—Morocco, Algeria, Libya, Tunisia, and part of northern Egypt—and South Africa, at the southern tip. The major climatic feature of the Mediterranean zone is the existence of two distinct seasons—a dry, long summer and a cold, rainy winter—with rainfalls at times exceeding 20 inches a year. Citrus fruits, grapes, apples, peaches, wheat, olives, cotton, rice, dates, and onions are grown in both Northern and Southern Africa's Mediterranean zones. Cattle and sheep flourish here, although desert winds from the southern interior called the Sirocco, khamsin, or Ghibli have been very devastating economically. Oil, natural gas, manganese, cobalt, lead, and mercury are found in the northern zone, whereas in South Africa, gold and diamonds are abundant.

Finally, the East African highlands found in Ethiopia, Uganda, Kenya, Mozambique, Tanzania, Rwanda, and Burundi constitute the best climatic zone for human habitat in Africa, with moderate to very cool temperatures. The land here is generally fertile, one of the reasons why Europeans preferred to live in this zone, as it is capable of producing a variety of crops, such as millet, sorghum, corn (or maize), cassava, bananas, potatoes, yams, beans, sugar, tobacco, coffee, tea, sisal, coconuts, sesame, and cashew nuts. The soil is said to contain diamonds, copper, gold, tin, beryl, soda, ash, tungsten, copper, phosphate, iron, coal, and uranium. Cattle, sheep, goats, and poultry also supplement the diet of the people who are fortunate to live in these areas where, compared to the rest of the continent, the most important soil feature is the high organic content. Mechanized transportation through the use of wheeled means has always been a major problem to the development of rapid communication. However, even though a modern wheeled transportation system did not exist in Africa prior to European arrival, does not mean that Africans were unaware of its use elsewhere in the world. Over the millennia, people have tried to tame the geography and the ecosystem of Africa, but the struggle has always been uphill. Soil erosion, deforestation, intermittent fires, desertification, pestilence, and the apparent rise in temperatures over the continent constitute perhaps the most serious problem Africans face regarding their continent. In this context, the many rivers and lakes notwithstanding, long distances to and from these waters present a major problem for at least 15 landlocked African countries that share a common legacy of colonial disinterest and neglect and continue to be very poor and underdeveloped. The GDP per capita income in Africa demonstrates this reality. In most of Africa, per capita income stands at less than $1,000, except, among the 54 independent states today, Seychelles, Equatorial Guinea, and Mauritania, which top the list at $16,319, $14,176, and $9,322, respectively. At the bottom of the list are CAR, Malawi, Burundi, and South Sudan where the figures fall as low as $365, $294, $284, and $210 respectively. Evidently, the geography of a continent determines, to a large extent, not only the type of its economic activity but also the wealth of its people and the trajectory of their history.

Conclusion

Africa is the second largest continent in the world but, despite its vast mineral and other natural resources, the problems that its geography presents to people and the animal kingdom are enormous: the Sahara and the Kalahari deserts, the thick forest in the center, and the high plateau of its topography are challenges that make life difficult. The tropical climate is also a favorable habitat for insects, such as mosquitoes and flies that are vectors of such diseases as malaria, yellow fever, sleeping sickness, and river blindness. Yet, Africans have been able to survive and strive over the span of cultures and the millennia and have proudly continued to join the community of modern nations, as the following section illustrates.

Material Culture

Africa and Its Encounter with the West

The forced interchange of goods and ideas between Europe and Africa due to colonization brought to the continent a myriad of modern benefits that were often designed only for the European population, its administrators, and its army. A major material cultural innovation in the interaction of Africa with Europe was clearly visible in the transportation system. With African labor, Europeans in Africa were able to build, for example, thousands and thousands of dirt, paved, and asphalt roads. The roads were designed not only to link sister colonies and towns but also to facilitate the transport of raw materials to the ocean ports and then on ships to Europe to feed the manufacturing industries, as was the case of the Uganda-Kenya railroad completed in 1901. The railroad system, initiated in the colonies during the 1880s, in the immediate aftermath of the scramble for Africa, was improved and considerably expanded following World War I, as the car industry was in its early inception. By the 1920s, however, even Chad, which never built a railroad on its own soil, had its first vehicle carrying for the first time the governor-general of French Equatorial Africa between Fort-Lamy (now N'Djamena) and Fort-Archambault (now Sarh), some 395 miles (or 557.1 km), 8.14 hours by car. At that point, the area that used to be called the Gold Coast had hundreds of lorries (trucks) on the dirt roads transporting cocoa products from the interior to the Atlantic coast, as other colonies were doing.

A firm belief existed among the astute administrators that if one wanted to colonize an area, a good and intricate transportation system was needed, which was thus expressed by King Leopold II: *"coloniser c'est transporter,"* or "to colonize is to transport." Likewise, Lord Frederick Lugard, twice governor of Nigeria, said in 1923 that "the material development of Africa may be summed up in one word—transport." On air transport for the colonial enterprise, an obscure but expert colonialist once said:

> People and nature may or may not have to be subdued, but remoteness must be subdued. Links are required to create and maintain an empire—to breach the horizons, spread into new land, occupy and unify distant territory, and then to manage, defend, and exploit it. Transport is a key tool of empire.[5]

By the 1940s, lorries and smaller automobiles were common in the relatively long roads of the British and French colonies, although less so in the Portuguese territories. It must be pointed out, however, that building the railroads took many African lives, as did the 270-mile line completed by the French in 1934. It ran from Brazzaville to Pointe-Noire on the Atlantic coast. The ten-year-long construction time (1924–1934) required over 120,000 African forced laborers annually, particularly the "dispensable" Sara of Chad and some Chinese recruits and porters, carrying a death toll of at least half of the workers resulting from work fatigue, accidents, endemic and epidemic diseases, and climatic changes. While in 1938, Nigeria had 168 miles of asphalt and 23,000 miles of dirt and gravel roads, French West Africa had built 30,000 dirt roads and the Belgian Congo some 27,000 miles. In Equatorial Africa, including Cameroon, the French had built 7,200 miles of earthen roads in the 1920s.

The steamboat, whose history of introduction in Africa is still in contention, became common in African rivers and facilitated the transport of goods and travelers, even though the African canoes continued almost unabated to serve the transportation needs of the Africans. The first steamboat on Lake Victoria dates back to 1900–1901, while reports claim that a smaller war steamboat may have been introduced in Africa by the British as early as the 1860s, prior to the scramble for Africa. Air transport came to Africa for the first time during the 1930s and was expanded considerably after the Second World War. Today, among the major airlines of the world, many fly to such African cities as Cape Town, Nairobi, Dar-es-Salaam, Abidjan, Cairo, Addis Ababa, Entebbe, and Accra.

The transportation revolution in Africa reduced reliance on camels, horses, and other animals such as donkeys, and the chariots adopted from the Middle East by the Egyptians. Improvements in the new transportation and communication system contributed to the following developments: introduction of the first telegraph line linking Durban, Cape Town in South Africa, Zanzibar, Mozambique, and other parts of Africa beginning between 1859 and 1879; the first telephone line (installed in South Africa as early as 1878); after independence, the television (first introduced

---

5   Quote in Kenneth Britton, Gianmaria Martini, and David Scott (eds.), *The Economics and Political Economy of African Air Transportation* (New York: Routledge, 2015).

in Nigeria in 1959); and recently, the vastly widespread computer and television advances. The cell phone, in particular, reached Africa in a stampede. It is estimated that at least two-thirds of sub-Saharan Africans own a mobile phone, even though, ironically, half of them do not have electricity at home.

The colonial interchanges transformed the economic life of the Africans exponentially, producing various cash crops that helped the colonized people pay taxes and profit financially. In Kenya, Cameroon, Uganda, Zimbabwe, and other former colonies, coffee, tobacco, sugar cane, corn, sisal, cocoa, cashew nut, bananas, rice, sweet potatoes, and many other farm products transformed the way people lived and the staples they were used to for centuries. While cattle raisers began using different methods of feeding the cows, milk and a variety of meats were sold in warehouses and butcheries that did not exist in mass quantities before colonialism. The new economic system forced Africans to embrace capitalism, even though they gained little benefit from it. Furthermore, European-modeled schools sprang up in the major towns, while biomedical hospitals introduced new types of treatment of the sick, although traditional physicians, using herbal curative recipes and ancient healing practices, continued to function side-by-side, even among the educated and Christianized Africans.

From the Church and European-forced imposition of their practices emerged the new musical instruments—organs, pianos, modern guitars—alongside centuries-old African entertainment tools and devices. Above all, Africans were compelled to master the European languages in school in order to survive in the colonial system, many of which became the national languages of the new independent states on the continent—English, French, Portuguese, Spanish, and Afrikaans. Cigarettes, pipes, imported new types of alcoholic drinks, such as wine and whiskey introduced as early as during the epoch of the slave trade, new warfare weapons and new types of entertainment, made, in a sense, Africa a distant mirror of Europe. As a result of the forced imposition of costumes and norms from Europe, African lives were changed forever, making the continent simply an exotic place in the eyes of many, including the rest of the world. Indeed, for many centuries, uninformed Europeans and Americans believed that no African lived in a house. By the 1960s, however, Africa had entered the age of globalization, which made the world and its people more interdependent. Yet, relatedly the role of the academy or that of the Western scholars and scientists in the cultural and political shaping of Africa, and its place and reputation on the world scene, cannot be ignored, as the following section demonstrates.

The often-imposed cultural exchanges of values and perspectives between Africans and mainly Europeans and educated Africans noted above had lasting impacts that transformed the continent and its people in their world outlook, their thinking, their values, and even their interaction as a people. Africans, for example, became accustomed to the prevailing foods introduced by Europe, even though the Europeans showed contempt for foods Africans had enjoyed for centuries as nutritious and good tasting. In some areas of the continent, Africans began to appreciate rice, drank European wines and whiskeys and other beverages produced and distilled in European cities, but the newcomers show no love for the African cuisine of such staples prepared by the Africans as sweet potatoes, manioc, or cassava. With time, Africans learned to appreciate the clothing and dressing style or attire of the White man, which was one of the preconditions for one to be considered civilized in an environment that was totally controlled by the Europeans.

African architecture began to be abandoned, at least at the beginning of the encounter and interaction between Europe and Africa, forcing the colonized to adopt the colonizers' home building styles, dotted by their stone and cement foundations, structures, and colors over the natural African landscape.

The old custom of bending and bowing in front of a visitor was replaced by a handshake and a hugging, reinforced by the kiss on the cheeks, as was the practice introduced by the Portuguese and the French in their 15 or more colonies in Africa. Biomedicine, introduced by the Europeans almost everywhere they resided, experienced a constant struggle with the prevailing traditional medical practices of the continent. Many of the cultural exchanges and impositions were reinforced by the teachings of the Bible, which created a myth among the Africans that the colonizer was invincible and therefore superior, who had the right to rule on the continent because God had so determined. The White newcomer convinced the forced host Africans that he was the only one to have created a civilization and a culture worthy of being spread globally. More critical and lasting European legacy from the enslavement and colonial domination of Africans was the inculcation of the concept of individualism contrasted to the prevailing continental system of communal living and sharing. The forced introduction of monogamy as opposed to the prevailing system of polygamy and extended family changed Africa beyond recognition in a matter of 50 years. Furthermore, the traditional subsistence economic system tied to family agriculture with the primary function of feeding the household began to wane quickly through **forced labor** and the introduction of a capitalist system whose highest aim in the life of the individual was profit at all cost.

Politically, one of the major results of the encounter and interchange between the Europeans and the Africans was the imposition of the concept of a multi-ethnic (but not a multi-language) nation because French, Portuguese, Spanish, or English had to be the sole means of official communication, whose allegiance would be on the president through a complicated electoral process Africans had never seen before. Unfortunately, this forced political system often led to nepotism, corruption, and mismatched priorities following independence during the 1960s and beyond. In sum, the whole African personality, the outlook of the people who had lived their own lives for over 3,000 years, was now completely changed by force whether the colonial system was **assimilation, indirect rule**, or a combination of the two. Unfortunately, throughout the forced changes made, the Africans were the losers at the hands of strangers who were more powerful militarily and highly cunning in every part of the world they had been, based primarily on a system of exploitation of man by man and the use of all local human and material resources to advance capitalism and world domination. It is therefore amazing that Africa was able to survive this ordeal for over 500 years and will continue to be a continent to reckon with in the centuries to come as it looks for its place among the world nations.

Conclusion

The material and cultural interchange between Africa and the rest of the world, particularly Europe, brought many changes to the lives of the Africans, including the new transportation system through, for example, the railroad, the concept of forced labor, the steam engine, new crops, taxes, a capitalist economy, European-modeled schools, new venues of worship in the form of churches and mosques, new languages, new medical or therapeutic practices supplanting the traditional healing system, new weapons used in warfare, new musical instruments, new technology, and new governance—all of which transformed Africa beyond recognition as it entered the twenty-first century.

Science and Technology

When the question about where Africa stands in science and technology compared to other continents of the world is asked, the answer is usually disappointing. One needs to simply visit a major university or medical school in Africa to surmise the state of the scientific advancement produced by African scientists. The limited research conducted by the most advanced, trained university faculty is not basic research but derived from the research of others conducted in the Western world or in China, South Korea, or Japan. Most of the true scientists were educated abroad and dared to come back and contribute to the development of science, technology, engineering, and mathematics in their own countries. Indeed, few advanced laboratories exist in Africa, and most do not have the equipment or the resources to pursue a specific scientific problem that someone in the West has not already tried. Students in the classroom spend most of their time taking copious notes from the instructor or memorizing what they find in books that are written abroad. Slavery, colonialism, a deficient educational system, siphoning national resources for the benefit of a few, and the topography are all elements that, unlike in other continents, has retarded Africa's modern developmental takeoff.

Indeed, Tom Kariuki, writing in *The Guardian*, notes that, in contrast to other continents, if the figures are to be trusted, there are only 79 scientists (some quote the figure of 92 to 198) per 1 million Africans, compared to 4,500 per million in a relatively medium-sized country as the United States. Furthermore, statistics show that the continent of Africa produces only 1.1 percent of the knowledge globally and that faculty research grants from abroad and domestic sources average only $20,000. This explains why research and clinical trials on the major diseases—malaria, HIV, and recently the Ebola virus epidemic, for example—are done either abroad or in Africa by foreign scientists, perhaps with African scientists as appendages. In contrast to the continent of Africa, Brazil, a developing country in Latin America, can boast 656 scientists per 1 million inhabitants, with India surpassing the "old continent" virtually a hundred times. If Africa invests any of its funds, these go mainly as a modicum of investment in economic development and security (the police, the army, and an illegitimate spy system to maintain surveillance over one's political opponents).

An anonymous survey of biologists, chemists, computer scientists, and engineers conducted by the *World Economic Forum* in 2016 found that 76 percent of the student and faculty respondents admitted that their institutions lacked adequate laboratory equipment for research, and 83 percent claimed that research equipment for future research was lacking, while most of their meager grants did not allow spending on these fundamental needs. The survey answers by students found that 91 percent noted that the undergraduate students did not have adequate equipment for hands-on training.

A major reason for the negligible state of science, technology, engineering, and math (STEM) is the insignificant number of students enrolled in higher or "tertiary" education in Africa, the lowest compared to that in other continents, where it is about 7.1 percent compared to 25.1 percent globally. Tunisia, Egypt, Algeria, Mauritius, Morocco, and Cape Verde topped the list as the best performers in this matter, followed by such countries as Botswana, Gabon, and Senegal. The next set of average improvement in enrollment in the study comprised the following countries: Liberia, 17 percent; Nigeria, 10 percent; Guinea, 9 percent; Namibia, 9 percent; Côte d'Ivoire, 8.4 percent; and Cameroon, 7.8 percent. Among the worst stand out Mauritania, Tanzania, Niger, Sierra Leone, Comoros, Eritrea, Chad, and Somalia. The lack of technological savvy and scientific achievements is underscored by the fact that Africa has never produced a car, a motorcycle, or even a bicycle, an airplane, a cell phone, a tablet such as an iPad, computer software, a railroad and locomotive, heavy construction equipment, or a television.

In fact, despite the abundance of oil deposits, Africa has been unable to extract and refine its own oil with its own scientists. The construction of highway roads and bridges is usually left to foreign nationals and firms, usually from China, Japan, and Italy. Simply put, all skills needed for such vital and daily national developmental tasks can be found only among expatriates. Needed equipment supplies are simply imported from Europe, Asia, Australia, or even Latin America. However, more recently, there has been an encouraging realization of the vacuum by African leaders and scientists through increased national rhetoric on basic research, science, and a technology-focused effort to build a brighter future for the continent. The newly founded Alliance for Accelerating Excellence in Science in Africa (AESA), for example, whose director is Tom Kariuki, has been established by the African Academy of Sciences and the African Union's New Partnership for African Development. Together these partners will contribute funds to provide research grants to universities and "…advise them on financial best practices and develop a science strategy for Africa"[6] to improve its scientific basis.

Conclusion

Notwithstanding the nefarious impact of the slave trade, European colonialism and imperialism, and the natural geographic barriers, Africans have survived and are catching up with the rest of the world in every sector of life, including the sphere of technology and science. Indeed, as one lands at an African airport, such as at Nairobi, Cape Town, Cairo, Kigali, Abidjan, Yaoundé, and Entebbe, one might be tempted to think that he or she is landing in Jackson, Mississippi, Pine Bluff, Arkansas, Baltimore, Maryland, or Louisville, Kentucky. Yet, the road to sustainable development is hard and long, but if things do not get better, African leaders have no one else to blame but themselves, given the continent's vast resources, such as oil and gas and the invaluable lessons they should have learned from colonialism, imperialism, and growing neocolonialist trappings, such as those presented by China's growing involvement in the continent's most critical developmental plans, which scholars, astute politicians, and enlightened citizens look at with guarded suspicion.

---

6   Tom Kariuki, "Africa Produces Just 1.1% of Global Scientific Knowledge—but Change is Coming." *The Guardian*, October 26, 2015: 1–3.

Gender and Sexuality

Gender Roles

The issue of gender roles, functions, and responsibilities assigned to men and women on the continent of Africa has been more of a concern among Westerners and educated Africans than among the majority of the Africans. The ascriptive roles determine one's opportunities and relationships in life. Most Africans, even today, including the women themselves, have traditional attitudes and norms that are so entrenched in their minds that at times they defend men who, for example, beat their wives and who force them to have as many children as possible, though they may be convinced that they cannot afford to educate or feed them. Yet, because the man wants it, they submit to his desires and may even tolerate his sexual escapades, whether known publicly or not. To begin with, one may point to the right to polygamy, namely, a man marrying more than one woman. Invariably, however, the woman has no such right or privilege, except figuratively in certain societies on the continent, and the reason is clear: men still have almost absolute power over women.

Following are the 32 countries that allow legal polygamy in Africa: Algeria, Burkina Faso, Burundi, Cape Verde, Cameroon, Central African Republic, Chad, Comoros, Democratic Republic of the Congo, Djibouti, Egypt, Eritrea (only for Muslims), Gabon (here, however, both men and women have the same right, even though only men are actually allowed socially to do this), Gambia, Guinea-Bissau, Kenya (where the law was enacted in 2014), Libya, Malawi, Mali, Mauritania, Morocco, Niger, Rwanda, São Tomé e Príncipe, Senegal, Somalia, South Sudan, Sudan, Tanzania, Togo, Uganda, and Zambia. Ghana prohibits polygamy under civil law but recognizes it by customary law. The courts and the civilian authorities that prohibit the practice look the other way when such cases still occur, especially in the countryside. In the urban areas, many educated and Christianized Africans feel embarrassed when their secret polygamous relationship(s) become publicly known since their church opposes them, lest they be excommunicated.

Interestingly—and ironically—several African leaders have publicly come out as living in a polygamous relationship. For instance, the late Moammar Ghaddafi of Libya is known to have had two wives; ousted president Jacob Zuma of South Africa had five wives before being forced out of office in early 2018; and Eswatini king Mswati III is known to have at least 14 wives and 96 children. Every time Mswati attends a celebration, he may choose any girl for himself and marry her. Former Gambian president Yahya Jammeh has three wives. Traditional King Goodwill Zwelithini of the Zulu in KwaZulu-Natal Province, South Africa, also lives with several wives. In Kenya, where the law allows polygamy, there is a man by the name of Akuku Danger who touts having the number of 100 wives. In general, chiefs and traditional kings tend to have a number of wives. For the common men who are polygamous, the relationship is usually in the form of bigamy or marriage to two women, as one has to be wealthy to afford more than two wives. The example of the African leaders, who often call themselves Christians and educated, makes the crusade against polygamy more difficult for those who think the practice should be eliminated.

In postcolonial Africa, a man is seen as the breadwinner who brings a salary home and pays for the education of his children, particularly the boys, and his brothers and sisters when he can afford it. This is a cultural offshoot from the practice of the extended family that has endured on the continent for the past thousand years. When the husband and wife work, the husband still expects to have priority over what the wife brings home, even though women are beginning to resist this patriarchal custom and practice. The husband is considered to be the head of the family, a practice that unfortunately is reinforced by the teachings of Christianity and Islam. It is important to note here that studies have confirmed that polygamy often results in the spread of infectious diseases, such as HIV/AIDS, because of men's multiple exposure that can easily increase the transmission of infections to co-wives. The issue of circumcision of men to avoid infections is not discussed here because the controversy over what the West has been imposing on male African children has not subsided.

In the rural areas of Africa, gender roles are clearly delineated. The woman works in the fields to sustain the family—which applies to between 60 and 80 percent of the African women. They plant the seeds, clear the shrub, and till the land; they maintain the farm productive; and they do the harvesting. The man, if he does not have a regular job, may cut the trees (usually still with an ax) and then rest throughout the year; he may hunt occasionally; tenders the livestock, a responsibility that is often entrusted to male children, as is the case among the Maasai of Kenya and Tanzania; or fishes, if the family lives near a river. When the household must move to another area, the men are generally responsible for building the new dwellings, but this occurs only occasionally, perhaps in ten years. In most of West Africa, women not only work in the fields using a hoe and are estimated to spend 50 percent more time at work than the men but may also sell their produce at the local open market and engage in what is called the informal business sector. Among the Nandi of Kenya, for instance, even though men and women cultivate the land for crops, the purpose varies—the men cultivate cash crops (tea, coffee, cocoa, and tobacco), while women grow the subsistence crops to help sustain the family. Studies have also shown that, among the Ibo of Nigeria, men grow the cherished big yams and women do cassava, perceived as an inferior and less delicate crop, perhaps because anyone can grow it, consume it, or sell it.

Fetching water is almost entirely a responsibility of the female members of the family, who also take care of the children when they are not in school, the case with millions of African children. Women sweep the compound, grind grain for flour, and prepare the meals for the husband, even if he has nothing to do during the day or when he spends his time playing games, such as the African chess, with his "buddies" under the shade of the compound trees. In East Africa, some women brew beer and sell it to get some cash. Girls are a prize for the family because they represent potential wealth, as in most societies, even today, the bride wealth (known in many parts of Africa as *lobola, lobolo*) must be provided to the parents for the marriage to take place. The type and size of bride wealth, determined only after negotiations have taken place between the two families, may be in the form of currency (upward of $1,000 at times in certain countries such as Uganda), livestock such as cattle and goats, or the groom's service to the future father-in-law for a certain period of time.

The issue of property ownership is always a major item of dissatisfaction and injustice. For example, overall in Africa, it is estimated that only 10 percent of the women own livestock. The bulk of it belongs to the men, who can use it to acquire more wives. The right to divorce is not applied to women but to men, who often may ask for their bride wealth back. This has become a source of major conflicts on the continent; it is the reason countries such as Uganda are trying to make bride wealth voluntary, if not a thing of the past by law. However, currently, a Ugandan court determined in one case that bride wealth must be allowed but not reimbursed when things go wrong in the household. Kenya has outlawed the practice, but people are still clinging to it, especially among the pastoral societies, where cattle have been the required medium to satisfy the requirement from the bride's family. Niger has ruled that the equivalent of about $80 should be the maximum bride wealth, while in Senegal and South Africa, the wealth provided is just symbolic. In Zimbabwe, families are encouraged to negotiate a realistic amount of the *lobola* obligation.

In most of Africa, when the man dies, his widow becomes the "property of the family," as is the case in Uganda and Mozambique, and most often loses any rights to inheritance and becomes the wife of the deceased brother, on the pretext that this arrangement will ensure her lifelong protection. In a nutshell, African women are almost powerless at home; they are objectified; they remain essentially a male possession; and they are simply treated as second-class citizens and can hardly leave the house—"backward" practices that activists, both men and women on the continent, are intent on eliminating sooner than later. Among the Muslims of northern Nigeria, once she is married, the wife is expected to be in the house, period. In one word, young women are therefore treated as the property of the "fathers, the husbands, and the members of the community," all of whom support this system of subordination and discrimination. Progress in changing the customs is occurring extremely slowly.

Sexuality

Sexuality is an abstract but concrete term that refers to one's feelings about their own biological sexual makeup, sexual behavior, sexual orientation, upbringing related to sex matters, sexual expression, sexual identity, sexual taboos and freedom, socio-sexual treatment, and sexual satisfaction in both physical and mental or psychological form. On the world stage, Africa has one of the most unique sex-related mores and norms that often appear to reduce a woman to a sex object in and outside the household. This section of the chapter focuses on the sexual acculturation and the standards of African men and women as members of their society and how they shape their perceptions and conduct as biological humans throughout their lives. Taken as a whole and compared to other people on the globe, the African continent appears to have some of the most resilient sexual norms and practices, when factors are looked at from the perspective of the scientific and cultural evolution of the world as upheld by the United Nations and its agencies, especially the World Health Organization (WHO) and UNESCO. Africans are now at the juncture of deciding whether or not all sexual mores and prescriptions need to be cherished and preserved, adapted to globally accepted practices, or abandoned entirely.

The first point that should be made about sexuality, specifically as it refers to female expectations in Africa, is that sex matters are part of long-standing taboos virtually everywhere on the continent. Thus, a woman is not expected to know, discuss, or show any signs that she enjoys intimacy or intercourse, even when she has reached maturity. As youngsters, females may be instructed by grown and experienced women about the rudiments of sexuality, as might happen during circumcision or the rights of passage, along with other girls of the same age, or when she reaches puberty. However, this is done in secrecy or very privately. Girls and wives are also told that they need to honor the husband's sexual wishes at all times because he is the head of the household and determines how large the family must be. The overarching norm impressed upon women is that their main role in society is to procreate and never to use sex as a part of life enjoyment, as their counterparts in the West do. In Sudan, for example, women who ignore these taboos are suscep-tible to severe sanctions, such as beatings and public humiliation, including open denunciation, and, at times, exile and divorce. There are few exceptions to this cultural standard, as is the case among the Tswana of Botswana and among the !Kung of the Kalahari Desert, where both men and women are allowed to carry on open conversations on sexual matters and openly discuss how enjoyable this private activity might be.

Simply put, in matters of sex and sexuality, nowhere in Africa can women be said to have rights yet. This has resulted in the overwhelming majority of men simply treating a woman as a possession, an entitlement, and an object of pleasure. When these attitudes are reinforced by religious teaching on the supremacy of men as a part of the resilient patriarchal tradition and the long-held belief of the inferiority of women, the abuses are rampant, and include domestic violence, rape, transmission of such infections as HIV (given the prohibition of condom use by men on the pretext that it prevents "flesh-to-flesh contact"), as well as what currently is called female genital mutilation (FGM). One study notes that all kinds of discrimination and unacceptable practices and conditions are prevalent in Africa, including: "the low status [of] women and male dominance in sexuality and economic relations; sexual abuse (particularly of young girls); historic and current separation of families from the migrant labor practices that result in multiple sexual partners; high use of sex workers due to single-sex quarters at the workplace; cultural resistance to the use of condoms; high rates of other STDs; and high levels of poverty and other inequalities, such as access to health care and education."[7]

The issue of the treatment of women, and especially spouse-beating, for example, is common all over the continent, even though some countries are beginning to heed the clamor from the rest of the world. Indeed, sexual harassment at work, school, and home by men, husbands, and even boys, forced and prearranged marriages are crimes that too often go unpunished. The same nonconsensual domestic sex occurrences are frequent but rarely seen as rape. Young women are often forced to marry before they reach the accepted marriageable age, which is between the age of 16 and 18 years, depending on ethnicity and geographic location. As the WHO noted in 2015, in rural Tanzania and Ethiopia, respectively, 56 to 71 percent of the women suffer from beatings or "other forms of violence by husbands and intimate partners." These forms of violence are varied. For instance, in some societies, as is the case of Zimbabwe and Zambia, dry sex is preferred, and women are forbidden from lubricating themselves prior to intercourse.[8] It appears that the reason held is that difficult penetration is more enjoyable to men and prevents women from being seduced too easily by other men, as the practice is painful to her.

As noted above, religion also reinforces the sexual subjugation of women because Africans are taught that "sex as pleasure is counter to fundamentalist or purist thinking that insists on sex as sin, sex as duty, sex as a marital right, and sex as male domination, male gratification and female

---

7   Siegfried John Ngubane, "Gender Roles in the African Culture: Implications for the Spread of HIV/AIDS." (South Africa: Stellenbosch University, unpublished MA thesis, March 2010), 1–64.

8   Diane Civic and David Wilson, "Dry Sex in Zimbabwe and Implications for Condom Use." *Journal of Social Medicine*, 42, 1(1996): 91–98.

procreation and is a sign of male power over female sexuality."[9] Unfortunately, studies have shown that, in 20 African countries, circumcision of girls occurs constantly and that surgery of young women's and girls' genitals is common. The aim of the surgery is to control female sexuality by "making intercourse painful and difficult," which activist, intellectual, and artist Z'étoile Mma sarcastically terms damaging and stupid "Black Pussy Politics" on the continent of Africa.

The unacceptable abuses and slow changes related to sexual conduct and societal expectations occurring in Africa were highlighted in 1998, when a Kenyan policeman by the name of Felix Nthiwa Munayo beat his wife Betty Kavata to the point of paralyzing her and damaging her brain, which led to her death five months later. The sad event galvanized the female community and the media all over the continent, and people began clamoring for respect for women's rights and dignity. As a result, Kenya passed a law against wife-beating and other forms of violence in 2003. However, currently the law is hardly observed, particularly in rural settings. Indeed, up to now, only 25 African countries have passed laws against domestic violence.

In 2018, for example, Somaliland, called in the past the stateless society, passed a law making rape, forced marriage, and trafficking for sexual slavery a crime—an important landmark in this part of Africa. Where the laws are in vigor, the woman must demonstrate signs of physical abuse to police officers, some of whom are among the worst offenders in this respect. Burkina Faso has distinguished itself as having passed laws against female genital mutilation, which, across the continent, still affects 130 million girls annually, causing injuries, infections, and sometimes death, as noted by such experts as the chairwoman of Kenya's Anti-FGM Board, Linah Jebii Kilimo. Rwanda has established "gender desks" in every police precinct to provide a rapid response and counsel to battered women.

The movement defending the rights of women in Africa started with the United Nations Declaration of the International Women's Year in 1972, which was followed by a major world conference organized in Mexico City in 1975 in which 136 nations and 144 international organizations participated. The conference called for the promotion of the "equality between men and women, to insure the full integration of women in the total development effort, and to recognize the importance of the increasing contribution of women to the development of friendly relations among states and the strengthening of international peace."[10] The cause of women's rights was further advanced in 1979 when the UN Convention on the "Elimination of all Forms of Discrimination against Women" (CEDAW) was announced as a universal goal, which was accepted worldwide in 1981. Furthermore, in 1992, any discrimination against women was characterized as a "violation of human rights" and a form of discrimination that "nullified their right to freedom, security, and life."

Finally, we must note, the issue of sexual orientation has continued to be controversial on the continent, as many African leaders claim that homosexuality, lesbian acts, and transgender practices and behavior have never been a part of African culture and have accused the West of trying to impose its own decadent cultural and "family values" on the developing world. The denial of

---

9   Ifi Amadiume, "Sexuality, African Religio-Cultural Traditions and Modernity: Expanding the Lies" (Thornton, Hanover, NH: Department of Religion and African American Studies, online article, 2006), 5.

10   United Nations. *Yearbook of the United Nations* (Boston: Martinus Nijhoff, 1987), 657.

rights, advocated by leaders and hundreds of church goers in such countries as Uganda, is preached and supported by the hundreds of evangelicals who land by the dozens every time a Boeing 787 or an Airbus 380 touches down at Entebbe and several other international airports in Africa. These are the same missionaries who used to tell Africans that God approved sexual intimacy only if couples used the "missionary position" and have recently urged the Ugandan government to pass inhuman anti-gay laws. Virtually all African countries have condemned these supposedly "alien" practices and some have passed stringent laws against same-sex relationships, including Nigeria, Uganda, and Kenya. Thus, by 2018, out of the 54 African states, 33 had passed laws forbidding such relationships that carry horrific penalties.

Fascinating is the fact that Kenya, whose constitution mandates that no one gender should have more than 2/3 of the total number of members in parliament, is in the process of attempting to fulfill the clause. On July 13, 2018, Kenya was the first country in Africa to promote a woman, Mrs. Fatuma Ahmed Mohammed, to the rank of major-general. She had been a brigadier general since 2015. Another encouraging development is a new local Nigerian airline, Air Peace, which just inaugurated its flights with an all-female crew, including the pilots. Worth noting is also the fact that Ellen Johnson Sirleaf, president of Liberia from 2006 to 2018 (Figure 5.3), was the first female in Africa to be elected for such a position, while Joyce Hilda Banda served as president of Malawi from April 2012 to May 2014 when President Binguwa Mutharika died in office. Noteworthy as well is the appointment of Zakia Hussein, holder of a master's degree in international relations from abroad, as the first and youngest Somali general and deputy police chief on August 16, 2018. These cases, however, do not represent a strong or generally approved precedent on the African continent.

FIGURE 5.3   Ellen Johnson Sirleaf, President of Liberia, 2006 to 2018.

Conclusion

In spite of the many obstacles still remaining in Africa, women's rights continue to be upheld slowly but surely every year by human rights organizations, outspoken **civil society**, the United Nations, and individual African men and women. In fact, women have become activists and vocal protesters even in such oppressive countries as Chad. Politically, their participation in elections and appointed positions in government continues to grow, especially in such countries as Senegal, South Africa, Namibia, Mozambique, Ethiopia, and Angola, where many have been elected to parliament or appointed to ministerial positions. Rwanda is said to have made more progress than any other African country in this arena with women, in 2017, occupying 40 seats out of the 80 in the lower house of parliament and 10 out of the 26 in the upper house, coupled with 9 female memberships in ministerial positions out of 19 nationwide. In fact, Rwanda is ranked the seventh globally in the provision of political opportunities for women.

War, Peace, and Diplomacy

For centuries now, every continent has experienced civil or international war (warfare), and Africa is no exception. Unfortunately, despite the frequency of wars on the continent, reliable studies on warfare have been minimal and sporadic, especially regarding pre-colonial wars because, as Mark Grotelueschen notes in *Oxford Bibliographies*, "many historians have tended 'to downplay the importance of military history and the role of conflict in the African historical experience.'" The reasons are not difficult to explain. Wars are painful events that humanity would rather forget due to the deaths they can cause, and writers often feel that, by approaching the subject, they have to take a stand against one of the parties involved. The issue is compounded in Africa by the

FIGURE 5.4   11th East African Division in Burma during World War II.

fact that prior to colonialism, interstate conflicts—for example, as was the case between ancient Egypt and its southern neighbor Kush or Nubia, between Ghana and Mali, or the conflicts in the lake area of East Africa—produced minimal casualties and did not linger as they did later on the African continent during the post-slavery period when relations had been drastically altered.

War and Peace in Pre-colonial Africa

It seems as if, through diplomacy prior to colonialism, the Africa of the past always rebounded back to peace. The other variable in the military realm prior to colonialism is that there was no clear demarcation between the role of the civilian and that of the military that could adequately answer the question about who the agent of war was—the civilian or the military. Timothy Stapleton puts it this way:

> In most of pre-colonial Africa, military structure—like many political and religious institutions—were very distinct from the rest of society. Those who formed armies when needed also had productive duties such as growing crops, clearing land, tending livestock, or building shelters. Leaders during war often had judicial, ritual, and other responsibilities. Though there were notable exceptions, most pre-colonial African states did not have professional militaries in the Western sense of a standing force meant to be constantly ready for conflict. African rules and subordinate rulers usually maintained a small core of specialist warriors at their residence and during times of war men would be called to leave their farms or fishing villages to form an army for a specific purpose.[11]

This meant that war could not just be declared at the whims of the civilian or military leader because there were local and internal consequences resulting from such a declaration given the various responsibilities "soldiers" or, better said, "warriors" had as civilians. From this researcher's studies of warfare in Central Africa, it appears that the newer war weaponry, of which Africans could avail themselves—including the weaponry they themselves manufactured—the more frequent wars appeared to be an initiative of the stronger, and the more violent and deadly the conflicts were. Since the fifteenth century, several African coastal rulers were able to import guns and gun powder, improve their use at war, and adjust the position of the infantry while perfecting the volleys, at times from stolen or confiscated cannons, even if the warriors were using spears and arrows. The effective use of the cavalry, however, was always a plus, despite the symbolism the horse represented in people's minds. Indeed, even with its wide use in this part of Africa,

> ... the horse lost some of its usefulness in the post-1860 period as firearms became more available and were more effectively deployed. The horse's natural advantage and usefulness, stemming from its use as a shock force against enemy troops, had always been offset by the costs related to its health and maintenance. In addition, because it was

---

11   Timothy Stapleton, *A Military History of Africa: The Pre-Colonial Period from Ancient Egypt to the Zulu Kingdom (Earliest Times ca. 1870)* (Oxford, England: Praeger, 2013).

associated with the nobility and theocratic warrior rulers and their slaving activities, the horse remained a symbol of oppression par excellence among virtually all non-Muslim populations in Central Sudan.[12]

Primary Source 1

The following excerpts from speeches by the first African presidents in sub-Saharan Africa, at times called the Founding Fathers of the modern states on the continent, are of special interest and weight because they reveal what many of these envisioned the future of the continent would be following the independence of the first sub-Saharan African country, Ghana, in 1957. The excerpts are declarations by the new leaders, listened to by the Africans of the era, and are authentic in that they have been kept intact in archives. In one word, primary sources are contemporaneous to the events that are known to have happened in the past and may be in the form of writings, witnesses, pictures, objects, voices, autobiographies, newspaper articles, diaries, memoirs, and official government documents. Students should understand that primary sources carry more weight than secondary or tertiary sources.

Visions of independence, then and now

The Early Years

"Dawn of a new era"

Kwame Nkrumah, first president of Ghana, 23 September 1960, at the UN General Assembly in New York

One cardinal fact of our time is the momentous impact of Africa's awakening upon the modern world. The flowing tide of African nationalism sweeps everything before it and constitutes a challenge to the colonial powers to make a just restitution for the years of injustice and crime committed against our continent ... For years, Africa has been the foot-stool of colonialism and imperialism, exploitation and degradation. From the north to the south, from the east to the west, her sons languished in the chains of slavery and humiliation, and Africa's exploiters and self-appointed controllers of her destiny strode across our land with incredible inhumanity without mercy, without shame, and without honor.

Those days are gone and gone forever, and now I, an African, stand before this august Assembly of the United Nations and speak with a voice of peace and freedom, proclaiming to the world the dawn of a new era. I look upon the United Nations as the only organization that holds out any hope for the future of mankind ... The United Nations must therefore face up to its responsibilities, and

---

12   Mario J. Azevedo, *Roots of Violence: A History of War in Chad* (Amsterdam, Netherlands: Gordon and Breach Publishers, 4, War and Society Series, 1988), 63.

ask those who would bury their heads like the proverbial ostrich in their imperialist sands, to pull their heads out and look at the blazing African sun now travelling across the sky of Africa's redemption. The United Nations must call upon all nations that have colonies in Africa to grant complete independence to the territories still under their control ... This is a new day in Africa and as I speak now, thirteen new African nations have taken their seats this year in this august Assembly as independent sovereign states ... There are now twenty-two of us in this Assembly and there are yet more to come.

"Hard work from every citizen"

Jomo Kenyatta, first president of Kenya, 27 May 1963, after he won elections and months before independence

On this momentous day, which set Kenya on the final stage before independence, I ask the cooperation of every man and woman in this land to help build a new nation. We aim to create a fair society, where no citizen need suffer in sickness because he cannot pay for treatment. We believe that no child should go without education merely because his family is poor. It will be the government's intention to do away with the terrible poverty of so many of our people. We do not expect to do all this from foreign charity. We are not going to compromise our independence by begging for assistance. The government will make it clear that our progress, our hope, our ambitions will only be fulfilled if we have hard work from every citizen.

"Honored and humbled"

Edward Frederick Mutesa II, first president of Uganda, 9 October 1962, independence address

I feel both honored and humbled ... because I have lived till this day when the British have relinquished power into our hands, after being under their protection for a period of 68 years [as a "protectorate" of Britain]. Now that we are independent, I appeal to you all to work with all your might in whatever you shall do, so as to bring glory to both our kingdoms and the state of Uganda. Let us not allow our differences in nations, religion and color to be a divisive factor among our people.

"Reorient the entire colonial heritage"

Ahmed Sékou Touré, first president of Guinea, 26 August 1958

We prefer poverty in freedom to opulence in slavery ... We do not confuse the joys of independence with separation from France, to which we intend to remain tied and with which we want to collaborate in building up our common riches ... Beyond a simple feeling of revolt, we are resolute and conscious participants in the political evolution of black Africa, a basic condition to reorient the entire colonial heritage towards and for the African peoples.

"We want to remain French"

Philibert Tsiranana, first president of Madagascar, speaking before the French National Assembly, 29 May 1958

We think it is better to have a well-prepared independence, since the anticipated political independence will lead us to the worst dependence possible, economic dependence. We will continue to have confidence in France and count on the French genius to find, when the time comes, a formula similar to that of the British Commonwealth. We Malagasies would never want to separate from France. We are of the French culture, and we want to remain French.

"Your suffering has not been in vain"

Félix Houphouët-Boigny, first president of Côte d'Ivoire, 7 August 1960, independence address

People of my country, let your joy burst forth. There is no other people that deserves its joy more. More than the others, you have long suffered in patience. But your suffering has not been in vain. You have struggled, but not uselessly, since today you know victory. The need for dignity that you carry within yourselves has finally been satisfied. You are free and with pride join the great family of nations.

"Independence was conquered through struggle"

Patrice Lumumba, prime minister of the Congo, 30 June 1960, independence address

Even though this independence for the Congo is being proclaimed today in agreement with Belgium, a country with which we deal as equals, no Congolese worthy of that name can ever forget that independence was conquered through struggle, a daily struggle, a fierce and idealist struggle, a struggle in which we spared neither our energy, nor our hardship, nor our suffering, nor our blood. ... Because of what we have gone through during 80 years of a colonial regime, our wounds are still too fresh and painful for us to chase them from our memories. We have known hard labor for which we were paid salaries that could not properly feed us, nor dress or house us decently, nor raise our dear children. We have been mocked, insulted and struck morning, noon and night because we are [black] ... The Republic of the Congo has been proclaimed and our dear country is now in the hands of its own children. Together, my brothers and sisters, we will begin a new struggle, a magnificent struggle that will lead our country to peace, prosperity and greatness. We will together establish social justice and ensure that everyone receives just pay for their labor. We will show the world what the black man can do when he works in freedom, and we will make the Congo a radiant centre for all of Africa. We will be attentive so that the soil of our homeland really benefits its children. We will review all the old laws and make new ones that are just and noble. We will end the suppression of free thinking and ensure that all citizens can freely enjoy the fundamental freedoms outlined in the [Universal] Declaration of Human Rights. ...

As you analyze the pronouncements of Africa's Independence Founding Fathers, can you discern the subtle differences between their personal philosophies and the common social and political thinking they aspired to despite the varied colonial legacy they inherited?

Discussion Questions

1. What are the salient and common points you detect in the speeches by these first leaders of independent leaders following colonial rule?
2. Select one Founding Father president and compare and contrast it with a new president elected during the 2000s on the African continent.

Primary Source 2

The author urges the students to consider the problems of inequality of women all over the world have experienced. Looking at women today, we must try to understand how far, even in the United States, we have come in the path toward guaranteeing human and citizens' rights to all people, regardless of gender, as advocated by the United Nations Declarations. Therefore, for Primary Source 2 to be useful, the whole class should read the excerpts and come prepared to discuss their importance in the classroom, pointing to the differences between these contemporaneous (primary) sources to women's struggles to be treated as human beings and not as second-class citizens. They need to compare these sources with those they may be familiar with, such as the television, and the voices of their own parents and those who fought to restore the dignity of all men and women on our planet.

Excerpts from the United Nations Fourth World Conference on Women
Beijing, China–September 1995–Action for Equality, Development and Peace

Platform for Action

Human Rights of Women Diagnosis

Strategic objective I.1. Promote and protect the human rights of women, through the full implementation of all human rights instruments, especially the Convention on the Elimination of All Forms of Discrimination against Women. Actions to be taken.

Strategic objective I.2. Ensure equality and non-discrimination under the law and in practice. Actions to be taken.

Strategic objective I.3. Achieve legal literacy. Actions to be taken.

I. Human Rights of Women

1. Human rights and fundamental freedoms are the birthright of all human beings; their protection and promotion is the first responsibility of Governments.

2. The Platform for Action reaffirms that all human rights—civil, cultural, economic, political and social, including the right to development—are universal, indivisible, inter-dependent and interrelated, as expressed in the Vienna Declaration and Program of Action adopted by the World Conference on Human Rights. The Conference reaffirmed that the human rights of women and the girl child are an inalienable, integral and indivisible part of universal human rights. The full and equal enjoyment of all human rights and fundamental freedoms by women and girls is a priority for Governments and the United Nations and is essential for the advancement of women.

3. Equal rights of men and women are explicitly mentioned in the Preamble to the Charter of the United Nations. All the major international human rights instruments include sex as one of the grounds upon which States may not discriminate.

4. Every person should be entitled to participate in, contribute to and enjoy cultural, economic, political and social development. In many cases women and girls suffer discrimination in the allocation of economic and social resources. This directly violates their economic, social and cultural rights.

5. Bearing in mind the Program of Action of the International Conference on Population and Development[14] and the Vienna Declaration and Program of Action[2] adopted by the World Conference on Human Rights, the Fourth World Conference on Women reaffirms that reproductive rights rest on the recognition of the basic right of all couples and individuals to decide freely and responsibly the number, spacing and timing of their children and to have the information and means to do so, and the right to attain the highest standard of sexual and reproductive health. It also includes their right to make decisions concerning reproduction free of discrimination, coercion and violence, as expressed in human rights documents.

6. Violence against women both violates and impairs or nullifies the enjoyment by women of human rights and fundamental freedoms. Taking into account the Declaration on the Elimination of Violence against Women and the work of Special Rapporteurs, gender-based violence, such as battering and other domestic violence, sexual abuse, sexual slavery and exploitation, and international trafficking in women and children, forced prostitution and sexual harassment, as well as violence against women, resulting from cultural prejudice, racism and racial discrimination, xenophobia, pornography, ethnic cleansing, armed conflict, foreign occupation, religious and anti-religious extremism and terrorism are incompatible with the dignity and the worth of the human person and must be combated and eliminated. Any harmful aspect of certain traditional, customary or modern practices that violates the rights of women should be prohibited and eliminated. Governments should take urgent action to combat and eliminate all forms of violence against women in private and public life, whether perpetrated or tolerated by the State or private persons.

7. Many women face additional barriers to the enjoyment of their human rights because of such factors as their race, language, ethnicity, culture, religion, disability or socio-economic class or because they are indigenous people, migrants, including women migrant workers, displaced women or refugees. They may also be disadvantaged and marginalized by a general lack of knowledge and recognition of their human rights as well as by the obstacles they meet in gaining access to information and recourse mechanisms in cases of violation of their rights.

Strategic objective I.1.

Promote and protect the human rights of women, through the full implementation of all human rights instruments, especially the Convention on the Elimination of All Forms of Discrimination against Women

Actions to be taken

By Governments:

a. Work actively towards ratification of or accession to and implement international and regional human rights treaties;

b. Consider drawing up national action plans identifying steps to improve the promotion and protection of human rights, including the human rights of women, as recommended by the World Conference on Human Rights;

c. Address the acute problems of children, inter alia, by supporting efforts in the context of the United Nations system aimed at adopting efficient international measures for the prevention and eradication of female infanticide, harmful child labor, the sale of children and their organs, child prostitution, child pornography and other forms of sexual abuse and consider contributing to the drafting of an optional protocol to the Convention on the Rights of the Child;

Strategic objective I.2.

Ensure equality and non-discrimination under the law and in practice

Actions to be taken

By Governments: [...]

a. Take urgent action to combat and eliminate violence against women, which is a human rights violation, resulting from harmful traditional or customary practices, cultural prejudices and extremism.

Discussion Questions

As you read and critically examine the United Nations Declaration of the Human Rights of Women, answer the following questions:

1. What do you think finally prompted the declaration advanced by the world community?
2. Why haven't all nations of the world signed and implemented the declaration?
3. What are the underlying shortcomings of the United Nations, and what do you think is the future of the declaration on women's rights?

It must be noted here that the military conditions in Africa did not differ globally from those in societies that were or had experienced the same socio-political developments and similar internal or external challenges, as was the case of several dynasties in Asia, including Japan, India, and China (Reid, *Warfare in African History*).[13]

---

13 Richard J. Reid, *Warfare in African History* (New York: Cambridge University Press, 2012).

Response to Colonial Occupation: War and Diplomacy

Following the invasion and conquest of Africa by the Europeans during the late nineteenth century, armed resistance spread over parts of continent during the 1880s-1890s, including the tax revolts in Zimbabwe; the Macossa uprisings against the Portuguese government in Mozambique; and the Mahdist Rebellion in Sudan against Egyptian rule. However, many of the violent occurrences were short-lived and of low intensity, and so little has been recorded about them in the colonial archives. These could be seen as attempts on the part of the conquered Africans at recovering their lost independence. During the colonial period and following the first cases of peaceful achievement of independence, violence was a rare occasion. Good examples include the former British colonies and some of the French territories during the late 1950s—Egypt, Morocco, Libya in 1956, and Ghana in 1957, and most of the French and British colonies and the Belgian Congo in the 1960s.

Violent resistance occurred in Angola, Guinea-Bissau, and Mozambique against the Portuguese (1960s–1975); Algeria against the French (1962–1964); Southern Rhodesia, now Zimbabwe (1974–1980) against the White regime; Namibia (1966–1990) against the White South Africans who controlled this former German territory in the aftermath of World War I (1914–1918); and Eritrea against Ethiopia (1956–1991), which led to the independence of the former in 1991. The Spanish territories (Equatorial Guinea and Western Sahara) did not resort to guerrilla warfare, even though some violent clashes occurred, especially in Western Sahara (now called the Sahrawi (Arab Democratic Republic) against Morocco, which has yet to achieve its independence, even though 44 countries at the United Nations and the African Union have recognized it as the 55th independent country in Africa. Equatorial Guinea became independent on October 12, 1968. The end of apartheid, or White separatist rule in South Africa occurred in 1992 after a protracted and sporadic violent resistance by the African National Congress and the Pan-African Congress. This paved the way for the first African government led by Nelson Mandela in 1994.

However, following almost three decades of African independence (1950–1980s), several military coups and attempted coups, most of which bloody, occurred particularly during the 1970s and 1980s. These revolutions were preceded by a totally unexpected but successful *coup d'état* of President Sylvanus Olympio in Togo on January 13, 1963, and the overthrow of the internally popular and internationally known President Kwame Nkrumah of Ghana in 1966. With its abundant natural resources, Nigeria, the most populous country in Africa, achieved its independence in 1960 and underwent several brutal military coups and rule of the military until the 1990s. Between 1967 and 1970, Nigeria experienced a major bloody civil conflict, the Biafran War, as it was called, waged by the Ibo of eastern Nigeria against the central government, then dominated by the Yoruba and the Hausa.

Historians and political scientists agree that between 1956 (when the first cases of independence began to surface, especially in North Africa) and the mid-1980s, there were 56 successful military coups in 26 sub-Saharan African countries; 14 experienced more than one coup; Benin had 6 and Ghana 5 (similar events took place in North Africa, as was the case in Egypt and Libya). Even though **civil wars** did occur in post-independence Africa, these were few and were based mostly on ethnic rivalries. The same may be said of the international wars on the continent: they have been few so far. Following is a list of the most important wars in post-independence Africa, with their causes briefly outlined, and a discussion of how diplomacy has been able to resolve them peacefully, sometimes through the United Nations or the African Union peacekeeping forces.

First of all, there has been virtually no inter-African war, except when one country has had to assist a neighbor threatened by the other. Second, most conflicts in Africa have been internal, as has been the case of the Democratic Republic of the Congo when they have flared on and off since 1998. Unfortunately, the civil war that started then but ended in a peace agreement in 2004 killed at least 5.4 million people. As a result of the deaths from this internal conflict and the fact that for the first time nine African countries (Democratic Republic of the Congo, Rwanda, Namibia, Zimbabwe, Angola, Ghana, Chad, Libya, and Sudan) banded together to defeat the enemies of the late Laurent Kabila, the self-appointed president of the Democratic Republic of the Congo. Observers have compared the struggle in the Congo with World War II, terming it the globe's most violent incident since 1945.

The war of independence of South Sudan against the Sudanese government lasted from the 1960s to 2005, ending through mediation by the African Union, the United Nations, and the United States government. Paradoxically, South Sudan has been engaged in its own civil war since 2013, stemming from former Vice President Riek Machar's defiance of the authority of the country's president, Salva Kiir. Serious peace talks took place in Addis Ababa at the request of Ethiopia's Prime Minister Abiy Ahmed and subsequently in Khartoum in June 2018. Yet, diplomacy did not bring an immediate peaceful resolution of the problem. However, in July 2018, the two enemies agreed to a cease-fire, allowing the former vice president to resume his responsibilities in a suddenly reconciled South Sudan. Whether this agreement will hold in the future is still an open question.

The civil war in Somalia has been raging ever since 1991, even though a new government was finally installed during the mid-2000s. Yet, the deadly attacks by the terrorist organization Al-Shabab have caused many casualties, particularly in the capital city, Mogadishu, the reason observers have dubbed Somalia Africa's "stateless" country. The Angolan civil war erupted immediately after independence from Portugal in 1975 between the two liberation movements—the National Union for the Total Independence of Angola (UNITA) led by Jonas Savimbi, and the Popular Movement for the Liberation of Angola (MPLA) led by Agostinho Neto first, and later, by Eduardo dos Santos. The MPLA finally emerged as the victor in 2012. The same scenario was repeated in Mozambique and came out of the liberation war victorious against the Portuguese in 1975. Two years later, the rule by the Front for the Liberation of Mozambique (FRELIMO) was challenged by the force of arms by the late Afonso Dhlakama and his Mozambique National Resistance (RENAMO) until a peace agreement mediated by the Catholic Church and the Italian government was signed in October 1992.

This war between the Front for the Liberation of Mozambique (FRELIMO) and the Mozambique National Resistance Movement (RENAMO) killed thousands of Mozambicans and destroyed much of the country's infrastructure. In Uganda, Yoweri Museveni helped oust Idi Amin when he joined a Tanzanian invading force in 1979 and seized power from President Milton Obote in 1986. Museveni has been president since then, with the distinction of having been elected five times. Since 1987, President Museveni has remained Uganda's strongman against the Lord's Resistance Army insurgency led by Joseph Kony. In fact, Museveni pursued Kony all the way into the Central African Republic, deciding to stop the operation (which received assistance from the United States) only in 2017 because, he said, the rebel leader had been completely weakened. Liberia has had two civil wars, one in 1987–1997 and the other in 1999–2003, in which Guinea became involved in favor of one of the rebel groups. Sierra Leone had two of its own civil wars in 1991–2002. In 2012, one of the most recent civil wars occurred in the Central African Republic, which saw the temporary intervention of Chadian forces and a UN peace keeping force to quell a Muslim insurgent group and a dispute over presidential elections. The situation was still precarious as late as 2019.

Rwanda experienced a short but bloody civil war in 1994 when a band of the Hutu people, calling themselves "those who attack together" (INTERAHAMWE) began slaughtering the Tutsi on April 7, 1994, in a move that has been internationally called a genocide attempt. In July 1994, however, a Tutsi militia, calling itself the Rwanda Patriotic Front, defeated the rebels. As a result of this deadly civil war, 2 million people sought refuge in the neighboring Democratic Republic of the Congo, partly sparking the second Congo War in 2003. In Rwanda, the number of dead from the carnage has been estimated at 500,000–1,000,000, 70 percent of whom are said to have been Tutsi. Chad, of course, has experienced coups and countercoups since April 1975, when François Tombalbaye was fatally shot by the army in 1975. His successor, Félix Malloum, was removed from office following a diplomatic initiative by Nigeria that created a national union government (GUNT) led by one of the rebel leaders, Goukouni Oueddei. In1982, Hissène Habré removed the latter from power using his own private army, the *Armée de Résistance Nationale*. In December 1990, the current President Idriss Déby Itno, benefiting from French tacit support, entered N'Djamena, Chad's capital, almost unopposed, as the new president. However, until a few years ago, about a dozen rebel groups have consistently threatened the government, particularly in 2008, but Déby has survived and has been reelected five times after changing the constitution to allow him to run for more than two terms.

Relatively speaking, however, as already noted, one can say that over the past 20 years, Africa has not seen major conflicts that have caused innumerable deaths, even though from time to time soldiers have toppled a government and people have been imprisoned, tortured, and even killed. Consequently, one can accurately posit that Africa has been relatively at peace, with the exception of the Democratic Republic of the Congo. Indeed, most of the conflicts have been brief and ended through diplomatic intervention by the African Union and the United Nations or through bilateral agreements. On the world stage, therefore, the continent is seen as peaceful, notwithstanding that many people have suffered from political persecution, internal social dislocation, and incredibly severe refugee conditions abroad. In fact, the United Nations estimates that of the 65,500,000 displaced people on the global scale, 26 percent—that is, over 17 million—are Africans found in and outside the continent. Many, for example, leave their homes through or from North Africa heading for Europe across the Mediterranean Sea on some of the most dangerous ships, boats, and ferries, on a voyage that has caused several hundreds of deaths, particularly in the wake of the Arab Spring in 2011. Infectious diseases, such as malaria and HIV, are also decimating millions of citizens, especially children under five, because the leaders, mired in rampant corruption, have had no clear vision for the future of the continent and have priorities that are completely mismatched with African realities.

Finally, this author feels compelled to mention here that the ravages by Al-Shabab in Somalia and Kenya, Boko Haram in Nigeria, Niger, Chad, Cameroon, the Central African Republic, and now in Northern Mozambique, and the terrorists allied to the Middle Eastern Islamist movements, such as Al-Qaeda and perhaps ISIS, in Mali, Libya, and Niger, have resulted in several casualties that have disturbed the peace of the region. However, through the action of local governments, assisted by such Western powers as the United States and France, the influence of terrorist organizations appears to be waning, and hopefully the future will be brighter.

Additionally, a word should be said about the so-called Arab Spring. The Arab Spring refers to a series of protests and demonstrations that began in North Africa, erupting between January and November 2011 and resulting in changes in the political and economic realms in Tunisia, Egypt, Libya, Yemen, Syria, and Bahrain, all countries that have been governed by authoritarian regimes. The movement started when an unknown Mohamed Bouazizi of Tunisia set himself on fire outside a government building following his arrest by police for running a vegetable counter without a license on December 17, 2010. The political commotion that followed his arrest was strong enough to force the president of Tunisia, Zine El Abidine Ben Ali, who had been in power since 1987, to resign and flee to Saudi Arabia on January 14, 2011. In Egypt, demonstrators gathered almost daily at Tahrir Square in Cairo, leading to the unexpected resignation of Hosni Mubarak on February 11, 2011. Mubarak had been president for 29 years. In Syria, there were democratic but peaceful protests beginning March 15, 2011, against President Bashar al-Assad, led by the group that called itself the Free Syrian Army. The movement precipitated the continuing current civil chaos in that country.

In Morocco, using brutal means, the police tried to quell the protesters on May 22, 2011. The result was the adoption of a new constitution that chipped away some of the king's power. In Egypt's neighboring country, Libya, demonstrations against Muammar Gaddafi, Libya's strongman for 41 years, were followed by angry protesters who gathered and attempted to take control of the city of Tripoli. American and French encouragement resulted in Muammar Gaddafi's assassination in a tunnel on October 20, 2011. By September 23, 2011, the Arab Spring had spread to Yemen, where people led a "Million Man March" demanding a democratic government. President Ali Abdullah Saleh resigned from power in February 2012, only to be killed five years later. In response to the demonstrations, while Tunisia held its first democratic parliamentary elections on October 23, 2011, Egypt held its own on November 28, 2011, followed by presidential elections in June 2012, with radical Mohammed Morsi being elected president. However, Morsi was removed from office by a military coup in July 2013. The army has since controlled the country.

The situation in North Africa resembles that of most of sub-Saharan Africa in its movement toward democratic governance during the 1990s. This means that North Africa is still going through the agony of authoritarianism, whose end is still not clear. Libya is in disarray caused by groups allied to ISIS and other rebel movements from the Middle East, which the present fragile government is attempting to defeat and restore law and order. Both Syria and Yemen are still experiencing a civil war that has killed thousands of people and caused many to seek refuge elsewhere in the world. Here, however, the military have been playing a role the population did not expect, despite the apparent strength of protesters and reformers who, unfortunately, could not unite to demand changes with one voice, and where the established structure was so deeply entrenched in governance even after the fall of the autocratic regimes—just as it happened in the rest of Africa decades ago.

Peace, Diplomacy, and Democracy

Multiparty Democracy: Africa's Second Independence

Prior to the 1960s and 1970s, independent multiparty systems were common in Africa, as was the case in Ghana, Nigeria, Tanganyika, Côte d'Ivoire, Algeria, Tunisia, and Chad. However, in the name of unity and as a strategy to prevent "tribal" or ethnic conflicts that could lead to the destruction of the new nations, the founding fathers, or the new African presidents of the time, including Julius Nyerere in Tanganyika, Jomo Kenyatta in Kenya, Félix Houphouët-Boigny in Côte d'Ivoire, Léopold Senghor in Senegal, and Kenneth Kaunda in Zambia, a single-party system was maintained, either through constitutional changes or by force. Notable exceptions occurred in Botswana and the Gambia, which had maintained a democratic system for decades. The growing outcry of civil society for a return to the multiparty system and the continent's economic hardships during the 1980s, particularly after the International Monetary Fund forced Africans to scale back their social programs, led Africans to try implementing more realistic and pragmatic policies. This environment was enhanced by the end of the **Cold War**, which saw both the former Soviet Union and the United States disentangle themselves from their sought-after spheres of influence on the continent and the growing demands by a new generation of Africans who had not experienced colonialism.

The military had already worsened the political and economic conditions with coups that in most cases brought more misery and violence to the continent, contradicting the very national pronouncements on the need for change from those who engendered the violent coups and countercoups that toppled civilian governments—namely, the military. From 1990 to 2001, a period called Africa's Second Liberation or Second Independence, the continent experienced 50 attempted military coups, 13 of them successful, despite the fact that several of the leaders had been elected and reelected following the changes brought about by the new wave of **multiparty democracy** that also determined the terms of office for the presidency and the parliament called the national assembly in the former French colonies. Yet, notwithstanding the obstacles, the ideals of a multiparty system with free elections, and the defense of citizens' freedoms and the demand for due process never died on the continent. Indeed, the political pressure has intensified in our own days, as underscored by the unthinkable ousters of the late 93-year-old strongman and dictator Robert Mugabe in Zimbabwe in late 2017 and that of 76-year-old Jacob Zuma in South Africa in early 2018. With these changes and others, coupled with relatively better economic performance since the mid-2000s, Africa seems to have ceased being the pariah continent, unlike Latin America and Asia, which achieved their independence during the nineteenth century.

As noted in this chapter, notwithstanding the political turmoil in the Democratic Republic of the Congo, most of Africa is at peace, while low intense conflict still exists in several of the 54 independent countries, including Mozambique, Burundi, Chad, Darfur in Sudan, and the Central

African Republic. The conflicts are exacerbated by corruption and graft, manipulation of election results, and persecution of opponents. What is needed now, to restore Africa's democracy and its rightful place on the international stage, is a stronger civil society; a younger and more visionary millennial generation; better use of the vast but wasted national resources that could assist Africans in feeding themselves; redoubling the effort to provide free education and free health care to the millions of Africans who are unnecessarily suffering and dying every day; and rescuing the crumbling infrastructure, especially in the rural areas. The 2011 Arab Spring can therefore be seen as a delayed manifestation of the same ideals that gripped sub-Saharan Africa toward a democratic governance frenzy that began during the 1990s.

As to the future of Africa and how the continent can come out of its political and economic quagmire, scholars from the Brookings Institution are right on target when they consider the year 2018 as a critical time for Africa to "unleash its inner strengths" if it wishes to join the international community with dignity. Its leaders are urged to strive for self-reliance through enhanced domestic resource mobilization, the sharing of prosperity with the masses "while tackling the stubborn human development challenges," scaling down the level of absolute poverty, and preventing the massive migration of people from the continent. The report further stresses the importance of new structural transformation that improves automation, challenges the failure of "scale up sustainable financing," and alters the course of the faltering progress and the continued "disempowerment of women," strengthened by an expansion of the tourist industry. Finally, the accelerated use of technology and innovation and the reshaping of policies and relationships globally, including those with the United States and China (the latter being seen in countries such as Kenya as introducing a new form of racist neocolonialism), must be pursued with deliberate urgency. Only the enactment of such priority goals and vision will allow Africa to play a major role on the world scene, nurturing a future that focuses on its people rather than on parochial interests that cater to the needs of the most prominent of its citizens, as is currently the case in most of the continent.[14]

Conclusion

Since the seventeenth century, humanity has experienced many unnecessary wars that could have been avoided through diplomacy: the Thirty Years' War, the Crimean War, the wars of the unification of Germany and Italy, World War I and World War II, the **liberation wars** in Latin America and Africa, and many others. The formation of new, modern, and permanent nation-states with the exclusive implications of the concept of nationalism was a major driving force behind the wars, as were the colonial and imperial designs of Europe and the impetus of the Industrial Revolution, which encouraged militarism and extreme nationalism. In the process, millions of people lost their lives or were displaced internally or became refugees in unknown lands. Yet, the rational tendency of the times had been the use of diplomacy, meaning dialogue and compromise. Unfortunately, most of the major international conflicts were resolved through war, and it was hoped that the world would see the value of human life and not resort to violent and deadly means.

---

14   Brookings Institution, "Foresight Africa: Top Priorities for the Continent in 2018" (Washington, DC: Thursday, January 2018), 1–8.

However, the hope in that concept was often dashed when a nation decided to declare war, as happened in World War and World War II and other violent confrontations, which also spread to the African continent when the concept of a European nation-state was imposed among the ethnic groups without careful consideration of their history.

Chapter Summary

This chapter focused on the most neglected, denigrated, and misunderstood continent of the world, Africa, the second largest in surface area and demographically the fastest growing on the globe. Most archaeologists and anthropologists are convinced that Africa is the cradle of humankind where the first lifestyles, such as hunting, cattle-raising or pastoral life, transhumance, and the pursuit of agriculture, appeared. Yet, the African continent and its people underwent so many unpleasant and excruciating experiences that situated them as if they were the curse of the earth—virtually a people without a history or culture that was worth preserving, vividly reflected in the imposition of slavery and the slave trade during the fifteenth century, followed by the European conquest. Through sheer resolve and use of its environmental and human resources, the continent was able to rebound and carve its due place in history, thus becoming a part of the international community.

Discussion Questions

1. Africa lags behind most continents in technology, inventions, and infrastructure. Can you suggest the reasons why, as you look at the development of Africa compared to other continents of the world, especially during the late nineteenth and mid-twentieth centuries? Do you agree with the late Guianese historian Walter Rodney, who, in his book *How Europe Underdeveloped Africa* (1982), blamed the Europeans?
2. In light of what you learned from the chapter, your own readings, and your professor's lectures, do you think most Africans are poor and live on less than $2.50 a day because of a lack of natural and human resources? Explain.
3. What do you think are the major natural obstacles to Africa's conquest of infectious diseases compared, for example, to the Western world, where most of them have been eradicated or at least controlled? Do you agree or not that prevention is better than treatment of disease? Would you say, as some do sarcastically, that the Ministries of Health in Africa are nothing more than Ministries of Disease?
4. Check the Internet and find out how multi-party democracy might be practiced in Africa and name some countries that have done better than others in this aspect. What are the signs that a country is democratically or autocratically governed?
5. How did social and natural scientists portray Africa to the world through what now are called stereotypes and myths that still linger within certain circles, including the academy? Do you think that Africans have done anything worth mentioning in the history of humankind? Elaborate with examples from the continent's material culture, resilience in the face of adversity, and international challenges.

FIGURE 5.5 Independent Africa's Founding Fathers: Fulbert Youlou, Congo-Brazzaville; David Dacko, Central African Republic (former Oubangui-Chari); Emperor Haile Selassie, Ethiopia; Jomo Kenyatta, Kenya; Unidentified; Joseph Sese Seko Mobutu, Democratic Republic of the Congo (the Former Zaire and Belgian Congo).

References

Using the Sources

Beyond the primary sources provided in this chapter, students will benefit from analyzing maps and images provided and additional readings and materials cited below. Students and instructors may find film and literary adaptations particularly helpful in the classroom or as additional assignments. References and suggested supplementary sources are provided.

Primary Sources

Africa Renewal. August 2010. "Visions of Independence, Then and Now." (See https://www.un.org/africarenewal/magazine/august-2010/visions-independence-then-and-now).

United Nations. 1995. Excerpts from the United Nations "DECLARATION OF THE HUMAN RIGHTS OF WOMEN." The United Nations. Fourth World Conference on Women. New York: United Nations. (See http://www.un.org/womenwatch/daw/beijing/platform/human.htm).

Secondary Sources

Abiola, Irele. 1990. *The African Experience in Literature and Ideology.* Indianapolis, IN: Indiana University Press.

Amadiume, Ifi. 2018. "Sexuality, African Religio-Cultural Traditions and Modernity: Expanding the Lens," 1–9.

Azevedo, Mario J. 1981. "The Human Price of Development: The Congo-Brazzaville Railroad and the Sara of Chad." *African Studies Review,* Vol. XXIV, 1(1981): 1–20.

———. 1988. *Roots of Violence: A History of War in Chad.* Amsterdam, Netherlands: Gordon and Breach Publishers, Vol. 4 (War and Society Series).

———. 2005. Mario J. Azevedo (ed.). *Africana Studies: A Survey of Africa and the African Diaspora.* Durham, NC: Carolina Academic Press, 3rd edition.

Britton, Kenneth, Gianmaria Martini, and David Scotti (eds.). 2015. *The Economics and Political Economy of African Air Transportation.* New York: Routledge.

Brookings Institution Report. January 11, 2018. "Foresight Africa: Top Priorities for the Continent in 2018." Washington, DC, 1–8.

Civic, Diane, and David Wilson. 1996. "Dry Sex in Zimbabwe and Implications for Condom Use." *Social Science and Medicine,* Vol. 42, 1(1996): 91–98.

Dudnik, Nina. "Stop Bemoaning Africa's Lack of Scientists—Start Funding Them." June 12, 2017. *World Economic Forum.*https://www.weforum.org/2017/africa-s-scientists-are-not-absent-they-just-need-the-right-kind-of- investment-b93066ad-8320-4f69-be60-e5, Retrieved July 5, 2018.

Flint, Karen E. 2014. *Healing Traditions: African Medicine, Cultural Exchange, and Competition in South Africa, 1820–1948.* Athens, OH: Ohio University Press.

Griffiths, Ieuan L. L. 1984. *Atlas of African Affairs.* Abingdon, UK: Methuen & Co.

Grotelueschen, Mark. 2017. *Pre-colonial Warfare in Africa.* Oxford, UK: Oxford Bibliographies (see also DOI: 10.1093/OBO/9780199791279-01490). Retrieved July 6, 2018.

Grove, A.T. 1989. *The Changing Geography of Africa.* London: Oxford University Press.

Hance, William. 1967. *African Economic Development.* New York: Praeger.

Harms, Robert. 2018. *Africa in Global History with Sources.* New York: W.W. Norton and Company.

Kariuki, Tom. October 26, 2015. "Africa Produces Just 1.1% of Global Scientific Knowledge—but Change Is Coming." *The Guardian,* 1–3.

Law, Robin. December 1, 2011. "Wheeled Transport in Pre-Colonial West Africa." https://doi.org/10.2307/1159117, online publication. Retrieved July 8, 2018.

Ngubane, Siegfried John. March 2010. "Gender Roles in the African Culture: Implications for the Spread of HIV/AIDS." Stellenbosch, South Africa: Stellenbosch University; Unpublished Master's Thesis, pp. 1–64.

Reid, Richard J. 2012. *Warfare in African History.* New York: Cambridge University Press.

Stapleton, Timothy J. 2013. *Military History of Africa: The Pre-Colonial Period from Ancient Egypt to the Zulu Kingdom (Earliest Times ca. 1870).* Oxford, England: Praeger.

Sterns, Peter, Michael Adas, Stuart Schwartz, and Marc J. Gilbert. 2015. *World Civilizations: The Global Experience,* 7th ed. Boston: Pearson.

United Nations. 1978. *United Nations Yearbook.* New York: United Nations, Office of Public Information.

Credits

Fig. 5.1: Source: http://un-maps.s3.amazonaws.com/package--1518103992077/4045%20Rev.%206%20 Original.pdf.

Fig. 5.2: Source: https://commons.wikimedia.org/wiki/File:Kilimanjaro_from_space_2016.jpg.

Fig. 5.3: Source: https://commons.wikimedia.org/wiki/File:Ellen_Johnson-Sirleaf3.jpg.

Fig. 5.4: Source: https://commons.wikimedia.org/wiki/File:Soldiers_of_the_11th_East_African_Division_crossing_the_River_Chindwin_by_ferry_before_moving_towards_the_village_of_Shwegyin,_Burma,_December_1944._SE923.jpg.

Fig. 5.5: Source: https://www.sahistory.org.za/topic/organisation-african-unity-oau.

Glossary

Abyssinia: Also known as the Ethiopian Empire, which stretched over parts of modern-day Ethiopia and Eritrea.

Africa: The second largest continent located between the Mediterranean Sea in the north, the Suez Canal and the Indian Ocean in the east, and the Atlantic Ocean in the west. The distance between north and south is about 5,200 miles and that between east and west is around 4,600 miles, with the total surface area of 11,730 million square miles.

African Diaspora: The movement of African peoples outside the African continent, notably during forced transport in the Transatlantic slave trade, in the mid-twentieth century during decolonization, and ongoing due to strife among groups in the modern African continent. The African diaspora led to widespread global transmissions of African culture.

Africanisms: A term that refers to African traditions found in societies and cultures of the African diaspora.

Afro-Eurasia: Refers to the landmass comprising Europe, Asia, and Africa. The term Afro-Eurasia reflects world historians' views that traditional geographical distinctions of continents do not represent world historical context because of the interconnectedness of traditions, goods, and people across Afro-Eurasia.

Age of Discovery: The period between the early fifteenth and seventeenth centuries has often been referred to as the Age of Discovery (or Exploration) in European history. In a world history context, scholars recognize that many peoples and cultures have their own significant periods—past, present, and future—of discovery and exploration.

Age of Imperialism: The European Age of Imperialism is often described as a period in the late nineteenth and early twentieth centuries (1870 to 1914) when the rapid growth of European empires, particularly in Africa, led to important global political and cultural shifts. In a world history context, many empires have practiced imperialism around the world over centuries, meaning that there are multiple ages of imperialism that a world historian could define.

Agriculture: A complex system of scientific, technological, and cultural practices human beings engage in to plant, grow, and process plants and to domesticate and raise animals for food and other uses.

Aircraft Carrier: A warship capable of launching and retrieving airplanes. First used during World War I, they were critical to victorious sea battles during World War II in the Pacific Theater.

Allied Powers/Forces; also Allies: During World War II, the Allied Powers, including the British Empire, France, and the Soviet Union, fought against the Axis Powers of Germany, Italy, and Japan.

Al-Qaeda: "The Base," a Sunni Islamist terrorist group best known for their 9/11 attacks against the United States. Founded to battle Soviet Russian invaders of Afghanistan in the 1980s, *Al-Qaeda* turned against Americans after the First Gulf War, arguing US forces, mainly non-Muslims, had no right to be stationed in Saudi Arabia.

Americas: The continents of North and South Americas as well as the Caribbean islands.

Anglicans: Members of the Church of England, the established English church. The Church of England is part of a worldwide Anglican Communion.

Annales [School]: A group of French historians and the progressive style of historiography they developed in the twentieth century.

Appeasement: Diplomatic concessions made to a hostile power to avoid military conflict. British prime minister Neville Chamberlain became infamous during World War II for his policy of appeasement toward Adolf Hitler.

Archduke Franz Ferdinand: Heir to the Austro-Hungarian throne. On June 28, 1914, Ferdinand and his wife, Sophie, Duchess of Hohenberg, **were assassinated** in Sarajevo by Gavrilo Princip, a member of the nationalist secret society the Black Hand. Ferdinand's assassination was the tipping point for tensions leading to World War I.

Armada: Fleet of Spanish galleons sent to attack England in 1588. Often called the Spanish Armada or the Great Armada. Bad weather and better tactics allowed British sailors to defeat the Armada.

Artisanat: French word that means artisan or refers to a craft industry. An artisan is a worker in a skilled trade, often making goods by hand as part of the craft industry.

Assembly Line: First popularized by automobile manufacturer Henry Ford, a series of workers and machines in which each is assigned a specific task before moving the manufactured good to the next worker or machine until the product is completed. The assembly line is seen as an efficient method of mass producing goods.

Assimilation: Refers to the adoption of another culture. In terms of modern world history, it usually refers to subjects' adoption of an imperial or national culture.

Austro-Prussian War: Also known as the Seven Weeks' War, an 1866 battle between Prussia and Austria as well as German states. Prussia's victory excluded Austria from Germany.

Axis (Powers): Germany, Japan, and Italy, who fought against the Allies in World War II.

Battle of Breitenfeld: 1631 Protestant victory during the Thirty Years' War which clearly demonstrated the superior tactics of the Swedish army under **Gustaf II Adolf**.

Battle of the Somme: Fought between July and November 1916, it was the bloodiest battle of World War I's Western Front. It serves as a stark reminder of the tremendous advantages of defense and the inability of generals to find a solution.

Berlin Conference: Also called the Congo Conference or West Africa Conference. In 1884–1885, Western powers, including Great Britain, Austro-Hungary, France, Germany, Russia, the United States, Portugal, Denmark, Spain, Italy, the Netherlands, Sweden, Belgium, and Turkey met to try to bring order to their presumed colonial claims in Africa. This meeting is seen as a marker for the late-nineteenth-century "**Scramble for Africa**," when virtually all of Africa was conquered by Western powers.

Big History: A historical and academic discipline popularized by David Christian. Big History uses a multidisciplinary approach to examine human history's relationship to the universe, Earth, and its diverse species.

Bloch, Jan: Polish banker who studied technology and warfare. He published a book in 1899 that argued modern war was impossible as technology made it so deadly.

Biopiracy: The act of co-opting indigenous flora and its uses for profit. European explorers, settlers, and scientists practiced biopiracy during their Age of Exploration and imperialism.

Black Hand: A twentieth-century secret nationalist Serbian society whose members fought for liberation from Austro-Hungarian rule. The Black Hand's assassination of Austrian archduke Franz Ferdinand (1914) was a catalyst in the outbreak of World War I.

Blitzkrieg: "Lightning war," a term popularized by newsmen to describe the rapid pace of warfare in 1939–1940, when German mechanized forces overwhelmed Allied defenders.

Bomba Kryptologiczna: Often called just *bomba*, a computing device invented by pre-1939 Polish scientists to assist their secret service in decrypting the Germans' Enigma machine, which produced very secure coded messages.

Bombard: Very large cannon employed in the 1400s–1500s, mainly to destroy defensive walls.

British East India Company: An English company given a royal charter in 1600 for the purposes of trade in India and Asia. From its origins as a trading company, it became heavily involved in politics, especially in India, where it acted as an agent of imperialism allowing British interests to penetrate, which led to formal British rule of the Indian subcontinent between 1858–1947. The company also expanded British influence in China, and British attempts to protect the company's trading interests are connected to events leading up to the American Revolution.

Boston Tea Party: On December 16, 1773, American revolutionaries dumped hundreds of chests of British East India Company tea into Boston Harbor in protest of British taxes on tea as well as what they saw as attempts by British powers to allow the British East India Company monopoly on the global tea trade. This event was a catalyst of the American Revolution.

Cacao (bean and tree): The bean, from a South American tree, is used to make cocoa, cocoa butter, and chocolate. Native to South America, the cacao tree now grows in Africa, the West Indies, and Central America.

Cahokia: An ancient great city where the Native American Mississippian culture thrived and spread over a large area in the modern-day United States. Based on the Mississippi River, Cahokia's ruins can be found in modern-day Illinois.

Capitalism: An economic system characterized by private ownership of goods and a free market system. Capitalism is often seen as a system developed in coordination with industrialization and imperialism and a system with social and economic inequities. While capitalism has been considered a Western development, global historians argue proto-capitalism was present in other early-modern societies and today is a dominant global system.

Carrack: Large three-masted European sailing ship from the 1500s–1700s. A tremendous improvement over older cogs (a type of ship), it allowed sailing across the globe. Carrack technology allowed Europeans to expand their influence along the coasts of Africa, India, and the New World.

Chattel Slavery: A system in which enslaved peoples are considered property and enslaved for life; these slaves' descendants are also considered the private property of a slave owner. This system, in its Western iteration, was legitimized by legal, social, and cultural norms.

Chuño: A type of freeze-dried potato first developed by indigenous peoples in the Andes (an immense mountain range along western South America) and used by the Incan Empire. Potatoes processed into *chuño* can last for decades. In a region known for its cold summer nights and sunny days, *chuño* was made by repeatedly freezing and thawing potatoes outdoors while removing the skins and liquids by crushing the potatoes by foot. *Chuño* continues to be used in Andean cooking.

Civil Society: Refers to a community of citizens with similar interests, usually separate from those of politics and business.

Civil War: A war between groups within the same nation, state, or society.

Climatology: The scientific study of climate.

Cold War: The period between 1945 and 1990 during which geopolitical tensions between the United States and the Soviet Union emerged. This war was considered "cold" because of a lack of outright military hostilities between the two superpowers. In world history, the Cold War is seen as a global conflict between the two played out on a global stage, resulting in bloody proxy wars instigated by US-Soviet tensions but fought outside their official channels and outside their borders.

Colonialism: A method of control over a land or people by an outside power that may include settlement and exploitation of resources at the expense of the indigenous residents.

Colony: An area of land controlled by a foreign power and/or that power's colonists (settlers in the colony).

Columbian Exchange: A term popularized by Alfred Crosby, it refers to the exchange of biological materials (flora, fauna, and microorganisms) between Afro-Eurasia and the Americas after European entry to the Atlantic World after 1492.

Commercial Revolution: Refers to a significant increase in commerce. Although often linked specifically to European experiences between 1300 and 1700 and a catalyst to the Industrial Revolution, commercial revolutions are found elsewhere in world history, including, but not limited to, China and the Middle East.

Communism: A political, economic, and, some suggest, cultural phase of human history that Karl Marx predicted would become a future apex of human society under a classless and stateless society created by a working-class revolution. Forms of Marx's original nineteenth-century descriptions of communism were developed in places including the Soviet Union, China, and Cuba in the twentieth century, although these systems modified Marx's proposed methods and theories substantially.

Conjuncture: A combination of circumstances or events that lead to a particular outcome. World historians use the term to argue that world history typically is not rooted in one catalyst but a combination of many factors, with diverse participants.

Conquistador: Generic name for Spanish adventurers who fought for "Gold, Glory, and God" in the New World during the 1500s–1600s.

Cortés, Hernán: Spanish adventurer and role model for the conquistador. His skillful diplomacy gained powerful local allies; combined with superior military technology, this allowed Cortés to defeat Mexico's Aztec Empire.

Cottage Industry: A home-based, small-scale business or form of production.

Cotton: A natural fiber and textile. Its use and production have an ancient history, originating in the Indus delta. From its ancient and smaller-scale use and production, cotton has become one of the world's leading industrial crops, and its path to global industrial use and production is associated with slavery, colonialism, imperialism, and capitalism.

Creole: Term applied to language, people, culture, and material goods typically rooted in a combination of cultural practices, specifically African, indigenous, and European in the Atlantic World.

Creolization: The process by which Creole history, languages, peoples, and cultures are created.

Criollos: South Americans whose ancestry is all, or nearly all, Spanish in origin, in contrast to peoples of mixed European, African, and/or indigenous descent.

Cultural Hybridity: A mixture of distinct cultures resulting in a new cultural identity.

Da Gama, Vasco: Portuguese navigator who left Portugal in July 1497 and arrived in India on May 20, 1498, making the first voyage any Portuguese or European had done by circumnavigating Southern Africa through the Cape and arriving in India in 1498, the famous source of "spices" and other products all Europeans had for so long sought.

De Vauban, Sébastien: French military engineer who designed very effective fortresses and developed tactics for attacking such. Also noted for his radical economic views.

Decolonization: The process whereby a former colony becomes independent from a foreign power or empire.

Dias, Bartolomeu: Fifteenth-century Portuguese explorer and the first European to navigate the Cape of Good Hope, opening routes through the Atlantic and Indian oceans to Asia.

Diplomacy: A formalized method of interacting in international affairs, characterized by professional skills and sensitivity to diverse cultures.

Disruptive Innovation: A business term coined by American academic Clayton Christensen. It warns investors that new technology has the power to completely overturn profitable companies, and that the rate of change has dramatically increased during the twentieth century.

Domestication: An often multigenerational cultivation of an originally wild plant or animal into one that can be raised in controlled circumstances by humans for human use.

Ecological Imperialism: A concept popularized by Alfred Crosby, which refers to European reshaping of land and resources from indigenous practices and uses for the benefit of Europeans. Crosby argues the colonization of land and natural resources (typically plants and animals) was a key factor in the rise of Western global power in the modern world.

Einsatzgruppen: Mobile death squads of soldiers and militarized police sent to kill civilians deemed unworthy of life in Adolf Hitler's Nazi Empire. They were mainly employed in eastern Europe and the Balkans.

Empire: A political or economic unit exerting control over diverse lands, peoples, or resources.

Enclosure: An area of land demarcated by natural or artificial barriers, e.g., fences. Enclosures may be associated with agriculture and political practices.

Enlightenment (Age of Enlightenment or Age of Reason): Seventeenth- and eighteenth-century intellectual movements that emerged as Europeans reacted to their increasing contact with the wider world. Enlightenment thinkers tended to embrace scientific, political, and philosophical thinking based on their understanding of human reason as a method to understand and explain the world around them.

Estates General: The representative assembly of pre-revolutionary France divided into three bodies: The elite clergy and nobility and a "Third Estate," which represented the majority population of common people.

Eurocentric: Focusing exclusively on European history and culture, often explicitly marking that culture as superior to others. Eurocentrism is often associated with European and Western ideologies of a special historical path and an exclusive identity.

Factory: A place where systems of division of labor and machines are used to create a finished product. The modern factory system developed in eighteenth-century Britain and spread around the world, replacing traditional methods of manufacturing.

Ferdinand II: Spanish monarch who united the kingdoms of Aragon, Castile, and Granada with his wife, Isabella I, in the late fifteenth century, creating Spain. Ferdinand and his wife also began Spain's entry into the modern period of imperial expansion. Their domestic efforts included the Spanish Inquisition and Muslim/Jewish expulsion or the conversion to Catholicism of Muslims. Their success at creating a unified Spain allowed them to support Christopher Columbus's voyages across the Atlantic Ocean.

Fertile Crescent: A region where some of the earliest groups of humans turned to settled agriculture. Its territory spanned the modern-day borders of Iraq, Israel, Palestine, Syria, Lebanon, Egypt, Jordan, Turkey, and Iran.

First Hague Convention: International meeting from 1899 that established "laws of war"; it banned weapons like poison gas or "dumdum" bullets.

First Opium War: Fought between 1839–1840, pitting the United Kingdom against China. It was a war for drugs, as the British championed their right to sell opium, and gained considerable advantages after defeating China.

Flintlock: A firing device where flint striking a steel plate created sparks, which ignited gunpowder charges in muskets. Flintlock could also be used to describe the musket employing this system.

Foodways: Foodways are the cultural, social, economic, and historical practices and interactions of human production and use of foods.

Forced Labor: The International Labor Organization definition states, "all [forced or compulsory] work or service which is exacted from any person under the menace of any penalty and for which the said person has not offered himself voluntarily." This may include slavery and bonded labor and is associated with the trafficking of human beings for labor or sexual exploitation."[1]

Ford, Henry: Controversial American inventor and business tycoon. Created highly efficient assembly line to produce his automobiles and was a major producer by the 1920s. Ford's name was synonymous with reliable, inexpensive cars, but he was also an anti-Semite.

Franco-Prussian War/Franco-German War: Fought between 1870–1871, in which a coalition of German states, led by Prussia, defeated France, resulting in a unified German state and diminished French power.

Frederick II: Eighteenth-century Prussian king sometimes dubbed "the Great." His tactical, strategic, and diplomatic skills enabled Prussia to become a great European power.

Frontier Mentality: A frontier may be a political or cultural border that in a colonial mindset marks the end of settled and civilized territory. The mentality formed from this understanding of a frontier assumes that metropolitan social norms may be absent or flexible on the frontier. It also assumes that what lies beyond the frontier may be reshaped at whim according to metropolitan sensibilities.

Geobukseon: "Turtle Ship," the world's first armored warship built in Korea during the 1500s. These were very difficult to attack with conventional wooden vessels and allowed Korean sailors to defeat larger Japanese squadrons.

Globalization: Coined in the 1930s, the term *globalization* became increasingly popular in the twentieth century; its basic definition is the interactions and interconnectedness of peoples,

---

1   International Labor Coalition, "C029—Forced Labour Convention," 29, 1930, https://www.ilo.org/dyn/normlex/en/f?p=1000:12100:0::NO::P12100_ILO_CODE:C029

cultures, and organizations in a global sphere. World historians may also use the term to describe world systems that occurred earlier in history.

Great Depression: A significant global economic depression from the late 1920s through the late 1930s. Often tied to the stock market crash in the United States in 1929, its catalysts and results were global and tied to the world wars.

Gribeauval System: Standardized cannons where specific models were built in the same shape and caliber, allowing France to have one of the better artillery systems of the late eighteenth century.

Grotius, Hugo: Dutch intellectual, diplomat, and economic theorist. His writings laid the groundwork for international agreements on limiting violence against civilians during wartime.

Guerrilla Warfare: Warfare performed by small groups typically using fast and nontraditional maneuvers against a larger, often state-sponsored, military. It is often used as a form of protest and has an ancient and global history.

Gustaf II Adolf: Swedish king whose military innovations influenced European military history during the 1600s. His intervention in support of Protestant forces changed the course of the Thirty Years' War.

Hakluyt, Richard: Born in England around 1530, Richard Hakluyt was an avid reader of geographic information and was elected to Parliament in 1558, where he continued to study world geography and to correspond with sailors, cartographers, and conquerors of new lands. Fascinated with the prospects of the British settling in the Americas, Hakluyt advocated the colonization of the New World, which, in his view, would be good for British trade and the evangelization of the Indians, particularly those living in Virginia. He died in 1591—as one historian notes—before the first slaves landed on a Dutch ship in Jamestown, Virginia, in 1619.

Hirohito: The Showa Emperor of Japan from 1926–1989. His controversial reign dovetails with World War II. Scholars still debate his role in the war.

Hiroshima: Japanese port city and target of the first atomic bomb in 1945.

Hispaniola: One of the largest islands in the West Indies (North Atlantic Ocean and Caribbean), today divided politically into the Republic of Haiti and the Dominican Republic.

Historiography: A term used by historians to refer to the study of the writing and methods of academic history and historians to trace how interpretations of history have changed through time.

Holocaust: As defined the United States Holocaust Memorial Museum: "The Holocaust was the systematic, state-sponsored persecution and murder of six million Jews by the Nazi regime and its allies and collaborators. *Holocaust* is a word of Greek origin meaning "sacrifice by fire." The Nazis, who came to power in Germany in January 1933, believed that Germans were 'racially superior' and that the Jews, deemed 'inferior,' were an alien threat to the so-called German racial community. During the era of the Holocaust, German authorities also targeted other groups because of their perceived racial and biological inferiority: Roma (Gypsies), people with disabilities, some of the Slavic peoples (Poles, Russians, and others), Soviet prisoners of war, and blacks. Other groups were persecuted on political, ideological, and behavioral grounds, among them Communists, Socialists, Jehovah's Witnesses, and homosexuals."[2]

Iberian Peninsula: The peninsula in southwestern Europe where modern Spain and Portugal are located.

Ibrahim, Axmad: Somali imam who directed a successful invasion of Ethiopia in the 1530s–1540s. A hero to Muslim Somalis but an archvillain to Christian Ethiopians.

ICBM: Intercontinental Ballistic Missile, which can carry a satellite into outer space or deliver a weapon of mass destruction to an enemy city. The ultimate weapon of the Cold War, it is still produced by many powers in the twenty-first century.

Imperial Methods: The varied methods, often cultural, that empires use to conquer and control colonies, as well as to manage an empire. These methods may include political, economic, military, and social means.

Imperialism: An action, policy, or ideology used to gain control of foreign peoples and lands.

Independence: Synonyms include self-government, self-rule, home rule, self-legislation, self-determination, sovereignty, autonomy, nonalignment, freedom, and liberty. It refers specifically to the act of gaining freedom from the rule of another country or empire.

Indian Ocean System: An important set of trade routes and interactions between Southeast Asia, India, Arabia, and East Africa.

Indigenous Peoples: A definition from the United Nations states indigenous peoples are "descendants … of those who inhabited a … geographical region at the time when people of different cultures or ethnic origins [began colonization]." Indigenous populations are found around the world.[3]

Indirect Rule: A form of colonial rule in which an empire uses indigenous peoples and localized power structures to maintain order.

Indochina (French Indochina): Refers to a portion of Southeast Asia inhabited mainly by descendants of Indians and Chinese controlled by the French government until the twentieth century, comprising Vietnam, Laos, and Cambodia. In 1940, the Japanese had occupied parts of Vietnam called Tonkin and Cambodia. However, the French kept their grip and influence in Indochina until March 1945, the year the Japanese made Vietnam an autonomous state. When the former surrendered to the Allied Powers in August 1945, the French still held Indochina as theirs but decreed that Vietnam would now become the Democratic Republic of Vietnam, equivalent to a quasi-independent state led by Ho Chi Minh. Laos and Cambodia were declared independent

---

2   The United States Holocaust Memorial Museum, "Introduction to the Holocaust," Holocaust Encyclopedia. https://encyclopedia.ushmm.org/content/en/article/introduction-to-the-holocaust

3   United Nations Permanent Forum on Indigenous Issues, "Indigenous Peoples, Indigenous Voices: Fact Sheet: Who Are Indigenous Peoples?," n.d. https://www.un.org/esa/socdev/unpfii/documents/5session_factsheet1.pdf

states in 1945–1950, but only following a Geneva Conference in 1954 were they recognized internationally as independent states, thus ending the conflict between France and the Viet Minh.

Industrial Revolution: A traditional definition focuses on the rapid growth of industrialism beginning in eighteenth-century England and spreading throughout Europe. World historians note that industrial revolutions occurred globally and continue today.

Industrialism: A system built on manufacturing and mechanized industries, as opposed to one built on agricultural or service industries.

Industrialization: The process of creating a system built on manufacturing and mechanized industries; specifically, the rapid growth of industries and industrialization in the eighteenth century called the Industrial Revolution originating in England and spreading worldwide.

Intermediaries: Refers to people who act as liaison between two systems; specifically, colonial intermediaries were indigenous people who acted as a link between colonizers and colonized people, either for their own benefit or for the benefit of indigenous groups. An example might be native Indians who worked for the British in the Indian (Imperial) Civil Service.

International Brigades: Volunteers from across the globe who fought to defend the Spanish Republic against the revolutionary forces of Francisco Franco.

Iran-Iraq War: Devastating Middle Eastern conflict of 1980–1988, which cost the lives of nearly 1 million people.

Isabella I: Spanish monarch who united the kingdoms of Aragon, Castile, and Granada with her husband, Ferdinand II, in the late fifteenth century, creating Spain. Isabella and her husband also began Spain's entry into the modern period of imperial expansion. Their domestic efforts included the Spanish Inquisition and Muslim/Jewish expulsion or the conversion to Catholicism of Muslims. Their success at creating a unified Spain allowed them to support Christopher Columbus's voyages across the Atlantic Ocean.

Island Story: Refers to a romanticized English national history periodized from Roman occupation to the modern day that focuses on a narrow interpretation of England's traditional national history.

Italo-Ethiopian (Italo-Abyssinian) War: The second Italian attempt at an invasion of Ethiopia, this time by Benito Mussolini, the self-proclaimed Duce of Italy, in revenge for the Italian defeat at Adowa in 1896, also known as the first Italo-Ethiopian (Abyssinian) War. In this second violent confrontation, assisted by Eritreans on October 3, 1935, Italian troops invaded Ethiopia from the north and from the east, Mussolini's troops were supported by the Libyans and the Somali. Even though Emperor Haile Selassie's army was larger in number, Ethiopia was not a military match for the Italian forces this time around. In 1936, Victor Emanuel III, king of Italy, proclaimed himself emperor of Ethiopia, forcing Emperor Haile Selassie to go into exile. Ethiopia was finally returned to the emperor by British admiral Andrew Cunningham, who defeated the Italians and entered Addis Ababa victorious on May 20, 1941. This allowed Haile Selassie to return home as emperor.

July Crisis: After the assassination of Archduke Franz Ferdinand in June of 1914, the series of rapid diplomatic and military actions over the summer of 1914 (particularly in July) across Europe, which led to the outbreak of World War I.

Karl XII: Swedish king from 1697–1718. A tactical genius who won many battles, but a poor strategist who could not win wars.

Koxinga: Also known as Zheng Chenggong, he was a pirate leader and Ming loyalist who defied the Qing Dynasty from his island bases. Also drove the Dutch out of Taiwan.

Kyoto Protocol: Adopted in 1997 in Kyoto, Japan, the Protocol, an international agreement linked to the United Nations Framework Convention on Climate Change, required committing parties to abide by international emission reduction targets.

Lake Chad: Located in west-central Africa in the area where Chad, Cameroon, Nigeria, and Niger meet; seasonally regarded as one of Africa's largest lakes.

Land of Gold: Located in ancient Ghana and Mali, two major kingdoms in West Africa. Between the eighth and twelfth centuries, the kingdoms played a major role in the Trans-Saharan Gold Trade, sometimes referred to as "the Gold Roads," north through the Sahara Desert into the Mediterranean.

League of Nations: An international organization formed in 1920 in reaction to World War I with a stated purpose of maintaining global peace through diplomacy.

Liberation Wars: Violent resistance to the denial of independence, specifically in reaction to failed independence efforts in European colonies.

Light Infantry: A military concept dating to ancient times. Picked men with limited gear could move more rapidly. During the 1700s, this idea spread to many Western armies, and light infantry were often elite troops.

Linen: A textile made from the flax plant and one of the oldest fabrics in the world. While superior to cotton, it is also more difficult to produce.

Louis XIV: The "Sun King" who served as a role model for absolute monarchs. Remembered for his fabulous palace at Versailles and disastrous wars that sowed the seeds for the French Revolution.

Manhattan Project: Code name for top-secret project to create American nuclear weapons during World War II.

Maori: The indigenous Polynesian people who migrated from eastern Polynesia by canoe and settled in New Zealand during the thirteenth century.

Marco Polo Bridge Incident: On July 7, 1937, a conflict broke out between Chinese and Japanese troops near the Marco Polo (Lugouqiao) Bridge located near Beijing. The conflict led to the occupation of Nanking by the Japanese and the Nanking Massacre, the Sino-Japanese War (1937–1945), and is considered a catalyst of World War II in Asia.

Maroon: A word used for Caribbean slaves who fled to mountains and other secluded areas to mount violent resistance as needed, against British slave masters during the seventeenth and eighteenth centuries.

Meiji Restoration: The culmination of political change in Japan between 1853–1867. It removed the Shogun and returned the emperor's authority. Japan's rapid modernization is often associated with this change.

Menelik II: Emperor of Ethiopia (called **Abyssinia** before the modern age), born at Showa in 1844. Menelik successfully expanded his northeastern African empire until his death in 1913. He also successfully protected Abyssinia from European colonialism during the nineteenth century, defeating the Italians at the battle of Adowa in 1896, which became an international humiliation of the Italians at the hand of the Africans. It is believed that Benito Mussolini, the Duce of Italy, invaded Ethiopia in 1935 as revenge against that historic defeat.

Merino Sheep: A breed of sheep that originated in Spain during the twelfth century, said to be brought into Spain by the Moors. Because of its fine wool, the Merino sheep was coveted in Europe and, at one point, unauthorized owners could be put in jail. The Merino sheep spread after the Spanish crown began to use it as a gift to royal family members and friends across Europe.

Middle Passage: Expression referring to the trading and the traumatic voyage of enslaved Africans crossing the Atlantic Ocean to the New World, including the Caribbean Islands, as well as what later became the American continents.

Militarism: Militarism refers to the tendency by European nations, most notably during the twentieth century, to resolve their disputes using force of arms rather than through diplomacy, even though not always successfully, during the previous centuries. The Industrial Revolution, which accelerated the manufacture of new weapons in the form of new types of more powerful and automatic guns, faster and more deadly gunboats, submarines, new napalm bombs, the Hiram Maxim, the grenade rifle, and later, airplanes, made the use of arms and the military more tempting to beat the enemy. At the turn of the nineteenth century, Germany, including the Prussian state before unification in 1870, France, and England were in the forefront of the movement to resort to a massive show of deadly weapons. Many historians hold the view that without this development, World Wars I and II may not have erupted or at least would not have lasted as long as they did.

Ming Dynasty: Also known as the Great Ming Empire Dynasty, which came about following the defeat of the Mongol-led Juan Dynasty, survived and ruled China from 1368 to 1644 from its elaborate capital at Nanjing. Among the main achievements of the Ming Dynasty was the Great Wall, along with impressive distinct architectural structures, new musical and visual artistic manifestations, and a new stream of literature genres.

Miscegenation: The mixing of races through marriage. Since the 1600s, Virginia, Maryland, and, later, other states passed strict laws that forbade interracial marriages, mainly to prevent blacks or white males from marrying blacks, whether still enslaved or freed. Some of these laws survived until the 1960s and beyond in several states, including Mississippi.

Multiparty Democracy: A type of democracy that accepts the principle of accepting the participation of more than one party in the governance of a country, as opposed to what is called a single-party system. Until the 1980s, most African countries had become single-party states immediately after independence, where the president invariably turned out to be a dictator or an autocrat. The reason presented by the supporters of a single-party system was that it would realistically curb the intrinsic tendency of Africans to be almost irreconcilably loyal to their own ethnic groups, which was called "tribalism," rather than to the idea of a nation.

Mussolini, Benito: Prime minister and leader of the Fascist regime in Italy during World War II.

Nader Shah: Eighteenth-century Iranian monarch who was a great fighter but held only limited strategic sense. His endless battles brought victories and wealth, but never a conclusion. Sometimes called the "Napoleon of Iran."

Nagasaki: Japanese city subjected to second atomic bomb attack in 1945.

Nanjing Massacre: Horrific event of 1937, hotly debated to this day. Nanjing was the capital of China. When Japanese troops marched into the city, their officers encouraged violence, rape, and theft. Japanese and Chinese argue over responsibility and numbers of victims; the latter number between 40,000 and 300,000, depending upon your source.

Napoleonic Code: Promulgated on March 21, 1804, by Napoleon Bonaparte, the Napoleonic Code, or the *Code Civil des Français*, was a compilation of all civil laws of France guiding the conduct of French citizens in matters of property ownership, civil rights, the country's colonial possessions, family and personal conduct, the Church authority, and overall governance. The code spread in western Europe and was later adopted by all continental Europe and Latin America.

Nasser, Gamal Abdel: Egyptian army officer who played a key role in overthrowing the monarchy in 1952. President of Egypt two years later and until his death in 1970. An Arab nationalist who maintained good relations with the Soviet Union, he fought, and lost, several wars with Israel.

National Assembly: Designation of the legislative body created by the French Revolution in France, which spread to other parts of the world, such as Africa. It is equivalent to Parliament in the United Kingdom, as well as in many of the developing countries in the world today.

Nationalism: A word whose usage began during the seventeenth century, exemplified by the causes of the Thirty Years' War (1618–1648), as the sense of belonging to a specific type of people or nation, determined either by language, forcible imposition, and/or local origin, who saw themselves as separate and distinct from everyone else who was different. During the past, extreme nationalism caused several wars throughout the world, as was the case of both world wars, when the Germans, the Italians, the French, and the Japanese decided to join the fight simply because they thought their nation was more important than any other.

Nemesis: An iron-hulled steamship of the East India Company navy. Used against the Chinese during the First Opium War, it was almost impossible to counter, as China's antique warships were incapable of catching the *Nemesis* or surviving its heavy artillery.

New Imperialism: To distinguish it from the expansion of the ancient world, such as that of Rome and Greece, the New Imperialism refers to the forcible conquest and colonization of parts of the world, especially Africa, Asia, and Latin America, by Europe, America, and Japan during the latter part of the nineteenth century and the beginning of the twentieth century. Most historians now hold the view the new expansion was spurred by a desire for raw materials, fulfillment of nationalistic ambitions, and the evangelization of the world, coupled with natural curiosity.

No-Man's-Land: Term used by Allied soldiers on the Western Front of World War I. It described the space between rival trench lines, a quagmire of shell craters, barbed wire, unexploded ordnance, and dead bodies. Attacking across this zone nearly always guaranteed high casualty rates.

North African Campaign: The North African Campaign refers to the 1940–1943 skirmishes and fierce battles in North Africa between British forces in Egypt, their protectorate at the time, and Mussolini's troops stationed in Libya, then an Italian colony. Fearing a defeat of the Axis troops, Hitler, Mussolini's protector, sent his "Afrika Korps" under the now famous General Erwin Rommel. What ended the campaign in favor of the Allies was "Operation Torch," a contingent of thousands of British and American troops that landed in western North Africa, forcing the Italian and German troops to surrender in Tunisia in May 1943.

Omdurman: Sudanese city and site of battle between Anglo-Egyptian forces and local Mahdists. A lopsided struggle as the Sudanese defenders had very few modern weapons, but still fought in traditional block formations. Terrible casualties resulted, magnified by Anglo-Egyptian troops killed and many enemies wounded. The Mahdist state collapsed as a result, and the Sudan became an Anglo-Egyptian condominium until 1956.

The Other: The word "other" is often used to exclude people from the mainstream, usually implying the socially inferior status of the person referred to as Other as opposed to Us. "Othering" is sometimes used as a verb.

Pathogenesis: The origin and development of a disease.

Palestine Liberation Organization (PLO): An asymmetrical force employing terror tactics to disrupt Israeli control of Palestine. Heroes to Palestinians, archvillains to their victims.

Periodization: The artificial chronological division of history into various periods, such as the Neolithic Age, the Middle Ages, the Renaissance, the Enlightenment, the Modern and Contemporary Eras, the Exploration Age, the Cold War Era, and the nuclear age. Periodization helps historians compress time and events that seem to relate to each other for a more focused and easier study and understanding of the experiences of making throughout the centuries.

Pikes: Long spears first used by Macedonian soldiers in ancient times. Revived by the Swiss during the 1400s, the pike was used by many nations in conjunction with slow-firing muskets during the 1500s–1600s.

Plantation: Usually a large farm owned by a slave owner who might have had between 20 and 100 enslaved Africans working for him in the house and in his outdoor property where critical crops were grown, including tobacco, cotton, indigo, sugar, and corn. Plantation life was miserable for the slaves as most of the masters treated them as chattel property and not as human beings. In the postbellum period (1865 and later), among the newly freed men and women, some former slaves left the plantation and were successful in finding employment. The majority, however, did not, and therefore could not leave. These remained behind and became sharecroppers, leading a life that was not much different from that experienced in slavery.

Plantation Agriculture: A form of agriculture where crops are grown for profit on a plantation.

Plateau: High elevated terrain in relation to sea level. The continent of Africa is often described by geographers as a high plateau, which is usually rugged and difficult to cross, presenting insuperable problems for effective economic development and a cheap and viable transportation system.

Polo, Marco: One of the most famous Western travelers to Asia, Polo (1254–1324) used the Silk Roads to explore Asia over a 24-year period. His subsequent memoir made a significant impact on Western understanding of Asia, although modern interpretations suggest that parts of his travelogue were romanticized, if not outright fairy tales.

Princip, Gavrilo: On June 28, 1914, the Serbian South Slav nationalist assassinated **Archduke Franz Ferdinand** and his wife **Sophie**. The assassination was a key catalyst in the outbreak of World War I.

Protectorate: Word used by the colonial powers during their partition of the world they conquered during the nineteenth century. A term used mostly by the British, a protectorate was a territory that was not conquered on paper but remained a territory under the tutelage or protection of the colonizer. Examples of protectorates included Egypt and Morocco under the British and the French, respectively, and Rhodesia under the British. Quite often, however, the word *protectorate* was simply a euphemism for colony.

Pulley Block: Wooden pulley blocks were vital for handling the many ropes that allowed ships to gather wind power for sailing across the oceans. Large warships might need upwards of 1000 pulley blocks.

Quakers: Essentially a religious sect promoted by its founder George Fox of England during the seventeenth century, also known as the Society of Friends or the Religious Society of Friends. Quakers derided the use of a clergy and did not believe in extensive routine religious ceremonies during services. They also had an aversion to war, even for self-defense, or any type of violence, and have therefore been known as pacifists. They preached equality between men and women and during the period of slavery joined the abolitionists. Consequently, Quakers were active in the women's rights movement during the 1850s and later. In the United States, most of the active Quakers lived in Pennsylvania, where they settled under their first leader, William Penn, whose name the state adopted. Today, Quakers number about 300,000, and most are said to be found in Africa.

Quartering Act: A 1774 punishment meted out by the British government on recalcitrant American colonists. It required locals to provide living space for British soldiers. Dubbed one of the "Intolerable Acts" by colonists.

Rillieux, Norbert: Born in New Orleans, Louisiana, and son of a White man, Vincent Rillieux, and a freed Black mother, Constance Vivant, Norbert Rillieux (1806–1894) is recognized as the inventor of the "multiple-effective vacuum operation" designed to better the processing of sugar. Having been sent to Paris by his enlightened father to study, he completed his studies and joined other scientists who were looking for the most effective sugar processing method, which he finally succeeded in developing in his factory in 1845. His related inventions were used for the processing of soap, condensed milk, gelatin, and glue.

The Rise of The West: The Rise of the West concept is mired in a dispute among historians who try to explain how western Europe became the dominant region in the world. Some believe the trend to dominance took place between 1450 and 1850, resulting from its territorial and political expansion around the globe, the Industrial Revolution, and the subsequent benefit it harnessed from the economic resources it amassed from the colonial possessions or the new imperial expansion. Those who hold this theory also claim that certain European cultural traits propelled the West to achieve the hegemony they have exerted over the past two centuries.

RMS *Lusitania:* British passenger liner sunk by a U-boat off the coast of Ireland in 1915. Over 100 American passengers drowned, and their loss altered public opinion in the United States.

Sack of Magdeburg: Terrible event from 1631, where enraged Catholic soldiers massacred most of the inhabitants of this German city after a long siege. Retaliations were swift, causing an escalation of violence on both sides.

Sahel: The peripheral area of the Sahara Desert in Africa, which is less dry and allows limited life and harvest of such crops as several types of nuts, and where some cattle raising is possible by those leading a nomadic and transhumance lifestyle. Many of the countries located in or bordering the Sahel, such as Senegal, Sudan, Chad, Niger, Nigeria, Mali, Burkina Faso, Mauritania, and even parts of Cameroon, often experience several periodic droughts that have caused famine.

Scramble for Africa: This expression refers to the effort and struggle among European nations to control Africa peacefully during the latter part of the nineteenth century. The scramble resulted in almost 99 percent of the continent being conquered and divided into some 50 colonies, territories, and protectorates, with the major share of the land and the resources having gone to Britain, France, Portugal, Germany, Italy, Spain, and Belgium.

Seed Drill: Invented and perfected by Jethro Tull (1674–1741) in 1714, the machine made farming more efficient by evenly distributing and planting seeds. It was an important agricultural tool of the Industrial Revolution's achievements.

Self-Determination: A basic right of all people to decide their own political status and pursue their own development. The concept of self-determination was part of the 1776 Declaration of Independence of the 13 American Colonies and enshrined in the Covenant of the League of Nations in 1919, in the French Declaration of the Rights of Man in 1789, and in the Charter of the United Nations in 1945.

Self-Government: The ability of a political community or a country to craft, live by, and master its own political affairs free from all external interference or control. Self-determination or self-government is often just a step toward political independence, as the French colonies in Africa were slated to be in the French Union as republics. Luckily for the oppressed Africans, this political compromise or trick was immediately rejected by the leader of Guinea-Conakry, Sékou Touré in 1958, who opted for outright independence, though embraced by the rest of the French colonies, only to be rejected as well in 1960 in favor of complete and absolute independence from France.

The Seven Years' War: Often known as the French and Indian War (1754–1763), the Seven Years' War was a major violent conflict between the British and the French regarding North America. The French loss was sealed at the Treaty of Paris in 1763. This treaty recognized most of North America as British, including all French territory east of the Mississippi River, as well as French Florida. Cuba was ceded to Spain.

Silk: A fiber spun by specific insects and arachnids, some of which can be used by humans to produce the fine fabric also known as silk. Most commercial silk is produced by domesticated silkworms originating in China.

Silk Roads: A series of trade routes begun during the Chinese Han Dynasty from 130 BCE to 453 CE. Traders dealt in such goods as glass objects, porcelain, textiles, horses, fruit, gunpowder, camels, perfumes, rice, spices, and honey. Marco Polo availed himself of this road and transportation network during his travels to the Orient during the thirteenth and fourteenth centuries.

Socialism: A social and economic system straddling capitalism and communism, which allows the state to involve itself in a country's economy to allegedly address national imbalances in wealth, control the national resources, and ensure that health and education are allocated as the right of every citizen.

South African War: The so-called South African War, also called the Boer War, pitted the British in South Africa against the Boers between October 11, 1899, and May 31, 1902. The cause was the attempt by the Transvaal Republic to become independent. The war resulted in many casualties among the Boers, of whom 115,000 had been interned in camps by the British. Out of this number, it is estimated that 28,000 died in the camps, 22,000 of whom were children. This elicited much world condemnation over the British handling of the war.

Spanish-American War: The war waged between the United States and Spain in 1898 because Cuba demanded its independence from the colonizers; this was supported by the United States, especially after the mysterious sinking of the battleship USS *Maine* in Havana Harbor. After a short war, the two nations signed the Treaty of Paris on December 10, 1898, at which time Spain renounced its claim to Cuba, which became independent, and ceded Guam and Puerto Rico to the United States as well as the Philippines, for which it accepted $20 million as the price of the deal with the United States. The ultimate outcome was Spain's permanent loss of its rule over its colonies in the Americas.

Stalin, Joseph: Soviet Russian Dictator, 1927–1953. His policies led to mass starvation, death camps, and a totalitarian nightmare. One of the great mass murderers of the twentieth century.

Steam Engine: A steam engine, as in a ship or train, begins in a water boiler that produces high pressure using a fire-tube or a water-tube. The fire-tube boiler, most popular during the nineteenth century, is a water tank perforated by many pipes. From the resulting pressure, hot gases from coal or wood fire heat the water in the tank, which creates an explosion that causes the engine to fire. Nowadays, in the more popular water-tube boiler, water goes through a "rack of tubes" from the hot gases coming from the fire producing stream, which in turn forces the engine to run. Today, however, many engines are designed to run using electricity rather than water or coal.

Subjects/Subalterns: Complex term(s) used by some scholars, including Marxists, who prefer to use them to denote people of lower class rather than the Marxist *lumpenproletariat* term. Among Chinese scholars, the two interchangeable words mean a second generation of migrant workers, such as the Diasi, or the Dalit in India. The concept appeared first among Indian scholars during the 1970s, who even developed the *Subaltern Studies* or *Subalternity*, a concept that was used by the famous scholar Antonio Gramsci, who defined it as the study of lower rank and marginalized populations, as noted in his book *Escritos Politicos*, under the social, political, and economic hegemonic control of the elite.

Suez Canal: A canal initiated by Frenchman Ferdinand de Lesseps in 1859 and completed in 1869. Linking the Mediterranean Sea with the Red Sea and then with the Indian Ocean, the Suez Canal is a major passage route for ships and other maritime vessels from Europe, Africa, and Asia. Its opening signified that no longer did the Europeans have to depend on the sea route successfully traveled by Bartolomeu Dias in 1487 and Vasco da Gama in 1498, through the southern tip of the African continent, to reach the Orient for commerce and trade.

Taino: Name of the original inhabitants of what now are the Bahamas, Puerto Rico, Haiti, the Dominican Republic, the Virgin Islands, the Lesser Antilles, Jamaica, and Cuba at the time Christopher Columbus landed on the Islands in 1492. The Taino were mainly farmers and lived in compounds or settlements of at least 3,000 people and spoke Arawakan. They were easily defeated by the Spaniards and virtually extinct along with their language by 1550.

Taiping Heavenly Kingdom Movement: A massive uprising that pitted Han versus Qing in mid-nineteenth-century China. A ten-year struggle, it was the deadliest conflict of the century.

Tarawa Atoll: A tiny island in the southern Pacific and scene of a hard-fought battle in 1943. Victorious Americans learned their Japanese adversaries were very unlikely to surrender and would rather fight to the last man.

Te Moananui-a-Kiwa Ngārimu: Born at Whareponga, New Zealand, in 1919, Ngārimu was a well-educated young man when he was called to enlist in the army. He was sent along with other young men on missions abroad, eventually joining the Maori Battalion that left to see combat in Greece, Tunisia, and Libya on May 1, 1940, after receiving further training in England and selected to perform intelligence duties. Ngārimu, a brave soldier, along with his battalion had to storm the German Post in Tunisia during the North African Campaign, called Point 209, where he was unfortunately killed on March 27, 1943. The Germans surrendered soon thereafter. Ngārimu's work and bravery were recognized by the army and the New Zealand governor-general. He was posthumously awarded the Victoria Cross for bravery, which was presented to his parents. His body, however, remains buried in the Sfax War Cemetery in Tunisia.

Tea Act (1773): The main purpose of the Tea Act was to help bolster the fortunes of the British East India Company to monopolize the tea trade in the British colonies. It further angered American colonists already opposed to taxes on tea, and this act pushed them toward active resistance, including the Boston Tea Party incident in December 1773. This act of rebellion was a precursor of the American Revolution.

Technical: A pickup truck mounting a large machine gun, rocket launcher, or cannon. These are found in Africa and the Middle East, where irregular forces and rebel groups cannot afford the cost of purpose-built fighting vehicles. Used with considerable skill by ISIS fighters in Syria and Iraq during the 2010s.

Third Estate: The representative body of the lower class, the middle class, and the working class, as one of the deliberating bodies of the French Assembly, along with the First Estate, or the clergy, and the Second Estate, made up of the nobility. It was the Third Estate that propelled the celebrated French Revolution in Paris in 1789–1794. The revolution eliminated the estates, as all citizens were declared equal and entitled (except women) to vote.

Thirty Years' War: Fought from 1618–1648 and causing widespread devastation in the Germanies. A religious and political struggle that had tremendous impact on the history of central Europe.

Trace Italienne: An Italian-influenced military architecture that called for thick, much lower walls and crisscrossed fields of fire making it very difficult to attack forts embracing this design. An American example of this system is Saint Augustine's Castillo *de San Marcos*.

Treaty of Sèvres: Through the August 10, 1920, Treaty of Sèvres, France and the victorious Allies forced Turkey to dismantle the Ottoman Empire and to renounce any rights over Arab Asia and North Africa. Armenia was declared independent and Kurdistan autonomous. The treaty was revised by the Treaty of Lausanne in 1932, following fierce resistance from young nationalist Turks.

Treaty of Tordesillas: Treaty signed at Tordesillas, Spain, on June 7, 1494, supervised by Pope Alexander VI, which settled the disputes over land in the New World between Spain and Portugal. A line was drawn, and all the land west of it belonged to Spain and areas east of it were given to Portugal. This is the reason Brazil became a Portuguese colony, while the rest of Latin America was colonized by Spain. The treaty did end the conflict between the two most important powers of the time and showed how powerful the papacy, represented by Pope Alexander VI, had become by the fifteenth century.

Treaty of Versailles: Treaty signed on June 28, 1919, at Versailles, near Paris, at the end of World War I (1914–1918) between the Allies and Germany and its own allies. It forced Germany to pay reparations and cede all its colonies, which were allocated to France, Britain, Belgium, and South Africa (i.e., southwest Africa). To preserve international peace in Europe and the world, the Allies established the League of Nations, spearheaded by Woodrow Wilson, the president of the United States. Unfortunately, Congress refused to ratify the league.

Tull, Jethro: An eighteenth-century English agriculturalist whose contributions included the seed drill (a mechanized device for planting seeds) and a horse-drawn hoe. His inventions contributed to the eighteenth-century British Agricultural Revolution and set a basis for modern agriculture.

Turquoise Trade: Previously little-known ancient and extensive trade item, a precious gem-, green-, blue-, and blue-green-looking stone known as *turquoise* from the Aztec of Mexico, discovered by archaeologists at Cerrillos, an ancient site in Mexico, also spotted in Colorado, Nevada, and southwestern California. Apparently, the ancestors of the Aztecs, the Puebloans, maintained the trade of this stone used for ornaments and simply as a precious stone to be owned and preserved, dating as far back as a few thousand years ago.

U-Boat: Short for *Unterseeboot*, German for submarine. Although every major power employed submarines during the Great War, Germany made the greatest use of this technology. U-boats terrorized surface shipping as they were very hard to detect, and their deadly torpedoes guaranteed a high chance of destruction.

United Nations (UN): The world organization founded and ratified in 1945 by European, American, and other nations of the world of the time, whose aim was to preserve the world peace severely threatened by World War II. The aim was to work together to stop any aggressor. Headquartered in New York, the UN is organized into a Security Council, the most important body, where each one of the five great powers—United States, Russia, China, France, and England—have the veto power, and the General Assembly, where each one of the 195 governments and state members have a vote.

Verdun: French city attacked by the Germans for most of 1916. Ended in stalemate despite tremendous losses by both sides.

Vikings: Also known as the Norsemen, the Vikings have remained partly a mythical and partly a historical group of people who occupied through war and plundering most of northern Europe or the Scandinavian countries of the time, namely, Norway, Denmark, and Sweden, eventually extending their domain to the British islands and as far as Baghdad in Asia from around 800 AD to 1066 AD. They were great warriors and terrorized the oceans as they had mastered the art of shipbuilding and were known as intrepid and successful navigators and avid traders in fur. One interesting detail that still needs to be proven convincingly is the claim that the Vikings may have visited America before Christopher Columbus, perhaps from their base in Greenland. This most likely myth relies on dubious Viking-looking sites in the northern tip of Newfoundland and other parts of Canada. If true, the Vikings can be compared to the Vandals, who devastated Europe beginning in 429 AD up to 533 AD after they had sacked Rome in 455 AD.

Volley Fire: Popular tactic in the 1500s–1800s, where groups of soldiers were ordered to fire all at the same time. The massive number of bullets let fly partially made up for inaccurate smooth-bore muskets.

Von Wallenstein, Albrecht: Skillful mercenary commander who served the Catholic Imperialists during the Thirty Years' War. Made a vast fortune until his ambitions led to his assassination.

Water Pump: Equipment that is designed to push or pull water for several purposes, such as irrigation and generation of power to propel engines. Beginning with the Egyptians, prior to the invention of electricity and gas, the water pump has had a long history and was instrumental in some of the inventions of the Industrial Revolution, including the steam engine and the locomotive. The organization Syntech Pumps of India provides the various types and functions of pumps that revolutionized the industry over the centuries. These include the Centrifugal, the Savery, the Axil Flow, the Jump, the Electromagnetic, and the Submersible pump.

Watt, James: Eighteenth-century inventor whose contributions to the advancement of the steam engine made significant contributions to the Industrial Revolution.

Weapons of Mass Destruction (WMDs): Per the United Nations, "Weapons of mass destruction (WMDs) constitute a class of weaponry with the potential to, in a single moment, kill millions of civilians, jeopardize the natural environment, and fundamentally alter the world and the lives of future generations through their catastrophic effects."[4]

The West: This word usually means Europe and people who live in the Western Hemisphere, usually seen as more economically, socially, politically, and scientifically advanced than the rest of the world.

Wool: Fiber obtained from hairy animals, such as sheep, goats, and camels used as cloth for man's protection against inclement weather and the sun before the invention of yarn by British knitters during the sixteenth century. At first, before its use spread, wool served mainly the middle and upper classes in Europe.

World Systems: Political-economic, socioeconomic and/or ideological regional or global systems; a theory developed by Africanist Immanuel Wallerstein that divides the world into two systems, the developed West, and the underdeveloped and dependent world. Whereas in the system's core Europe is the dominant capitalist world that benefits from the periphery, surviving through the exploitation of the economically and militarily weaker parts of the globe—also known as the Third World. The developing world will continue to be forever dependent unless a popular revolution changes the balance of power. Wallerstein's book titled *The Modern World System: Capitalist Agriculture and the Origins of the European World Economy in the Sixteenth Century*, 1974, is no longer as relevant as it once was given the demise of almost all Communist countries.

World War I: One of the most tragic wars in the history of Europe, it spread to the African colonies. World War I (1914–1918) was a culmination of the many unresolved problems among the nations of the time, brought about by extreme nationalism, militarism, and imperialism. However, what triggered the beginning of the war was the assassination of the heir to the throne of the Austro-Hungarian Empire, Archduke Franz Ferdinand, by nationalists from Serbia on June 28, 1914, when he and his wife visited Sarajevo. With encouragement from unified Germany, Austro-Hungary sent a stern ultimatum to Serbia. The latter eventually rejected Austrian

---

4   "Weapons of Mass Destruction," United Nations Regional Centre for Peace and Disarmament in Asia and the Pacific. http://unrcpd.org/wmd/

demands. As a result, Austro-Hungary declared war on Serbia exactly one month following the assassination, namely, on July 28, 1914, encouraged by the serfs, including those in Russia. Slowly, most of the European nations, such as Serbia, Bulgaria, and the Ottoman Empire, sided either with Austro-Hungary and Germany, officially known as the Central Powers, or with the enemies of the latter, France, England, joined by Russia, Montenegro, and Belgium, along with the African colonies, Canada, and Australia, as the Triple Entente. Austria and its allies lost the war after the Americans joined in 1917, which ended with the Treaty of Versailles in 1918–1919. The treaty demanded that Germany relinquish all its colonies to France, Belgium, England, and South Africa, the return of Alsace-Lorraine to France, the cession of Eupen-Malmedy to Belgium and Memel to Lithuania, and the Hultschin District to Czechoslovakia.

World War II: War triggered by Adolph Hitler's invasion of Poland on September 1, 1939, which forced France and Britain to declare war on Germany, eventually forcing Europe and other parts of the world to join either the Allies (France, Britain, the United States, and Russia) or the Axis powers (Germany, Austria, Italy, and Japan, among others). The war resulted in part from Germany's resentment over the Treaty of Versailles, the **appeasement** policy the West followed towards Hitler's blatant aggression in Europe, and the issue of extreme nationalism present in the Europe of the time. The war ended in 1945 after Germany's unconditional surrender, leading Hitler to commit suicide. To weaken the aggressor, Germany was divided among the Allies and the Soviet Union, had to pay reparations, and constitute a new democratic government.

Yellow Fever: Virulent disease of the tropics, sent from Africa to the New World by the Columbian Exchange. Mosquitoes spread yellow fever, and before the late nineteenth century, there was little medical science could do to treat this disease. It caused very high death rates for first-time victims.

Yi Sun-sin: Korean scholar and self-taught admiral who deployed ironclad warships plus artful knowledge of coastal waterways to defeat larger Japanese fleets in the 1500s.

Zheng He: Famous and intrepid commander of Chinese expeditions in Asia and Africa. He was born of a Muslim father in the Chinese province of Yunan around 1371 and given the name of Sambao, later to be changed to Ma He, when he began working for Emperor Jianwen of the Ming Dynasty. Captured in his adventures as a young military man, Zheng He was captured and castrated during one of the expeditions. He grew up to become a diplomat and a naval commander who made seven trips around the world between 1431 and 1433, at times carrying a fleet of 62 ships of close to 30,000 men. Records seem to provide evidence that he reached the Indian Ocean and sailed to the southern tip of the African continent, even before Bartolomeu Dias in 1487 and Vasco da Gama in 1498. He died in Calcutta, India, in what became his last expedition. The record seems to hint further that he went to Mecca in pilgrimage and that perhaps he contracted a disease while there.

Appendix

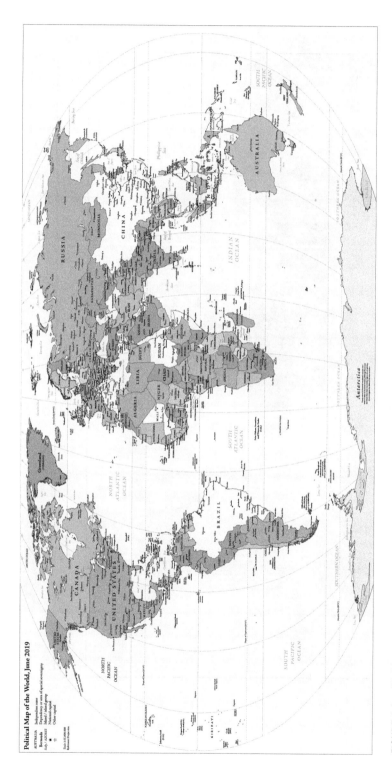

FIGURE A.1   World.

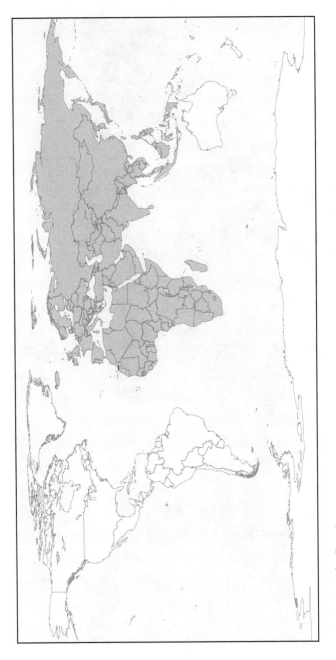

FIGURE A.2   Afro-Eurasia.

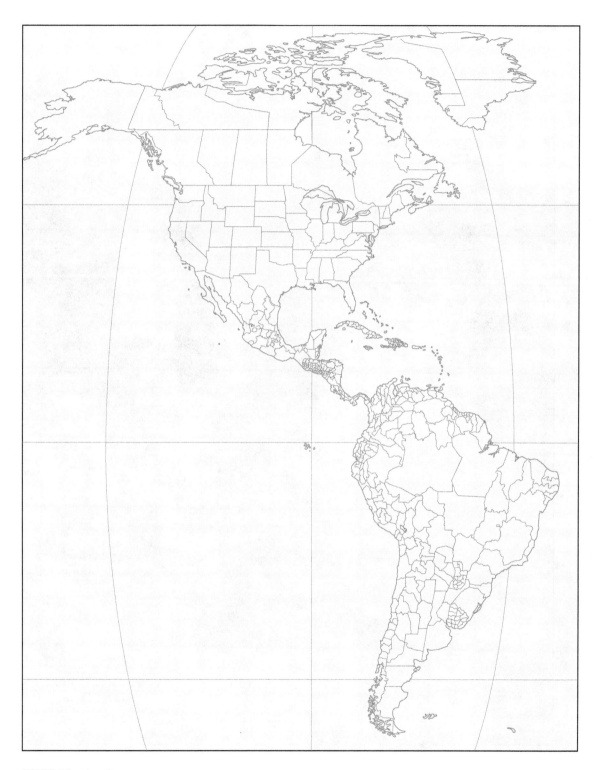

FIGURE A.3   Americas.

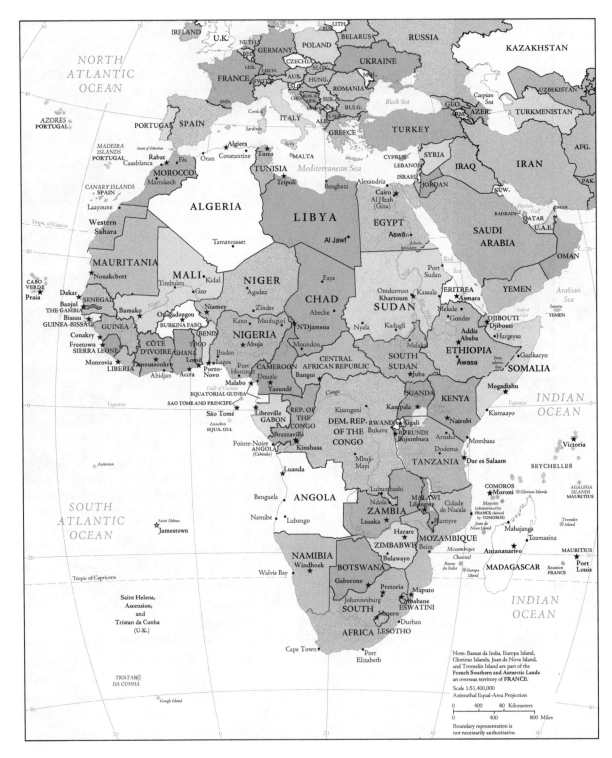

FIGURE A.4   Africa.

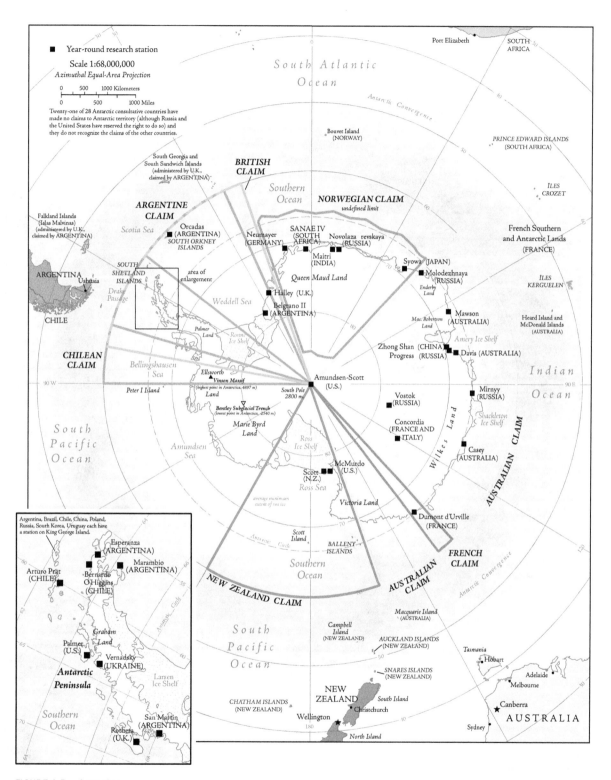

FIGURE A.5   Antartica.

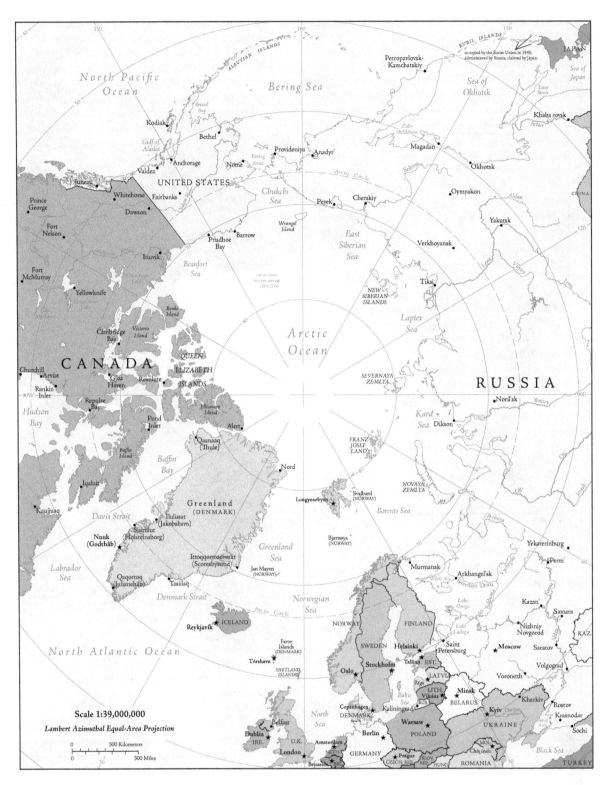

FIGURE A.6   Arctic.

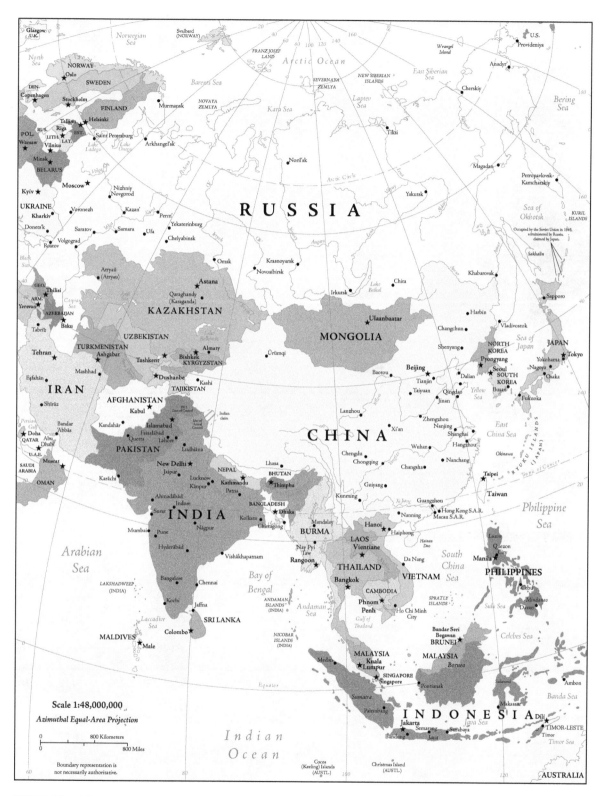

FIGURE A.7 Asia.

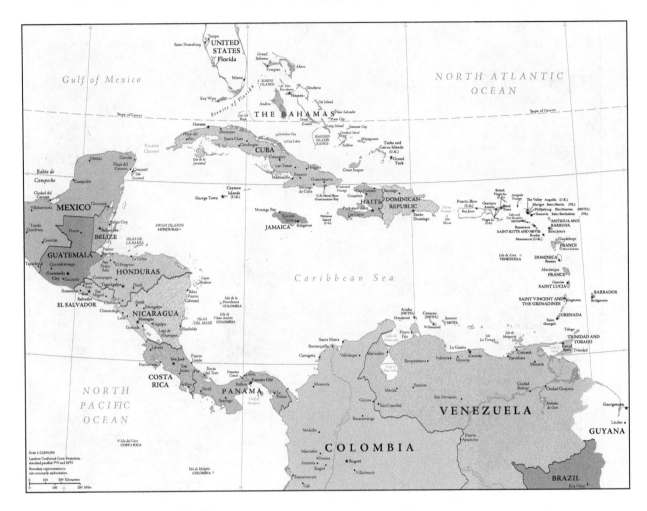

FIGURE A.8   Central America and Caribbean.

FIGURE A.9   Europe.

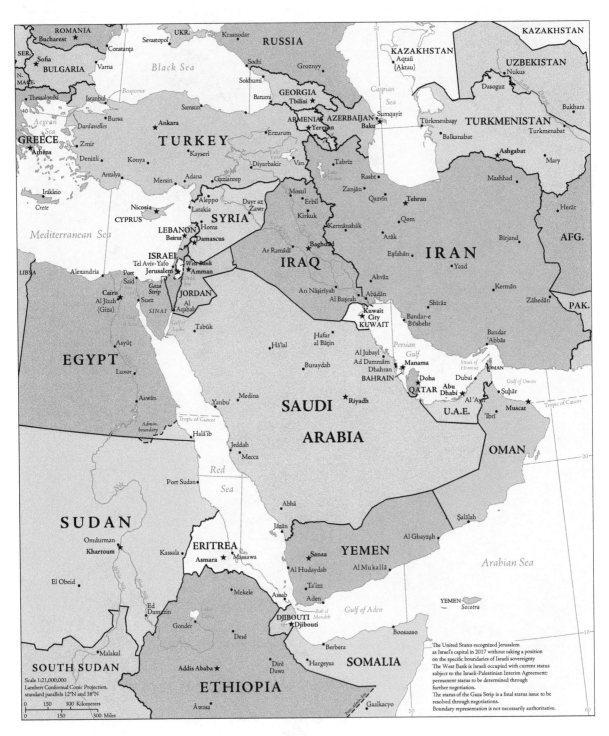

FIGURE A.10   Middle East.

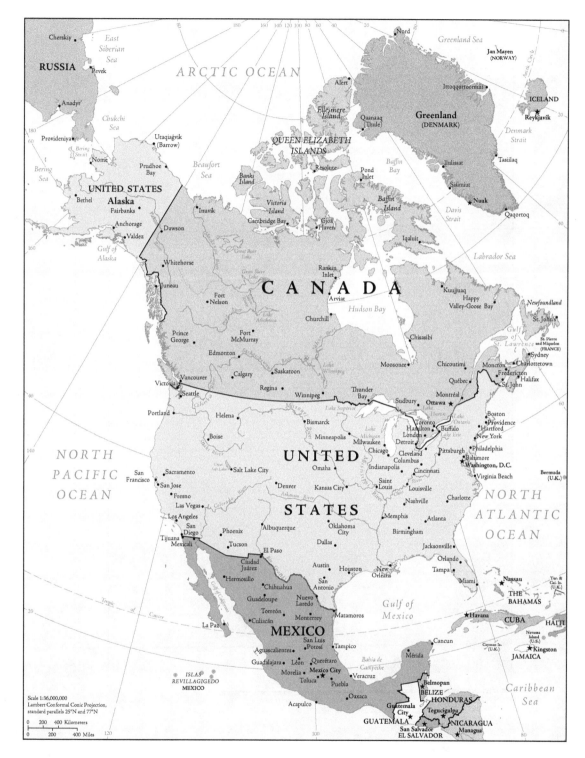

FIGURE A.11 North America.

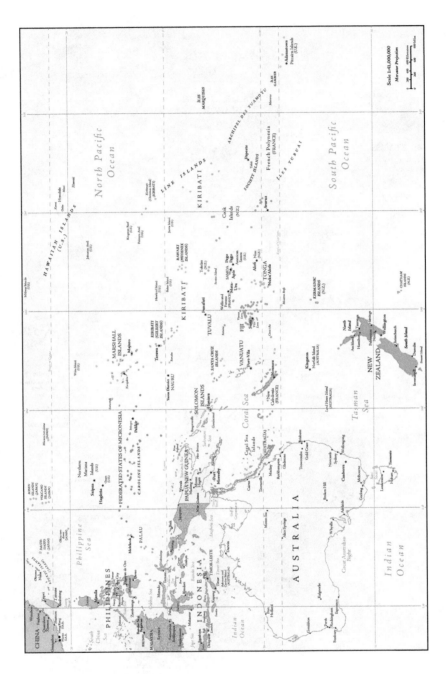

FIGURE A.12   Oceania.

FIGURE A.13   South America.

Credits

Fig. A.1: Source: https://www.cia.gov/library/publications/the-world-factbook/attachments/images/large/world-political.jpg?1561571042.

Fig. A.2: Copyright © by TUBS (CC BY-SA 3.0) at https://commons.wikimedia.org/wiki/File:Afro-Eurasia_in_the_World_(red).svg.

Fig. A.3: Copyright © by Milenioscuro (CC BY-SA 3.0) at https://commons.wikimedia.org/wiki/File:Americas_blank_map.png.

Fig. A.4: Source: https://www.cia.gov/library/publications/the-world-factbook/attachments/images/large/africa_pol.jpg?1558019449.

Fig. A.5: Source: https://www.cia.gov/library/publications/the-world-factbook/attachments/images/large/antarctic_region-political.jpg?1547145647.

Fig. A.6: Source: https://www.cia.gov/library/publications/the-world-factbook/attachments/images/large/arctic_region-political.jpg?1547145647.

Fig. A.7: Source: https://www.cia.gov/library/publications/the-world-factbook/attachments/images/large/asia-political.jpg?1547145648.

Fig. A.8: Source: https://www.cia.gov/library/publications/the-world-factbook/attachments/images/large/central_america-political.jpg?1561570741.

Fig. A.9: Source: https://www.cia.gov/library/publications/the-world-factbook/attachments/images/large/europe-political.jpg?1547145650.

Fig. A.10: Source: https://www.cia.gov/library/publications/the-world-factbook/attachments/images/large/middle_east_pol.jpg?1558019563.

Fig. A.11: Source: https://www.cia.gov/library/publications/the-world-factbook/attachments/images/large/north_america-political.jpg?1561570875.

Fig. A.12: Source: https://www.cia.gov/library/publications/the-world-factbook/attachments/images/large/oceania-political.jpg?1547145653.

Fig. A.13: Source: https://www.cia.gov/library/publications/the-world-factbook/attachments/images/large/south_america-physical.jpg?1547145654.

Index

CPSIA information can be obtained
at www.ICGtesting.com
Printed in the USA
BVHW010216111121
621212BV00002B/8